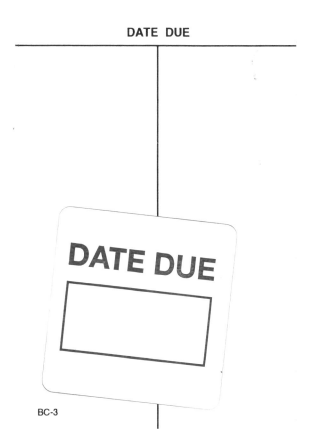

APR 12 '97

AFZ8488-5

# NOTES OF A
# RACIAL CASTE BABY

**CRITICAL AMERICA**
**General Editors: Richard Delgado and Jean Stefancic**

# NOTES OF A
# RACIAL CASTE BABY

COLOR BLINDNESS
and the
**END**
of
**AFFIRMATIVE
ACTION**

BRYAN K. FAIR

NEW YORK UNIVERSITY PRESS
New York and London

NEW YORK UNIVERSITY PRESS
New York and London

Library of Congress Cataloging-in-Publication Data
Fair, Bryan K., 1960-
Notes of a racial caste baby : color blindness and the end of
affirmative action / Bryan K. Fair.
p.     cm.—(Critical America)
Includes index.
ISBN 0-8147-2651-8 (alk. paper)
1. Affirmative action progress—United States.   I. Title.
II. Series.
HF5549.5.A34F336     1997
331.13'3'0973—dc20          96-25394
                                        CIP

New York University Press books are printed on acid-free paper,
and their binding materials are chosen for strength and durability.

Manufactured in the United States of America

10 9 8 7 6 5 4 3 2 1

for Dee

# CONTENTS

ʮ

## A NOTE TO THE READER

......................................................................................................................................

**M**ost Americans think their government is the best in the world. Each of its branches—legislative, executive, and judicial—is an essential component of the Constitution established by the states more than two centuries ago. Then, after the Civil War, compromises regarding the nature and scope of the government's powers were reached, giving Americans in large measure the government they have today. Nonetheless, many people still look at the federal government as too big, too wasteful, too powerful, and even evil.

Some critics want to redesign the government in the tradition of Thomas Jefferson; others champion state or individual rights. Both groups, however, see the government as overgrown and overintrusive and believe that it should be recreated. But is the federal government the sole source of America's many ills, as some people insist? Would Americans want the government to give up its traditional role of providing for the nation's general welfare?

I, like many African Americans, view America's government differently. For example, I am suspicious of many of its detractors, especially those who, having amassed fortunes as longtime insiders, now seek the cloak of reformer. And because I have read some of Thomas Jefferson's writings—especially on blacks' cognitive limitations—I'm skeptical of anyone who holds him up as a role model.

Some of the criticism of the government is directed at its funding of welfare, social security, education, health care, or other social programs, that is, the government's withdrawal of power. Fewer complaints are directed at the expansion of government power. Consider, for example, the proposals to ban abortion, to make English the nation's official language, to prevent flag burning, to permit school prayer, to stiffen criminal laws and hasten executions, to balance the budget, and to repeal affirmative action programs. Do such proposals add up to less government? Would they reduce the national budget or the federal deficit? Or would they simply offer Americans a national government with a different agenda, which is what some would-be reformers want. Such people really don't want less national government, they want one with different priorities: fewer taxes and regulations on business, fewer entitlements for the poor and elderly, more state autonomy, and so on.

The point is not that all criticism of the government in the United States is groundless or motivated by partisan interests. Rather, we simply should be careful to direct our criticism at real problems, not those that a politician or special-interest group has created in order to divide and suppress us. Thus, even though I too recognize bureaucratic waste and corruption, I would attack the problems of $300 hammers or toilet seats, political corruption, and inefficiency by means of reform measures aimed specifically at them. I do not blame the federal government for every problem facing America or assume that individual states will resolve them more efficiently.

Indeed, many state officials tolerate similar waste and corruption. Moreover, all the states' representatives in Washington try to grab as much federal money as possible and then complain to their constituents that the federal government is killing them with regulations and taxes. Does it surprise you that Speaker of the House Newt Gingrich's Cobb County district is heavily subsidized by the federal government? Gingrich and others who deliver local dollars have been rewarded with long terms in Washington. Would a more appropriate target of criticism be the people who have been running the government for ten, twenty, or thirty years? Perhaps our inefficient government—federal, state, and local—is the result of ineffective, self-serving individuals, not its constitutional design.

Without subsidies from the federal government, most of the states would be in far worse shape, and the national infrastructure from which all Americans benefit would likely collapse. Who would maintain the roads, bridges, and national parks? Who would help the victims of fires, floods, hurricanes, and earthquakes? The farmers? The depositors in failed savings and loan banks? Who would control the states' economic rivalries or subsidize international business development to the tune of $100 billion? Who would help the millions of children living in poverty? Can the states provide for the general welfare and defense of the nation? The framers of the American Constitution didn't think so.

Even worse, many state officials have demonstrated repeatedly that they will not protect the rights of political, religious, or racial minorities from abuse, even when mandated by law to do so. When the states have failed to prohibit racial discrimination in public accommodations, housing, education, voting, and employment, the federal government has been the great defender, periodically vindicating the American constitutional promise of equality. All the civil rights laws enacted in the 1960s had one aim: to halt racial discrimination by whites against blacks and other minorities and also gender discrimination by men against women.

At that time, the federal government specifically addressed discrimination by employers or institutions receiving federal contracts, requiring that they make good-faith efforts to employ qualified minorities and women. Their failure to do so could result in termination of their federal contracts, which today run into the billions of dollars annually. This corrective, remedial affirmative action and its expansion beyond employment have caused a steadily growing outcry throughout the United States. Some of these critics, persons who previously did not have to compete with minorities and women because of race and gender monopolies, believe that the government has gone too far. Thus, along with the antigovernment mood sweeping the United States is an unprecedented assault on remedial affirmative action programs.

This book is a defense of remedial affirmative action, a policy that seems to be the only fair and workable solution to the chronic problem of racial caste in the United States. Other—often compelling—books use moral or philosophical justifications, but few of them discuss affirmative action both personally and in light of American history or legal precedent.

As a teacher of American constitutional law, I regularly discuss race and gender discrimination cases with my students. In one of my courses, I have the students interview a grandmother, mother, aunt, sister, or female friend about gender discrimination in their job. For many of these students, reports of gender-based discrimination meant little until they affected close family and friends. Indeed, more than anything else we do during the semester, this assignment convinces my students that gender discrimination is pervasive, and only then are they able to discuss possible solutions.

Americans desperately need to talk about their racial experiences. But right now, they aren't able to hold a conversation; they just shout at one another. On some level, Americans—all Americans, of all races—need to shout, but they also need to listen. Only by hearing one another's stories can we reach an agreement regarding the importance of remedial affirmative action.

This book examines the significance of race and racial caste to my life, the benefits of affirmative action, and also the historical and constitutional legitimacy of remedial affirmative action. This self-examination has deepened my commitment to eliminating educational and occupational segregation and my belief that remedial affirmative action is the most effective strategy for achieving that goal. It has also helped me see that all white men in the United States are not angry, that some of them support remedial affirmative action, that some minorities and women do not, that remedial policies are limited, and that they benefit women, racial minorities, and poor whites.

I support race-based remedial affirmative action because it promotes racial opportunity and inclusion, still in short supply in America. It mandates racial sharing in light of the historic refusal of many white men to do so in the absence of such policies. Affirmative action operates directly to eliminate pervasive racial caste caused by educational and occupational segregation and tracking. My hope is that whether or not my readers agree with me, this book will promote their racial awareness, cross-racial affinity, and active participation in this important discussion. In the end, Americans may discover that the chasms among them are too great and that their trust is too weak. I hope not. But Americans owe it to their children to try to eliminate the scourge of racial caste.

## ACKNOWLEDGMENTS

This book would not have been possible without the generous support of many people, especially colleagues and friends at the University of Alabama School of Law. I am grateful to Dean Kenneth Randall, former Dean Nat Hansford, and the Alabama Law Foundation for generous financial support for research during the summers between 1991 and 1996. Those funds made it possible for me to spend time reading, thinking, speaking, and writing about race and American law.

I owe enormous debts to many of my teachers and all of my students. Several teachers at each stage of my training told me my life mattered. They showed me a special kind of caring and sacrifice; they gave me a chance at a different life. All my former students, especially those at the University of Alabama School of Law, have challenged me to think carefully and speak forthrightly about the great American constitutional issues of the day. We have listened to and learned from one another.

My colleagues at Alabama have encouraged me to say what I think, without fear of reprisal. They have embraced me as an equal citizen. I am grateful for their support, guidance, and constructive criticism. Pam Bucy, Pat Hermann, Ken Randall, Martha Morgan, Tony Freyer, Susan Randall, Beverly Thorn, Ron Turner, Bill Andreen, Wythe Holt, Tim Hoff, Jerry Hoffman, Tom Jones, Bill Brewbaker, and Norman Stein read early drafts of this book. I am honored to work with such an outstanding community of dedicated teachers. Tim Coggins, Paul Pruitt, Penny Gibson, David Lowe, Diana May, and Robert Marshall provided exceptional library services.

I also received invaluable support from my colleagues at the Southwestern/Southeastern Teachers of Color Legal Scholarship Conferences. From them, I have learned that our world is not bipolar and that race matters not just to blacks and whites but to all Americans. I benefited, as well, from discussions of this book with friends at the Seattle University School of Law. Previous versions of some parts of this book were published in the *National Black Law Journal* 13 (1993) and the *University of San Francisco Law Review* 28 (1994), and I am grateful to each for permission to publish expanded versions of those earlier works.

My friend Patty Lovelady Nelson worked extra and late helping me learn to use my computer and revise drafts. Michelle Monse and Aaron Estis offered detailed comments from the very beginning and helped me stay focused. Nina Sethi, Grace Rai, Jennifer Fonner, Ray George, Angela Turner, Valerie Phillips Hermann, Rejeana Lavender, Lori David, and Darnell Coley all provided expert research assistance.

Finally, I must give heartfelt thanks to Jean Stefancic and Richard Delgado and the editors at New York University Press, especially Niko Pfund, who encouraged me to share my thoughts, in my way.

ꙮ

## PREFACE: TELLING STORIES

I am the eighth of ten children of a single mother, born in a black ghetto in Columbus, Ohio, in 1960. Since my siblings are close in age—the youngest within fifteen years of the oldest—we lived at home at the same time for a significant period. My mother sometimes had two jobs, but still, her wages were low, she received no job benefits, and none of our fathers helped her. We certainly did need welfare; I can't imagine what we would have done without it. Even with it, my family went weeks without regular meals at home. Each month we ran out of food and ate sugar or mayonnaise sandwiches until they too ran out. Sometimes, in order to get something to eat, I had to steal.

Even though each of our houses was old and small, rent in the ghetto was high. We occupied every square foot of space: bedrooms, basement, and attic. We never had our own bedrooms and frequently shared our beds. I shared one with two younger brothers, and the tensions among us ran high. We drew imaginary lines in the bed that were not to be crossed. And when they were, battles broke out until my mother or one of my older siblings threatened punishment. Our house was poorly insulated and infested with roaches and rats. I remember sitting on the couch at night, afraid to put my feet on the floor for fear a rat or mouse might scurry across them. Our campaign against roaches was futile: they were the permanent residents, and we were the transients, moving every couple of years in search of cheaper rent or when we fell behind in our payments to the landlord.

Sometimes during the frigid, below-zero Ohio winters, my family had no gas heat. We never knew ahead of time that our utilities would be disconnected. Instead, we found out when we got home and the temperature inside was not much different from that outside. To stay warm, we huddled under blankets and slept in our clothes. To bathe, we either took icy showers or boiled pots of water on our electric single-burner hotplate. A few times my mother could not pay the electric bill either. I thought we were the poorest people in Columbus. We were not.

When I was seven, I started hustling jobs, and for the next eleven years, after school and on weekends, I ran errands, shoveled snow, cut grass, cleared trash, cleaned bathrooms, swept floors, cooked, stocked groceries, sold candy, and cleaned animal cages. My survival depended on those jobs. They enabled me to buy food, a few clothes, and school supplies and to help my mother pay bills.

I attended elementary school regularly and earned A's and B's in most classes. But when I participated in a voluntary busing program during junior high that moved black kids from the ghetto into predominantly white schools, the work seemed much harder and my grades fell. I couldn't read well, and I had to struggle to finish my homework. Now I was only a C student. When I started high school, one of my teachers told me that although I had an appealing personality, I didn't know very much. To help, he gave me history and literature books to read. Without constantly looking up in the dictionary the many words whose pronunciation and meaning I didn't know, I couldn't make sense of them. I was scared and angry, and I felt trapped.

Many blacks in Columbus and elsewhere in the United States are born into conditions like those I have described, and most remain there. I escaped. I am now a lawyer, a professor of constitutional law, a university administrator, and a published author. I am not poor or dependent on welfare. Neither are any of my siblings. I support myself and help support my mother. How did this happen? One important factor was remedial affirmative action. It helped me move from the ghetto into more rigorous schools and increasingly nurturing environments. So no one can tell me that affirmative action does not work. It did for me, as it has for many other Americans.

One of my reasons for telling this story is to make clear that remedial affirmative action is not the same as the whites-only, racial caste–producing legislation that has often prevailed throughout America's history. My life experiences have convinced me that remedial affirmative action and hard work, plus the support and direction of many people, are what— even though the odds were decidedly against me—enabled me to escape from that Ohio ghetto. Without the educational opportunities, I would have been imprisoned by circumstances and conditions beyond my control.

## RECASTING REMEDIES AS DISEASES

Everywhere you turn in the United States, remedial affirmative action is under assault. "Innocent," "angry" white men insist they are victims of "reverse discrimination," unfairly losing their jobs and other opportunities because of minority or gender preferences. Randy Pech, owner of a Colorado-based construction company that lost a highway guardrail contract to a minority-owned company that benefited from a federal affirmative action policy, took his claim of reverse discrimination all the way to the United States Supreme Court, which once again showed that it is far more receptive and responsive to whites alleging race discrimination than it has been to minority plaintiffs, especially blacks.[1] The Rehnquist Court has embraced the white victim rhetoric that is sweeping the legislative councils, corporate boardrooms, and courts throughout the United States.

Politicians and activists are questioning state and federal affirmative action policies: Both President (and Democratic presidential nominee) Bill Clinton and former Senate Majority Leader (and Republican presidential nominee) Bob Dole commissioned a national study of all federal affirmative action programs. Two apparently angry white guys, Tom Wood and Glynn Custred, along with the support of a third, Speaker of the House Newt Gingrich, organized a voter initiative campaign to repeal all state-sponsored affirmative action programs in California, insisting that such programs have outlived their usefulness. Other challenges seem imminent.

Public discussion in the United States often portrays affirmative action as primarily those policies that help "unqualified" blacks or other racial minorities attend school, gain employment, or elect representatives of their choice. Little is said or written about the numerous remedial policies that help white women overcome centuries of economic exclusion or policies that aid small businesses operated by socially or economically disadvantaged persons, including many white men.

Critics also ignore the fact that remedial affirmative action was instituted by white Americans in response to massive demands for remediation of the discriminatory conditions under which minorities and white women were forced to live because of quotas for white males. They say even less about the privileges that continue to accrue to white male elites by virtue of legacies, old-boy networks, custom, seniority, and the like; this kind of affirmative action for the rich or connected seems less offensive to many Americans. Rather, the principal target for many white men and a few blacks is race-based remedial policies.

Many blacks in America view this selective attack on race-based remedial affirmative action policies with disbelief, seeing it as just one more example of white arrogance and the latest lesson on white supremacy in the United States. They observe that white men still run America. They know that white women have benefited as much, if not more, from remedial affirmative action as they have. Yet most of the affirmative action "tragedies" that we hear about center on the costs of race-based policies, identified as stigma, polarization, incompetence, and the like.

Today, America's racial problems seem little improved from a century ago, when a rigid color line—a line favoring whites over blacks—was the rule of law or local custom. Now as then, a majority of the Supreme Court has turned its back on darker-skinned Americans by construing the Constitution in a way that permits subtler forms of racial discrimination to pass unchecked and in a way that constrains efforts to eliminate racial caste.

For decades the Supreme Court told blacks that it was helpless to do anything about slavery, segregation, or other policies of white supremacy in housing, voting, employment, public accommodations, or education, because that discrimination was either sanctioned by the Constitution or beyond its reach. Just before the Civil War, in the landmark opinion in *Dred Scott v. Sandford*, Chief Justice Roger Taney told blacks—whether free or enslaved—that they were not citizens under the Constitution and therefore could not sue in the federal courts. That decision only made visible the law's endorsement of white supremacy.

Even after the U.S. Constitution was amended between 1865 and 1870 with three sweeping provisions and Congress enacted new federal statutes prohibiting white supremacy, the Court was unwilling to interpret the new amendments and laws as they were intended, namely, to prevent whites from keeping blacks in slavelike conditions. Instead, the Court read the Citizenship Clause and the Privileges and Immunities Clause of the Fourteenth Amendment as either meaningless or constitutionally redundant, so that neither clause nor any other provisions of that amendment gave freedmen any federal protection of their civil rights. Likewise, even though the Fifteenth Amendment explicitly forbade voter discrimination on the basis of race, the Court held that government officials could still prevent someone from voting on the basis of other qualifications such as gender, age, property, or educational status, enabling some states to deny blacks the right to vote until well into the 1960s.

To add the proverbial insult to injury, the Court told blacks that there was a constitutional difference between social and political equality, that separate was in fact equal. The Court even went so far as to intimate that the Constitution could do nothing to remedy distinctions between whites and blacks that were based on color, that white superiority was natural. As a result, for much of the next sixty years, the Court sat by as white elites arranged every area of life to suit themselves, in ways that were almost always separate and almost never equal.

Because whites had access to the United States' best educational resources, it followed that they would also win its best jobs, highest incomes, and best housing. To make sure, many whites adhered to private practices that guaranteed their superior status. For instance, some signed contracts agreeing never to sell houses to blacks or other minorities. Some turned away blacks from the polls through threat, intimidation, or trickery, and others refused to consider blacks for certain jobs. In some places, blacks could not eat or sleep in the same public accommodations, drink from the same water fountain, use the same toilet, or be buried in the same cemetery as whites. Few whites even pretended to be color blind. Under the guise of separate but equal, color meant whites only or whites first. Blacks and other people of color got the leftovers, if there were any.

By 1954, the Court, led by Chief Justice Earl Warren, seemed poised to lead the United States away from racial caste, holding for the first time that segregated public schools were inherently unequal and unconstitutional and later expanding that ruling to all areas of public life. Congress and the president followed, enacting more federal laws prohibiting discrimination by whites against blacks in public accommodations, education, employment, voting, and housing. Those laws permitted, and in some circumstances required, remedial affirmative action. For a short period, it appeared that each branch of the federal government was committed to eliminating racial caste.

By the mid-1970s, however, following the assassination of Martin Luther King Jr. and the rise of black nationalism, a new majority formed, with a modified definition of racial discrimination. Now the Supreme Court maintained that only intentional *invidious* discrimination violated the Constitution. This meant that de facto segregation, the kind that occurred without the force of law, was not illegal. Similarly, a policy's racially disproportionate impact was, by itself, not proof of intentional discrimination, so to prevail, plaintiffs had to prove that government agents had adopted policies for the intended purpose of their discriminatory effect. Accordingly, blacks protesting policies that disproportionately burdened their political and economic rights were turned away, with no recourse.

Then in 1974 and afterward, along came Marco Defunis, Allan Bakke, and other white Americans insisting, in many cases successfully, that they were victims of *reverse discrimination* and that remedial affirmative action was no different from past policies of discrimination against blacks. This argument has always found some support in the Supreme Court, despite the obvious distinction between policies that promote white supremacy and those that eliminate it.

It took black people more than three centuries to persuade white Americans to eliminate official white supremacy, but it has taken a few whites only two decades to recast history and convince the Supreme Court that race-based remedial affirmative action must go. Five of the current justices have agreed that race-conscious affirmative action programs are usually illegal, and four seem ready to prohibit any race-conscious policy in the name of color blindness.

## COLOR-BLIND JUSTICE

The United States Supreme Court has already accepted the usefulness and constitutional legitimacy of remedial affirmative action in solving the problem of gender caste. Because of those victories, women, especially white women, have made substantial economic and political gains during the past thirty years. For that reason, their silence in the current debate over race-based affirmative action is disappointing.

Just as disconcerting is the Supreme Court's unwillingness to extend to matters of race the same constitutional theory and judicial sensitivity it applied to reduce gender caste. There is only one equality provision in the Fourteenth Amendment, and nothing in it points to one meaning in disputes between men and women and another meaning in disputes between racial groups. But this duality of meanings is essentially what the Supreme Court has confirmed. And this is perverse and wrong, especially since there is little doubt today regarding the purpose for adopting the equal protection clause: to prohibit discrimination against former slaves. If the federal government can eliminate gender caste without running afoul of the Constitution, it can do at least as much to eliminate racial caste.

The Supreme Court's deliberate failure to see what is apparent to most blacks reveals, as the late Associate Justice Thurgood Marshall wrote in his final dissenting opinion, that "power, not reason, is the new currency within this Court." [2] Indeed, this attack on remedial affirmative action is a lesson about power and who wields it in America. The Rehnquist Court intends to dismantle race-based remedial affirmative action policies in the same way that its predecessor emasculated the Civil War amendments and supporting federal civil rights laws. When that happens, blacks will once again have been shown that the inscription atop the Supreme Court Building—Equal Justice Under Law—has an unwritten qualifier: except if you are not white.

The United States has never adopted any policies designed to promote white caste. No current remedial affirmative action policy has the *invidious* purpose or effect of excluding whites from public accommodations, voting, employment, education, or housing. Rather, such policies were enacted because of their remedial effect, thereby making reverse discrimination a travesty.

Many white Americans believe the fairy tale about racial equality in the United States, which, in turn, rests on myths about traditions of fairness and color blindness. Few blacks and other racial minorities in this country, however, subscribe to such ideas.

To accept this fairy tale, Americans must ignore the true history of white racial privilege:

> For [more than] two hundred years the United States has been operating under a rigid quota system. This quota system has insisted on and got a 90 to 100 percent monopoly for white males in all the principal centers of power in government, business, and the professions, and in the competition for jobs at every level. [3]

In reality, the quotas most important to an analysis of modern remedial affirmative action are the invisible ones never talked about, those that have given white Americans, especially white men, virtual monopolies over all the means of acquiring wealth: education, employment, land acquisition, and political participation. Opponents of remedial affirmative action say little about this historical quota system.

Many Americans know from their own experience that legal traditions in the United States do not rest on racial equality, equal opportunity, or equal justice under law. Nor are those traditions color blind or based on merit. Instead, America's traditions have been ones of unabashed, shocking, and widespread race consciousness and white privilege. The result is modern racial caste and racial enmity throughout every sector of the United States, which began long before remedial affirmative action was instituted.

Critics of affirmative action insist that the American Constitution cannot make races equal. Why not? Why can't the Constitution do for racial equality what it once did for racial inequality? It was amended to reverse its original sanction of white supremacy, so why can't it eliminate racial caste?[4] And why don't more white Americans realize that eliminating racial caste is a national interest of the highest priority, one that is in their children's best interest?

In his celebrated dissent in *Plessy v. Ferguson*, Justice John Marshall Harlan wrote that "our Constitution is color-blind, and neither knows nor tolerates classes among citizens."[5] To understand what Harlan meant, it is instructive to look at the text preceding this often-quoted statement:

> The White race deems itself to be the dominant race in this country. And so it is, in prestige, in achievements, in education, in wealth and in power. So, I doubt not it will continue to be for all time, if it remains true to its great heritage and holds fast to the principles of constitutional liberty. *But in the view of the Constitution, in the eye of the law, there is in this country no superior, dominant, ruling class of citizens. There is no caste here. Our Constitution is color-blind, and neither knows nor tolerates classes among citizens.*[6]

Harlan, the former Kentucky slave owner who after the Civil War repudiated slavery, believed that the Fourteenth Amendment prohibited government-sponsored racial caste, and therefore he concluded that it was unconstitutional for Louisiana to adopt a statute that treated blacks as a subject race. He also believed that Congress had broad powers under sections 1 and 5 of the Fourteenth Amendment to enact legislation against racial caste.[7]

More recently, Justice Lewis F. Powell Jr., a Virginia corporate lawyer who reluctantly accepted his second nomination to the Court, in his opinion in *Regents of the University of California v. Bakke,* articulated another vision of the color blindness principle. Powell wrote that "[t]he guarantee of equal protection cannot mean one thing when applied to one individual and something else when applied to a person of another color. If both are not accorded the same protection, then it is not equal." Powell concluded that constitutional color blindness prohibited the use of race as the sole factor in governmental decision making, declaring (with four others) that instead, race could be one of many factors.[8]

Justices Harlan and Powell each contended that his color blindness principle was derived from the Fourteenth Amendment's equal protection clause. Yet their opinions in *Plessy* and *Bakke* at times appear contradictory regarding the constitutionality of race-based remedial affirmative action. The conflict between their opinions is one of form, however, rather than substance: Harlan emphasized the elimination of racial caste through affirmative action striking down Jim Crow laws and conditions, whereas Powell wanted to do the same through affirmative action striking down educational and occupational segregation and tracking. Therefore, unlike several current members of the Supreme Court, Harlan and Powell understood the difference between policies designed to promote white supremacy and policies designed to eliminate racial caste. Nonetheless, now when one encounters a reference to color blindness rhetoric, as in *Adarand v. Pena,* it often is unclear whether it has the meaning espoused by Justices Harlan and Powell or one that would prohibit remedial affirmative action.[9]

Therefore, the problem of the twenty-first century will be the problem of color blindness[10]—the refusal of legislators, jurists, and most of American society to acknowledge the causes and current effects of racial caste and to adopt effective remedial policies to eliminate them.

Americans should interpret their Constitution to prohibit policies that advance racial supremacy, not to repeal policies designed to eliminate America's legacy of white supremacy. They cannot pretend to be color blind. To do so will only extend white supremacy and black caste into the next century. To paraphrase former Associate Justice Harry Blackmun, to get beyond racial caste, Americans must take account of race. And to take account of race in this way does not promote racial supremacy, as did prior historical practices in the United States favoring whites only.

## THE DESIGN OF THIS BOOK

This book has three parts. Part 1 is the story of my own life and how it has influenced my thinking about racial caste, color blindness, and remedial affirmative action. I explain why I support race-based remedial affirmative action, in addition to gender- and class-based policies, and why I am not an advocate of color blindness.

Part 2 discusses significant moments in America's history of racial privilege for whites and color-based subordination of blacks. I describe the historical origins of racial classifications in the United States, including the racial attitudes of whites toward blacks during the colonial period and the codification of slavery. I also examine the records of the 1787 Constitutional Convention in Philadelphia, during which the framers drafted a constitution containing race-conscious preferences for whites and discrimination against blacks. Next, I look at how the rights and racial privileges of whites expanded between 1787 and the early 1960s while the rights of blacks were rigidly circumscribed. Last, I consider the color blindness principle to show that it is unrealistic, ahistorical, and antithetical to advancing racial equality in the United States. Today, some Americans have transformed the color blindness principle into a doctrine that tolerates and encourages racial caste in a way similar to the pernicious "separate, but equal" philosophy of *Plessy*, which Justice Harlan so rightly rejected.

Part 3 presents the mid-twentieth-century backdrop for the federal government's adoption of remedial affirmative action. I look at the justifications for adopting federal affirmative action programs for minorities and women in contracting and employment during the 1960s and 1970s. I then review the landmark Supreme Court decisions on race-based affirmative action since *Bakke* to illustrate that the Court has concluded repeatedly that such affirmative action is constitutional, explicitly rejecting a rigid color blindness rule. I offer a summary of current affirmative action policies, the most common arguments against affirmative action, and my responses to them.

Finally, I return to Justice Harlan's concern about racial caste and demonstrate how pervasive it is today. I propose that the Court—whose duty it is to declare what the Constitution means—endorse the distinction between remedial affirmative action and laws that endorse racial supremacy. The Court can do this by embracing Justice Powell's diversity approach in *Bakke* or by treating race-based affirmative action under the same analytical standard it applies to gender-based policies.

# NOTES OF A
# RACIAL CASTE BABY

〜

# PART ONE

## A PERSONAL NARRATIVE

### NOT WHITE ENOUGH

I have lived in Ohio, North Carolina, California, and Alabama. In each place, most blacks, whites, and other minorities live separate lives. Most blacks are poor and live in isolated, self-contained slums. They attend segregated schools that are poorly funded, overcrowded, and in need of repair. Most whites live away from them, in other sections of the cities or in the suburbs. Most of them attend better-funded, less crowded, newer schools. Other racial enclaves buffer or border those of whites and blacks. Daily contact between whites and blacks is limited, except in employ-ment settings where whites supervise blacks. Social clubs and churches are often hypersegregated. Residential property values seem to be driven by racial demographics, with the degree of whiteness in the community in proportion to the price. Each community has its own consumer ser-vices, whose quality varies with the community's color.

Similar patterns prevail across the United States. Even the poorest whites and blacks live separately, suggesting that economic status alone does not explain housing segregation. Yet in most of the country, I hear barely a whisper publicly about these differences in the lives of whites and blacks. Behind closed doors, however, racial groups hurl epithets and accusations. How did Americans arrive at this state? Is there something peculiar about blacks that locks most of them in America's ghettos? Are white folks responsible? Is there anything Americans can do to eliminate racial caste? I want to answer these questions in light of my own experiences.

I was born in Ohio. Even though this state was not organized as a slave state, its early judicial cases indicate that by law, whites had numerous rights that blacks and mulattoes were denied. The Ohio constitution restricted voting privileges to white males, and its statutes limited common schools to white children. When a white person was a party in a case, blacks and mulattoes could not be witnesses, and they also could not serve on juries.[1] Presumably, most Americans today would admit that such policies were racist and unfair. Nonetheless, Ohio is not generally thought of as a racist state, at least not in the way that many Americans view, say, Mississippi or Alabama. Indeed, many communities outside the South are seen as free of the racist tradition that defines the South for many non-Southerners. This assumption makes the South—specifically a place like Alabama, where I now live—appear worse than it is, and the rest of the country better.

But is this reputation deserved? Long before I was born, Ohio had relegated most blacks to caste by law and custom. Many early judicial cases in Ohio were brought by parties claiming some proportion of white blood, which, they insisted, entitled them to all the privileges of whiteness. For example, Polly Gray, who appeared to be "a shade of color between mulatto and white," had her robbery conviction reversed because the trial court had permitted a black witness to testify against her in violation of state law. The appellate court found that a person "of a race nearer white than mulatto . . . should partake in the privileges of white." In another case, the court had to determine whether the children of an all-white mother and a three-quarters white father were white under the law. The court held that because the term *white* described blood and not complexion, the children were white.[2]

Other cases in the Ohio courts focused on whether those having a mixture of any blood other than that of "entirely white" persons could vote. The courts ruled that all persons nearer to white than black were entitled to enjoy every political and social privilege of the white citizen. *Monroe v. Collins* is a good example. In this case, the Ohio Supreme Court examined the constitutionality of a state law assigning to elected judges the duty to question any person with a distinct and visible admixture of African blood who was trying to vote under state law, about his or her age, place of birth, parents' marital status and whether they had African blood, whether in this person's community he or she was classified and recognized as white or colored, and whether his or her children attended schools for white or colored children. The court found the statute to be unconstitutional, not because the vote was denied to blacks, but because persons nearer to white than black were denied their constitutional right to vote. Many similar cases required judges to decide the rights of fugitive slaves who had fled to Ohio, the rights of their alleged masters seeking their return, or the criminal liability of those who aided the fugitive slaves' escape.[3] The judges accepted what they believed was their legal duty: to determine whether Ohioans were white enough to enjoy various rights or privileges.

*Van Camp v. Logan*[4] best describes Ohio's early race rules. A divided state supreme court held that Enos Van Camp's children—who were three-eighths African and five-eighths white and who appeared and were generally regarded as colored—were not entitled to go to the white children's schools, notwithstanding prior statutes and judicial opinions to the contrary. This case indicates the elusive meaning of whiteness; that is, in the middle of the nineteenth century, the meaning changed.

According to Judge William V. Peck, before 1848, no law in Ohio provided for the education of any but white children. Then in 1848, Ohio law for the first time provided for the education of colored children, directing a tax for that purpose to be levied on the property of colored persons to support separate schools for them. This statute proved ineffective, however, because it did not generate sufficient money to fund a separate school, and Ohio continued to refuse to divert any of the common school funds to educate colored children.

In 1853, the Ohio legislature repealed this earlier statute, replacing it with one that maintained racially separate schools but gave colored youth their full share of the common school funds, in proportion to their numbers. But when the village of Logan did not maintain a school for colored youth, because of insufficient numbers, the court found nothing illegal, declaring that it was a matter for the legislature, not the judiciary.[5]

The court's divided opinions contain a revealing exchange among the judges regarding what the Ohio legislature intended when it used the term *colored* in the 1853 statute. The majority held that the term was used to create two classes, *white* and *colored*, thereby changing the problem from the proportion of white blood to the presence of any nonwhite blood. Based on this reasoning, a person was either entirely white or colored. The court used Webster's dictionary to define *colored:* "black people, Africans or their descendants, mixed or unmixed.... A person having any perceptible admixture of African blood, is generally called a colored person." The majority therefore decided that the 1853 statute was intended to place in one school all the white youth and, in the other, all who had any visible "taint" of African blood.[6]

Judge Milton Sutliff, for himself and the chief justice, wrote in a bitter dissent that "caste legislation is inconsistent with the theory and spirit of a free government, asserting all men are created equal."[7] He concluded that prior constructions of Ohio law precluded the decision reached by the majority. But Sutliff was unwilling to extend the disabilities assigned to colored youth any further than those that had been applied to blacks and mulattoes—an emphasis on caste legislation that presaged the writing of John Marshall Harlan at the end of the nineteenth century.

While I was growing up in Ohio, I never learned anything about its racial history or its traditions of racial privileges for white Ohioans. None of my teachers mentioned that Ohio law had given precedence to whiteness. We never discussed why schools were segregated in the first place or why white parents did not want their children to attend schools with black children.

*Logan* and similar cases throughout the country were used to construct the meaning of being white, that is, a person without the "taint" of black blood. Whiteness was defined in opposition to blackness; in short, whiteness meant nonblack.

Contemporary writers criticize modern remedial affirmative action as a racial spoils system. But this system was established in places like Ohio in the early 1800s when legislatures and courts were claiming that white blood was somehow better than black, thereby entitling whites to privileges denied to blacks and other Americans of color. This, of course, is the essence of white supremacy: the presumption that white blood or whiteness is, by some unknown measure, better than other blood or racial identities.

Notice the circular logic here: whites receive privileges because of their special blood, and since they receive privileges like education, employment, and voting, they are superior. If whites are superior, then nonwhites—namely, blacks—must be inferior. Racial superiority, then, is a social construct too, a myth created to express certain beliefs and acts.

If there were no such thing as white blood, would there then be no such things as white and black? Was James Baldwin correct when he wrote "color is not a human or a personal reality, it is a political reality"?[8] Is it possible that racial blood groupings were devised to allocate benefits to select Americans? As Ian Haney López writes, "Put most starkly, law constructs race."[9]

I wish I could state that these concepts—whiteness and white superiority—were nothing but flimsy houses of cards, but even if this were true, it would not change America's current political reality. As Cheryl Harris argues, the law's construction of whiteness defines and affirms critical aspects of white identity (that is, who is white), of white privilege (what benefits accrue to that status), and of property (what legal entitlements arise from that status).[10]

Being known as or appearing white has given select citizens, in Ohio and elsewhere in the United States, political and economic advantages over blacks, mulattoes, and other colored persons, as well as poor whites, especially white women. Successive generations of whites have accumulated and passed down wealth derived in part from racial privilege. In turn, these advantages have placed persons who were not known as or who could not pass as white into a racial caste. For them, white privilege meant deprivation, little wealth to accumulate or pass down. White supremacy denied them equality of opportunity, destroyed their families, and relegated them to enclaves of despair. In American neighborhoods today, the results of racial privilege for whites and racial caste for blacks and other racial minorities are evident. The United States today is at least two nations.[11]

For Ohioans of color, the law has not been color blind; indeed, color determines status and rights; it means everything. Some of those colored folks who could not pass as white Ohioans were my dark brown ancestors who migrated to Ohio from Virginia and West Virginia at the beginning of the twentieth century, barely a generation from American slavery. My maternal great-grandmother, Julia Clay Woods, moved from Talcutt, Virginia, to Columbus with her five children: Faye, Gertrude, Sadie, Bessie, and Alexander, my grandfather. Victoria Smith Casey and Pank Casey, my other maternal great-grandparents, moved their twelve children from coal-mining company towns in Bluefield and Wyco, West Virginia, to Columbus. Their daughter Elizabeth Casey married Alexander Woods. My maternal grandparents had four sons and one daughter: Alexander, Jerry, Ralph, Earl, and my mother, Dolores.

## DEE

My mother, known as Dee, was born in Columbus, Ohio, in 1929, the oldest of five children, in the midst of the Great Depression. The crash of the stock market was only a prelude to a general collapse of the American economy. As many as fifteen million Americans were unemployed, and the national income dropped by more than 50 percent. Farm prices fell nearly 60 percent, and business failures and mortgage foreclosures led to the failure of more than five thousand banks. Congress and President Franklin D. Roosevelt responded with sweeping federal legislation to rescue the economy and to protect industries and workers from financial ruin and starvation. After the Depression came World War II, also requiring the guidance of a strong national government.

Neither President Roosevelt's New Deal nor the war effort was color blind. Consequently, blacks living through those crises had to contend not only with economic insecurity but also numerous forms of racial discrimination and violence. For instance, relief payments for blacks were often several dollars less than those for whites, and blacks did not receive the same employment opportunities as whites did under the Works Progress Administration (WPA). Black servicemen, regardless of their education or experience, were forced to live in segregated facilities and serve in segregated units. In fact, many felt freer when they were overseas than when they were at home. And the federal government's economic bailout from the Depression did nothing to eliminate racial caste in the United States.

Dee's father, Alex, was a chauffeur and janitor. For a brief time he worked in the WPA. Her mother, Elizabeth, cooked in restaurants. During World War II, she worked with other women at the War Depot, but their jobs were returned to men when the war ended. Even though neither of my grandparents was lazy or held unacceptable values, their economic opportunities were restricted by educational and employment policies favoring whites.

In 1950, my mother married Sylvester Eugene Fair. Like Dee, he was tall and striking, with a rich, dark brown complexion. He worked in the railroad yards in Columbus. They had two children, Butch and Theresa, but then divorced in 1952. Dee never remarried. By 1965, she had eight more children: Sheila, Bettye, Jayme, Duncan, Kimberly, me, Mark, and Brett. All of us took my mother's married name, Fair.

I do not remember many of Dee's jobs. She worked in grocery stores and bakeries, but mostly in restaurants and bars. She complained all the time about her jobs, how hard the work was and how little she earned. Sometimes when she disagreed with an employer, she simply quit and started looking for another job. She changed jobs frequently, sometimes working both during the day and at night. When she was working at restaurants and bars, she did not get home until after midnight, and so my older siblings were in charge. With so little supervision, I came and went as I chose, staying away from home as much as possible.

Sometimes I went to work with my mother and helped her wash glasses, clean bathrooms, or scrub floors. The bars were all the same: dark, smoke filled, and dilapitated, with a juke box, a cigarette machine, a small pool table, and an old, overused kitchen. Men and a few women came and went throughout the day. When I finished my work, I played pool or listened to the juke box and watched Dee's interactions with the customers.

Dee often had to work alone, serving drinks, cooking, and cleaning. She usually prepared a daily special, such as fried chicken, pork chops, or meatloaf, accompanied by vegetables and white bread. Occasionally, she cooked pig's feet or chitterlings. The customers loved Dee's cooking. Nobody had her ability to make food look and taste exquisite, at least not anyone working on Mount Vernon Avenue or Long Street. I had seen her work miracles with food at home. She made meals from almost nothing and could make bologna or beans and wieners seem special.

I remember how easy it was for Dee to make conversation with her customers. A few of them were friends that came to our home, but most lived and worked nearby and frequented the bar or restaurant. She didn't treat any of them as strangers. They talked about local news or politics, as well as the latest stories from the *Call & Post*, the black newspaper. She asked about their work or families and listened to their stories. Some were in between jobs or recently divorced. Others were sick from high blood pressure or sickle cell anemia. Dee was their confidante. She could console them or make them laugh. She never talked about our family or herself. As far as they knew, Dee and her family were fine. I remember being surprised by her kindness and sensitivity because at home she seemed like a different person.

At home, the demands on Dee as the breadwinner for our large family caused enormous stress. At times she worked several jobs at once, but none of them paid more than the minimum wage plus tips. She never had enough money to pay our bills. The warm, friendly disposition that I observed when Dee worked rarely appeared at home. Instead, conversations were short and pointed: "No, I don't have any money!" or "Tell the landlord I'm not home!" Scraping together barely enough to survive took its toll. Her ten kids were an overwhelming burden. I don't know whether she was ashamed of our poverty, but she often seemed very unhappy at home. I noted her vastly different personalities and hoped to emulate the one from work.

Unlike some of my siblings, I do not know who my father is. For years when people asked about him or his occupation, I just made something up or said he was dead. I was ashamed to admit that I didn't know because I didn't want to be different from my friends who did know their parents. It also was embarrassing to tell lies or to explain how my mother tried to make ends meet. I couldn't tell anyone how little we had, why I had to work so much, or why I stayed away from home. I hated my father for not caring about me and not helping my mother support me.

When I was a teenager, I had several awkward conversations with Dee about my father's identity, but they usually ended with one of us screaming. So I decided not to ask her about him anymore, but my resolution only increased my anger toward him and Dee. Why couldn't she tell me who he was? Was she protecting him? Would he hurt her? And why didn't he reveal himself? Why didn't they understand my need to know? Even though I never again broached the subject, I had to free myself of feelings of shame, and it was not until high school that I was mature enough to acknowledge that I did not know my father. I decided, therefore, that I would not lie about my relationship with my father, that I had no reason to be ashamed, that I was not responsible for the choices he made. Now when people ask about my parents, I say that my mother has been a single parent all my life.

Not having a father taught me many things. First, I didn't want to repeat his actions. I would not have a child until I was ready, and under no circumstances would I abandon my child. Another lesson was that children need nurturing and guidance to prepare to make life's choices. When I reached puberty and became curious about girls, I didn't know what to do or not to do. I didn't know what a condom was until I was sixteen, well after my initial sexual experiences at age eight. The closest I ever came to getting guidance at home was when I once overheard Dee tell one of my older brothers to keep his penis in his pants. But those words mattered little when I was pressing myself against a girl. I needed information about pregnancy, contraception, and sexually transmitted diseases, and I needed it from responsible, informed people. My not-so-much-older siblings were of little help, as we all were on our own and had to learn from experience. It's a miracle that I didn't get some child pregnant.

I cannot remember a time when any of the fathers of my siblings helped Dee support or rear us. Their absence made our lives much more precarious, coming on top of the general poverty and racial caste in Columbus. For us there was only Dee. She never left us. She kept us together and provided for us as best she could. The eleven of us journeyed through the ghetto, collectively and individually, a loose but strong confederation, the older kids supervising the younger ones when Dee was working.

## BLACK COLUMBUS

The dangers of racial caste in America are real and growing worse. By the time I was born, in 1960, all of Ohio's earlier official racist policies had been repealed, but racial caste remained nevertheless: inadequate food, clothing, and shelter; substandard schools, illiteracy, and high dropout rates; few occupational opportunities, two-digit unemployment figures, and poverty wages; households headed disproportionately by single working mothers and inadequate child supervision; insufficient sex education and consequent teen parenting; poor health care, exposure to harmful chemicals and toxins, and disproportionately higher mortality rates; crime, drug-related violence, and communities under siege by police who often seem unable to distinguish between lawful citizens and criminals; and racial animus in the criminal justice system that causes many black defendants to receive punishment disproportionately greater than that for whites convicted of similar offenses. No one can endure such conditions for long without becoming angry, hardened, and bereft of hope.

Life is desperate in a black ghetto. Children's basic needs go unmet. Rather than spending time in school, in community centers, or at camp, they are in the streets hustling whatever they can, just to get by. Some see no choice but to sell themselves. As they grow older, they acquire few skills for which industry will pay them a living wage. They attend school but struggle to learn to read. For some, their greatest concern is obtaining food and/or shelter. Their role models are not teachers or ministers but drug pushers or pimps who make more money and have nicer possessions than most black people they know with lawful jobs. To some, crime seems to pay, and to many, the constant deprivation creates anger and racial hatred.

Americans living in a racial caste often think they have a better chance for success and material wealth by peddling dope or stealing. And because they don't value their own lives, they don't value others'. In such a situation, no one is safe. The advent of crack cocaine in the ghetto and the spread of gangs and guns in cities large and small have exacerbated other symptoms of racial caste. Car jackings and drive-by shootings have become regular events in many communities throughout the United States.

Sylvester Monroe's book *Brothers*, Jonathan Kozol's *Savage Inequalities*, and Alex Kotlowitz's *There Are No Children Here* describe the horrid conditions under which blacks and other minorities live, attend school, and die in places like Chicago, New York, and East St. Louis. Monroe's return to the Chicago projects where he grew up explains why racial caste is handed from generation to generation and why few blacks can escape it. Several of Monroe's childhood friends were killed before reaching adulthood. Others became "child parents" with no means of supporting a family. Kotlowitz dispels any belief that the life chances for the typical young black child are the same as those for most white children. He describes the gauntlet, the war zone that many black children must negotiate. More and more black children see their peers die and come to doubt that they will even reach age eighteen. Kozol shows that ghetto schools kill the dreams of minority and poor children who learn at an early age—from how they are treated in those schools and how they live—that they are not important.

Black Columbus, too, was a bleak world, encompassing two large ghettos on the east and north sides of the city, where racial caste reigned supreme. My family lived mostly on the east side off Fairwood Avenue, near both Livingston Avenue and Main Street, where small local businesses, grocery stores, restaurants, barber shops, and bars peppered the area for twenty blocks between Nelson Road on the east and Ohio Avenue on the west. Mount Vernon Avenue and Long Street were similar strips at the north end of my ghetto. Alongside and between those businesses were large and small churches and mosques: Apostolic, Baptist, A.M.E., C.M.E., Catholic, and Black Muslim. Behind those thoroughfares were the tenements and near-slums where most blacks resided. On a few streets, a handful of blacks had restored large old houses to their original grandeur. Most homes, however, showed the weight of time and little structural maintenance or repair.

On Fridays and Saturdays, especially at night, blacks dressed in their best polyesters, gabardines, and fake leather, their floor-length coats and stylish hats, and headed to one of those avenues. The streets came alive, with the restaurants and bars the social centers for adult entertainment.

What I remember best about those days and nights are the scores of drunken black men, whose only ambition was another bottle of Ripple or Wild Irish Rose wine, and the scantily clad women strategically placed on certain corners. The dirty, vomit-smelling men in ragged, soiled clothes, awakening along Main Street after a long night or weekend of drinking, terrified me. They appeared deranged, stammering to themselves in slurred tones, stumbling down the street, or, worse, sitting or standing in vomit, urine, or feces, their mouths and noses encrusted, their bodies emaciated and shrunken, their eyes glassy and bloodshot.

These men gathered and sat or stood in groups outside pool halls, corner stores, or abandoned buildings, passing a bottle, asking for change, or doing nothing at all. If I could avoid walking past them, I did, but there were so many that this usually was impossible. Merchants regularly chased them from in front of their businesses. The faces of these walking dead men revealed their shame, the only remaining sign of human dignity. I didn't know how they had gotten this way, but I prayed it wouldn't happen to me.

The prostitutes fascinated me. How could they do what they did, and so publicly? Why did they work for a pimp? Why didn't they have normal jobs? Why weren't they in school? Exactly how much did it cost to have sex with them? I had many questions. Usually, two or three women worked a block, strolling provocatively until a client approached. When they leaned through the car window, you got an eyeful.

Most of the prostitutes looked old, were overweight, and showed the strain of their profession. Many wore heavy makeup, colored wigs, and clothing two sizes too small. They looked rough, sagging beyond their years. But others were strikingly beautiful, with smooth, creamy brown skin, their own hair and teeth, and shapely bodies. Their clothes varied from the shortest skirts, shorts, and halter tops to fitted, revealing jumpsuits. Often you could see the outline of their nipples and high up the front and back of their thighs.

Some wore the scars of their work, wounds from pimps who beat them if they didn't turn enough tricks. All the pimps in black Columbus must have studied under the same trainer. Each was a sketch, a carbon copy, of the others, driving the biggest pink or yellow Cadillacs in the city and wearing bright, flashy clothes and jewelry, with hats that arrived before they did. Each wore a signature silk scarf tied around his neck, falling just above the opening of a nylon or silk shirt. They were black men of every hue, many with processed hair. They all strutted with a decided limp, almost as if one leg were shorter.

I was terrified of the pimps. Their reputations for ruthlessness were borne out on the faces of the prostitutes. I didn't understand how the women, especially the beautiful ones, ever got involved with them. Were they conned or terrorized? Could anyone *choose* to be a prostitute? I felt sorry for the women and detested the men who ran them.

By Sunday, Main Street, Long, and Mount Vernon Avenue were littered with beer and wine bottles and other trash from the weekend's revelry, as well as some semiconscious men. Nonetheless, by eleven o'clock, the churches were overflowing with black families giving thanks for their blessings. From my vantage point, I didn't understand exactly what blessings they meant. Dee never talked about religion and did not attend church. Whether I went, therefore, was solely up to me.

I sampled a number of churches, especially a Catholic church, and later joined a Baptist one. The Catholic church was an imposing structure, just off Main Street, within two blocks of where I worked and lived. Adjacent to the church was a playground with a basketball court, apparently intended as bait for the kids. When we played there, the white priest came out and invited us to services. Inside, the church was dark, cavernous, and ornate. Candles provided the primary lighting. High above the altar hung a large cross on which was a carving of a white-looking man, his face testimony to the anguish from the nails piercing his flesh.

The congregation was mostly white, from nearby communities just across the railroad tracks or the highway bypass to the east and south of the ghetto. I guessed that they had once lived in the old houses that blacks now occupied. The services were formal. The congregation became the choir, singing two or three hymns before reciting the Lord's Prayer. Between each event the worshipers dropped to their knees on cushioned pads to pray. The sermons never lasted more than a few minutes, and the entire ceremony was over in an hour. I liked that.

Like many of the storefront churches and businesses, housing in the area was old and blighted. There was little new construction here, except when someone added a room or screened in a porch. Some people owned houses, but most lived in rentals, duplexes, or apartment buildings, which also showed their years of wear and no repair. Some structures, long boarded up and abandoned, served as temporary quarters for the homeless, for criminal activity, and for rats the size of small cats.

In black Columbus, single mothers did the best they could to sustain their children in the face of truancy, teen pregnancy, crime, drugs, alcohol abuse, and poverty. While their mothers were away working, the children sampled everything the ghetto had to offer: Some smoked reefer, drank beer, hung out in pool halls, and had sex. Many had children before they finished high school. Others died before they had a chance at life, in gun accidents or tenement fires, or from slower deaths from drugs or alcohol. Very few people escaped black Columbus.

Recognizing the symptoms of racial caste is only the first step, however. Crucial to any understanding of ghetto life are the many factors that lock most blacks into a racial caste, even without specific laws to do this. What has kept most Columbus blacks in dilapidated neighborhoods, substandard schools, and low-wage occupations? Are these conditions random, the result of private economic choices? Or is there a direct link between Ohio's earlier commitment to racial caste and the predicament that most blacks living there face today?

History does not take place in disconnected segments, and communities don't just evolve, they are planned. People decide the topology—where things will go. They determine where the houses will be built and what kinds they will be. They plan where apartments, adult theaters, gas stations, malls, liquor stores, and chemical or industrial plants can locate. They choose where to build new schools, parks, and community centers. Much of this planning is done by zoning councils, in conjunction with school boards, city government, local developers, and banking interests. A primary factor in such decisions has historically been racial prejudice.

In Columbus, communities were segregated by design. After whites abandoned communities, blacks could move in. Technically, blacks could live anywhere they could afford. But in reality, most could afford only black Columbus. Given their education and employment opportunities, very few blacks could escape the ghetto, and those few who could were powerless when their new white neighbors hastily moved out. Black schools collected fewer funds and, therefore, offered a substandard education compared with the white schools. Some of the black schools were staffed by teachers that no one else would hire. In addition, race and gender stereotypes and customs restricted employment opportunities. Black men did the dirtiest manual labor for the least pay. A few worked in better-paying black jobs like sanitation. Black women were domestic servants for whites or were cooks in part-time, low-wage jobs. Local banks did not operate branches or make many loans in black Columbus. In their absence, alternative lending businesses flourished, charging small fortunes for standard financial services. Few supermarket chains opened stores in black Columbus, and those that did eventually closed or moved away. As a consequence, the grocery stores and other businesses that did operate there sold their wares at inflated prices, knowing their clients had few choices. Why, then, would anyone choose to live in the ghetto? The answer is that no one would.

Some decisions that disproportionately affect blacks—such as the location of a new school or library, public housing, or a waste incinerator or whether to locate a supermarket or bank branch in a particular neighborhood—might appear on the surface to be race neutral. But if one looks more closely, white privilege emerges as a significant factor in decisions by whites to place new businesses, shopping malls, and schools in white communities and to locate waste sites or prisons in or adjacent to black communities. Because few—and often no—blacks hold decision-making positions and because blacks are a numerical minority in most American cities, whites in Columbus and elsewhere have been free to arrange governmental and private policies to favor themselves and their interests. Blacks have gotten Columbus's leftovers. Fed on scraps, two large black ghettos emerged.

## RACIAL POVERTY

In Columbus, race is largely a proxy for economic status. Some blacks in the city belong to the middle class and have gone to college and perhaps graduate or professional school. A handful of black doctors and lawyers have practices, and some blacks operate small businesses, on Mount Vernon, Long, Main, or Livingston. Others include teachers and ministers. But most blacks live in one of the ghettos. It is hard to separate race and poverty in black Columbus; they have blended into racial poverty. By contrast, many whites belong to the middle or upper class, living in essentially all-white communities like Bexley, Upper Arlington, Berwick, or Westerville. Thus, if you are black, you aren't expected to be there, especially after dark, and the local police see to it that suspicious (that is, black) people are questioned.

For most of my childhood, my family required Aid for Families with Dependent Children (AFDC), or welfare. But it was not nearly enough for food, housing, and clothing. Part of the welfare money was spent immediately on food stamps. Under the food stamp program, a welfare recipient can buy an allotment of food stamp coupons for less than their face value. For example, one can buy $200 in food stamps for about $125. That may sound like a windfall, but anyone who has lived on AFDC and food stamps, especially in a large family like mine, knows that the stamps and food always run out well before the end of the month.

For the first two weeks of each month we had milk and cereal, peanut butter and jelly, and plenty of bread. For dinner we ate spaghetti, chili, or Hamburger Helper. Occasionally, we had pot roast or stew. As the month passed, we ate lots of liver and onions over rice, neck bones, or navy beans and corn bread. We also ate luncheon meat, hot dogs, and beans. Except for watermelon on the Fourth of July and oranges at Christmas, we didn't eat fruit. We rarely had balanced meals.

Balanced or not, all too soon the food ran out. Sometimes with ten or more days remaining in the month, we had no more food stamps. The menu then consisted of mayonnaise, sugar, and syrup sandwiches. Among the eleven of us, we could almost always scrape together enough change for bread. We flavored it with whatever we found. Occasionally, we drank sugar water to fill our stomachs. Once, while foraging through the cabinets, I found what I thought was a chocolate candy bar, which I hastily gulped down. But it turned out to be ExLax, a laxative, with predictable, counterproductive results.

If our school had free breakfast or lunch programs, we had at school what was, on some days, our only meals. At other times, I ate at the homes of schoolmates. But sometimes I was too ashamed to accept their parents' offer, even though my stomach ached from hunger. Ironically, few people talk about the stigma or shame of poverty. Instead, they talk about the supposed stigma or harm of remedial affirmative action that can eliminate poverty. Without AFDC, some free meals at school, and generous friends and their parents, I would have gone hungry more often and would have been even more malnourished. That was true for my siblings as well, but we rarely talked about it. Beyond anger, frustration, and hunger, an empty stomach provides little incentive for conversation.

All across the United States every day, millions of people wake up and go to bed hungry; such is life in "the richest nation in the world." Many days and nights, I sat up hoping that Dee would bring home something, anything, to eat. The voices of teachers talking about the importance of abstract educational skills were often hard to hear over the distracting growling of my stomach.

Even with welfare, there was not enough money for basic clothing or adequate shelter for my family. Dee never had money for clothing or shoes. We didn't have hand-me-downs either. I will never forget the humiliation of either having to wear my sister's shoes to school or not go. Local charities occasionally gave clothing and shoes to needy families. Charity Newsies was one of the largest aid groups in Columbus, and every couple of years, Dee took some of us to a local warehouse where Charity Newsies stocked its clothing: shirts, pants, coats, and shoes. We could pick out three outfits, a coat, and shoes. Usually the selection was limited to two or three styles, colors, and patterns. We reluctantly wore these clothes to school, knowing that some of the kids would recognize where they came from. Nevertheless, we wore those clothes until they were tattered. Even though I was always embarrassed when we went to the warehouse, I was grateful for the charity's help. As I grew older and began working, I proudly bought my own clothes.

After buying food stamps, most of the rest of the welfare check went to pay part of the rent. Rent in the ghetto is artificially inflated because so many blacks are competing for the same slum tenements and because few can afford to live elsewhere. Rich people rarely allow low-income housing in their communities, using zoning restrictions to keep out undesirable housing and people, a practice that also artificially inflates the value of their property. Zoning is another way in which the law upholds white privilege.

My family lived almost exclusively on the east side of Columbus, in older housing. We almost always lived in houses because apartments were simply too small. Occasionally, we lived in houses owned by the local housing authority. We had to move often in search of cheaper housing, in some cases when we couldn't get any more extensions from the landlord. In my twelve years of school in Columbus, we moved seven times, all within the same ghetto.

Each house that we lived in was at least fifty years old, really just a shell providing only minimal protection from the elements. Some had leaking roofs, others holes that welcomed rats and field mice. None was large enough to accommodate eleven people. We always shared rooms and sometimes beds, depending on the number living at home. I shared a room with my two younger brothers until I moved in with my oldest brother and his wife during my final year of high school.

Our large number was a test for any house, but much greater for one that was small, poorly insulated, and infested with roaches and rats. We had no money for repair, maintenance, or exterminator services. If the landlord didn't pay for them, we did without them. At night, after most of the lights were off, the roaches took over. When we switched on the lights, they scattered for cover. Sometimes, a rat or mouse scurried past in the shadows cast by the blue light of the rented television. When we saw a rat, Dee would bring home traps and place them strategically around the kitchen, some more conspicuous than others. Eventually, while checking the traps, one of us would discover a rat still struggling to escape, or after a few days, the stench confirmed a kill.

Dee never had enough money to pay our high utility bills. She regularly did mental gymnastics to determine which bill was the most urgent, nearest the disconnection stage. Telephone service was a luxury we could only occasionally afford, and our service was often restricted to local calls. After it was disconnected, the telephone company required a deposit and reconnection fee. To avoid those costs, Dee arranged for someone to give her a gift telephone package that had no additional fees. Eventually, the phone company recognized the scheme, and we went without a telephone.

Money was sometimes so short that we had no gas heat or hot water during frigid Ohio winters. At those times, racial poverty became surreal. How could there be no heat when the temperature was below zero? The only way to stay warm then was to wear layers of clothing, even in bed. I dreaded the mornings. Each time I stepped into the icy shower, I was sure I would break my neck from jumping around. In the summer a cold shower is bracing but refreshing; in the winter it leaves you trembling, almost numb. I often brooded over how little we had.

Racial poverty was the constant feature in my life in black Columbus. At an early age I was an expert on racial poverty. When I should have been learning to read, write, and play with other kids, I was hungry, cold, and learning about being black. When I should have been developing cognitive skills, I was learning that if a person is hungry enough, he or she will steal for food. Before I could read, I learned how to case a store, locate its clerk, grab something to eat, and walk out without paying.

Jequeta's, M&R's, Demler's, Lawson's, Big Bear, Kroger's, and other stores along Livingston or Main were my training ground. Occasionally, when I slipped up, clerks chased me through streets and alleys. I'm lucky no one ever shot at me. I never wanted to steal; it was not a game. But sometimes I was so hungry that I didn't know what else to do.

At times, we look to others to blame for our difficult circumstances, and I did, too. I was ashamed of my racial poverty. But I didn't blame the "white man," and since I didn't know my father, I blamed Dee. For years my relationship with my mother was strained because I blamed her for not telling me who my father was and for all that we didn't have. But Dee was not responsible for my father, and she wasn't lazy or idle. She had graduated from high school and had gone to work. But not every occupation was open to her. I didn't understand then that in Columbus and elsewhere black women could work in only certain jobs.

Undoubtedly, some readers will ask why Dee had ten children. I don't know why she did. But I do know that some states have restricted access to contraceptives and have criminalized abortion. And I do know that Dee's family did not have access to general health care. I assume she couldn't afford or didn't want to have an illegal, back-alley abortion. I also suspect she didn't realize she would have the sole responsibility for all of us. As her eighth child, I'm glad, of course, that she didn't stop at seven. Yet even if I believed that having ten children was a bad decision—a point that I'm not willing to concede—it was a decision aggravated by her educational and employment limitations: Dee did women's work for women's wages, and any number of jobs for which she might have qualified were simply closed to her. Dee was not to blame for those constraints. The costs of gender tracking and the devaluation of women's labor are enormous for families headed by single women, forcing most of them into a standard of living below the poverty line. For minority women, race and gender discrimination intersect, pushing even more families into poverty.

Those of us living in the ghetto were not destined for poverty because of inferior genetics or poor values. Rather, we were poor because we had limited opportunities as blacks and because of our circumstances. When I left the ghetto in the seventh grade, my life took a new direction. Escaping black Columbus also taught me that whites are not superior to blacks in regard to genetics or values. If you locked whites in ghetto conditions and denied them rewarding opportunities, most of them would be poor, too. Indeed, in pockets of the United States, some of the poorest citizens are white. It is the self-serving racial rhetoric of white elites in America that has kept blacks and poor whites, including many white women, divided, largely by pitting them against each other and convincing poor whites that by virtue of the color of their skin, they too are superior to blacks.

Critics often charge that welfare itself creates dependency, a peculiar claim because AFDC was started in the 1930s for the opposite reason: to ease the dependency of poor children. To qualify for it, one already had to be dependent. How, then, can welfare create dependency? Some of welfare's critics believe that the current guidelines increase the number of households headed by single women by threatening to terminate benefits if a father or adult male lives in the home. If this is the case, why not change just that part of the policy? Do these critics believe that welfare payments are so large that rational people would rather receive welfare than work? If so, then why don't more Americans choose welfare's "easy street?" Do the critics think that welfare recipients have the luxury of choosing either to work for poverty wages in dead-end jobs with no medical benefits or to receive public assistance with limited benefits? Or do they think welfare is a legitimate option because some Americans don't earn a living wage?

AFDC did not make Dee idle or dependent; she needed it for her dependent children, not herself. Dee did what so many others have done in similar circumstances: she turned to a government that claims not to permit dependent children to go without food, clothing, or shelter. Unfortunately, most of the time we were on welfare, we did not have sufficient food, clothing, and shelter.

Welfare programs currently provide only marginal subsistence for the millions of children they are supposed to aid. The first priority of welfare reform, therefore, must be to ensure that the money spent adequately feeds these children and puts clothes on their backs. In 1990, the federal government spent $14 billion on the Food Stamp Program while spending $10 billion on criminal justice. In 1996, fourteen million people (two-thirds of them children) received AFDC, for which the federal and state governments spend nearly $23 billion a year.[12] The money we invest in our children's health and educational development now is far less than what, without this investment, we would spend for additional law enforcement and prisons.

Despite the prevailing assumptions, federal spending on AFDC amounts to less than 1 percent of the national budget; yet some politicians and the media lead us to believe that once we "fix" welfare, the huge federal deficit will disappear. Unfortunately, many of the people talking about welfare seem to know very little about it and seem not to care about our most vulnerable citizens: poor children. If they really do want to reform welfare, they should talk to the real "experts": those kids going without food at the end of the month.

I now regret feeling ashamed and embarrassed about my family's racial poverty and especially rue blaming my mother for it. Only now do I understand how hard it was for her to see us live as we did. Unfortunately, we are not born with knowledge and skills to negotiate such feelings, nor are there enough accessible institutions to help poor people cope with such feelings or provide them with guidance to move out of racial poverty. Plans for welfare reform must increase the funding and accessibility of such agencies–such an agency could have helped my family a great deal. Under our extraordinary circumstances, Dee was the best mother we could have had. Although she was smart and talented, she had accumulated few material possessions to show for it. Nonetheless, she fashioned an existence for us out of almost nothing, and she never seemed consumed by despair, hers or ours. As a result, I never lost hope. She never talked about hating whites or the men who had abandoned her and her children. Although we had very little, Dee taught us to take care of what we did have, and she made it clear that she expected each of us to help the family whenever we could. I was my siblings' keeper. We all helped out, and Dee stayed and struggled with us. I don't know why she didn't leave, but it never once occurred to me that she might.

### MAN-CHILD

Being poor, hungry, and on welfare did not make me idle or dependent. I was never lazy, and I was dependent only when I was a child. Instead, racial poverty drove me to work hard to escape it. In any case, work was not optional; it was a matter of survival. I began working at age seven, running errands, doing yard work, or shoveling snow for neighbors.

My first steady employer was a white guy named Ed Rollins who ran the Bonded gas station on Livingston, one block east of my house. He paid me fifty cents to walk to the Donut Hole for hot coffee and fresh donuts. Six days a week, hundreds of people headed to the Donut Hole on their way to work to buy freshly baked glazed, stick, or cake doughnuts and coffee. The name of the store was appropriate for its size. You could hardly find a parking place, and when you entered the store, the customers were elbow to elbow—some standing, some sitting—savoring assorted delights. Ed always ordered a large hot coffee and two stick doughnuts. I walked by his station every day, hoping he would need me to make a run. In addition, if I swept the floor or took out the trash, he paid me another fifty cents. Every dollar postponed hunger.

One day when I arrived at the station, the police were there. Ed was nowhere in sight. Another white guy told me that Ed would not be working there anymore. The rumor was that he had stolen the previous day's cash and simply left. I never saw him again, and I missed him. He had been nice to me, and I secretly hoped he wasn't in jail. The station closed shortly thereafter, but I continued to find clients, expanding my coffee-and-doughnuts customer base.

When we had no food and I could not find work, I resorted to stealing. This required finding a store whose checkout counter was not next to the exit. I looked for stores with long aisles and checkout counters far enough from the exit so that if necessary, I could get a running start. My technique was always the same: first I entered the store and walked around to identify who was working and how many people were in the store. After I felt sure I could pull it off, I picked up a large package of cookies or potato chips and slowly walked toward the exit. I pretended to browse the shelves, as if I were looking for another item. As I got near the exit, I glanced at the cashier. When the clerk's attention was distracted by another customer, I slipped out the door. Once out, I ran as fast as I could to safety. Then I hurriedly ate my take.

By age nine, after we had moved twice more, I worked at Napper's House of Ribs, a local Coney Island hot-dog-and-rib joint located on Main Street, three blocks from where we lived on Franklin Avenue. Charles and Sharon Napper had converted a house into a take-out restaurant catering to black Columbus, especially on the weekends when Main Street took on a carnival-like atmosphere. My brother Duncan, who was eleven, had worked for the Nappers for a year when I started. He helped me get the job and served as my supervisor. The Nappers worshiped him almost as much as I did, treating him like the favorite son they never had.

Initially, my job was to clean up waxed-paper wrappings, soda cans, and other trash left by customers who ate their food standing in the front of the restaurant. For three days each week, I spent a couple of hours cleaning the yard. Then I began to make and serve coneys. For twenty hours of work, I made $50 cash.

On a slow day, Napper's might sell five hundred coneys. At any one time, there were five large pots of boiling water brimming with hot dogs. Behind them were another set of pots stuffed with ribs. By consensus, Charles made ribs to die for, the best on the east side. Duncan was his protégé, watching his every move. After cooking the ribs for a short time, Charles seasoned them with salt, pepper, and paprika and put them into a deep brick oven for an hour. He sold wet or dry ribs by the slab, small or large end plates, and even rib tips; usually the meat fell off the bone. When Charles wasn't there, Duncan cooked the ribs.

On Fridays and Saturdays, when black Columbus had a little more cash, there was a line at Napper's out the door until after midnight. Slabs and coneys disappeared in record numbers. We could not cook the food fast enough to keep up with the orders. One day in the frenzy to serve customers more quickly, I knocked a pot of hot dogs off the stove. They splattered everywhere, forcing Duncan and Charles to leap out of reach of the boiling water. They looked at me with frustration, told me to pick them up, and go to the kitchen. I complied—under the watchful eyes of the customers, making sure that none of these fallen hot dogs became part of their order. Charles later told me he would have to deduct the cost of those hot dogs from my pay, but he never did. Duncan was more blunt. He cussed me out. If you didn't know, you would have thought Napper's was his business. With him, there was no room for error. I never spilled anything again.

Occasionally, I had a day off from Napper's, which I looked forward to because then I could see my friends, go to a dollar movie, or maybe go downtown to Mr. Lee's, a men's store selling all the latest urban fashions. The clothes were always made from some synthetic material that never looked the same after one washing. The store advertised on the black radio station, and it seemed that every day brought a new sale. Mr. Lee's had a lay-a-way policy that made it possible to pay for a new outfit over sixty or ninety days. I bought most of my clothes that way.

I cherished my time off; indeed, my career at Napper's ended when Duncan fired me for refusing to work on my day off. He insisted that I work, but I had other plans. I was eleven, he was thirteen. He didn't think I would refuse to work; I never thought he would fire me.

Between the ages of eleven and fifteen, again after school and on the weekends, I sold candy door-to-door all over Ohio and worked at St. John's Grocery, a neighborhood store, across the street from Napper's. All together, I worked four to six days a week, three to four hours each day. With school and work, my days began early and ended late, sometimes after eleven o'clock. During the summers, I worked at least twice as many hours.

I sold candy a couple of days each week for two white guys, first Tim Lapish and then Mike Neff, through a business called A Better World. The business was "designed to take kids like me off the street and keep them out of trouble." That phrase was part of my sales pitch to each household. Tim or Mike would arrive in my neighborhood in a van about 4:30 p.m. and pick up a crew of six to ten boys. Most of my brothers also worked for Tim and Mike, as did a few other friends, like Effley Brooks and Mark Barbour, and after Napper's folded, Duncan became one of the drivers for Mike. We traveled to one of the white residential communities throughout greater Columbus. On the way, we grabbed some fast food.

Tim, Mike, or Duncan would drop us off in pairs, one on each side of a residential street. The driver then crisscrossed the neighborhood, picking up, restocking, and dropping off groups until about 8:30 p.m. when we totaled up the number of boxes sold and how much we owed. In three hours, I usually sold twenty to thirty boxes, including the one that I ate. We earned about 50 cents for each box we sold for $2 to $3. Most nights I netted $10 to $15, plus tips, which moved my total closer to $20. On Saturdays, when we worked for eight to ten hours, I could sell more than fifty boxes. I often took home $35 or $40.

On some weekends, especially during the summer, we traveled to Akron, Tiffin, Dayton, Athens, Cleveland, Portsmouth, or Cincinnati to sell candy. Those trips were my first away from Columbus. Tim or Mike would reserve a block of rooms in a motel, and we would spend two or three days working ten hours per day. At night we gathered in one of the rooms and played tonk for money or watched television. At least once a year, we had "dollar days," on which we received a dollar for each box we sold. Kids who never sold many boxes found hidden talent on those days. Some of the older kids sold incredible amounts, and with tips, a dollar day could mean nearly $100. A lot of white people bought candy from me. A Better World did make a difference.

My main job was at St. John's, where I spent three to four hours a day, three to five days each week. Margaret St. John owned the store with her husband Paul, who was dying of cancer. She employed half a dozen men to work with her from seven in the morning until midnight. Two of them were her sons, Joe and Jesse. After Duncan fired me, I went to Joe and asked if he could use more help. He asked me about school and my grades. I was only in the sixth grade, but Joe seemed impressed that I had good grades, even though I worked. Nonetheless, he was concerned that I not ignore school. I assured him that I went to school every day but that I also needed to work. I was hired two days later.

I was the youngest St. John's employee by a quarter century. Except for Mrs. St. John and her husband, everyone else had at least one other job. Joe sold insurance. Cecil Thompson worked for Battelle Memorial Institute. Skip Skidmore was a local construction subcontractor. Jesse was a drug addict and a thief, working his way toward prison.

St. John's was more than a corner liquor store, selling not only cheap beer, wine, and cigarettes but also potted meat, Spam, various luncheon meats, sliced cheese, soda, potato chips, canned goods, milk, juice, cereal, candy, and a few toiletries and cleaning supplies. Its clients were mostly poor blacks living just off Main Street, who came there rather than going to a supermarket for only a few items. Some were drunks addicted to Ripple, MD 20–20, Boones Farm, or Wild Irish Rose. Others were neighborhood kids seeking a sugar fix or a cold soda. Black Muslims—members of the Nation of Islam who had a mosque nearby—frequently bought papaya juice during their weekly fast. They dressed like business-men, were always clean shaven, and carried copies of *Mohammed Speaks*. The women were covered from head to toe, exposing nothing but their faces. A few members of the Columbus chapter of the Black Panther Party, in their black turtle-necked shirts, army fatigues, and black berets, also were in and out of the store.

My duties ranged from dusting off the shelves and the tops of old canned goods, to sweeping, mopping, and cleaning out the freezers, stocking soda, beer, and wine, slicing meat or cheese, and going to the warehouse for supplies. Within a year, I could do everything in the store, including operate the register, an old NCR machine that required you to enter the amount for each item. When others ran the register, I raced them to add the costs of each customer's groceries. My accuracy amazed everyone.

Mrs. St. John also paid me in cash. I earned $2.50 per hour, or about $60 each week. With my earnings, I bought clothes, shoes, and school supplies. I also had to help Dee pay our bills or give her money for food. At times Mrs. St. John allowed me to take advances on my pay in the form of food. Although the store's selection was limited, I designed many family meals from its stock of canned stew and canned beans, as well as bologna, bread, cheese, soda, and assorted snack foods. I worked at St. John's until the business fell off and my hours were cut. When its debts mounted, St. John's closed for good.

Between selling candy and working at St. John's, I ate sweets all the time, but I had no dental care coverage. Over time, I got bad cavities, which caused debilitating pain and awful breath. On my first trip to the dentist I had to have four teeth extracted. I also needed two root canals and several fillings. I was only fifteen. The dentist told me that if I didn't take better care of my teeth, I would lose them all.

Throughout high school, I worked at Battelle Memorial Institute in the animal research labs, cleaning and changing animal cages. I got that job not because of any special talent or test, but because Cecil, whom I had worked with at St. John's, was a supervisor there. Since Cecil was certain I could do the work, he pushed through my application and persuaded his boss, Al York, that I was a hard worker and a good student.

I worked four- to eight-hour shifts, usually with a crew of six to eight people, twenty-five hours per week, including some Saturdays. My job was to move the various lab animals, mostly rats and mice, into clean trays or cages, replenish their food and water, clean the soiled trays, and hose down the cages. We processed hundreds of trays each day through a large sanitizing washing machine. It was almost like working at a car wash, except that we wore green medical scrubs, latex gloves, and protective masks and we worked inside. Cecil, Bill French, or Al supervised the crew. All of them were black. They appeared to be the only blacks at Battelle who were supervisors. Each one seemed pleased that I was earning straight A's in school and planning to go to college, and so they allowed me to work flexible hours.

I was paid biweekly, for the first time by check. After taxes, my earnings added up to more than $140. I joined the credit union and saved as much as I could. I had more money than ever to buy clothes or school supplies. I ate better and continued to help Dee. After a year I even bought my first car, a 1966 sky blue Volkswagen, for $300 cash.

I have no memory of being idle or, for that matter, of anything resembling a childhood. I worked my way through school: elementary, junior high, and high school. I went to school because Dee made me, but I worked in order to survive. Work was far more important than school. Without the earnings from the former, I probably could not have stayed with the latter. One reason I was able to escape from the ghetto was that I worked with caring, nurturing adults who encouraged me to do well in school and who provided me with invaluable examples of hard work and discipline. They helped me believe that I could achieve high goals. Of course, the time I spent working was time away from school and homework, but I never thought I had a choice. If I didn't work, I might not eat.

## COLORED MATTERS

In the first grade, when I got into a fight at Deschler Elementary School, I began to learn that being classified as "black" mattered. Deschler was located in what then was a racially mixed, working-class community in southeast Columbus. The school was likewise mixed, with six out of ten kids being white. My first teacher, Mrs. Hufstedler, was a gentle, pleasant white woman who won awards for her achievement in teaching young children. One of my special friends at Deschler was a white girl. We played together in class and during recess. We sat near each other during story time. Her brother, a year older, did not approve of our friendship, and he told me to stay away from his sister, a request that I didn't understand. He explained that his parents did not want me around her. I asked why, and he said that because of my race, his sister and I could not be friends. I was "black," and she was "white." "But why can't we be friends?" I protested. "It's just wrong," he told me. Of course, he couldn't explain why it was wrong or what his parents thought was wrong with me. By age six, my lessons on race etiquette had begun: blacks were unfit for whites to associate with.

Neither his sister nor I understood what the problem was, so we continued to play together until her brother told me that he planned to beat me up. At school, word of impending fights spread fast. They were never private matters. Throughout that day, my black classmates reminded me that I had been challenged by a white boy. Color was important to them, too. The fight took on a life of its own, symbolizing to some of the children a contest between all whites and all blacks. But I only wanted to keep my friend and defend myself.

That day after school, he and I fought. I recall a large, racially divided, multiage crowd gathering to watch. Some of my brothers and sisters looked on, making it even more important that I not lose. Otherwise I would have to answer to them—especially Butch, who as the oldest, thought it was his prerogative and duty to teach his younger brothers how to box. He terrified me. So I won that fight, hammering my opponent with blows to the head and body, but I lost my friend. I didn't have another white friend for a long time.

I also learned from my relatives that race was significant. I never knew my mother's parents, but I spent time with some of their sisters and brothers. My great-aunts and great-uncles—especially Gertrude Woods and Faye Woods, my grandfather's sisters; Lilly Casey Gore and Frank Casey, my grandmother's sister and brother; and Gert's son, Harry Woods—shared with me pictures of and stories about my grandparents, what they were like and where they came from.

I spent the most time with Gertrude and Harry. Harry owned a modest house about a block from Deschler. Most mornings when I passed by it on the way to first grade, Gert met me with a treat, usually a baggie containing four vanilla creme cookies and a nickel for milk. Gert was about five feet tall and weighed one hundred pounds. She was already in her early sixties when I began to spend time with her. Harry had served in the segregated U.S. Army in the 1940s and worked until retirement for the Defense Construction Supply Center in Columbus.

Twice each month Harry went to the market for Gert and Faye, and I sometimes went along. Watching him was like seeing Sidney Poitier or Paul Robeson. He was organized and meticulous in everything he did. He walked with confidence and dressed with elegant assuredness. He was charming and personable and spoke with careful diction. He greeted all passersby, white and black. With a list in hand for each household, we moved from aisle to aisle in the store until we had gathered everything. We then took the groceries to Faye's apartment before returning to his house.

I also helped Gert and Harry around their house with small chores. Sometimes they wanted me to clean up after their dogs, cut the grass, or clean the basement after a party. Harry loved to entertain. Half the basement was set up for parties with oversized chairs and sofas, a television, a stereo, and a well-stocked bar. Duncan and I helped him paint it when he remodeled it. He had friends from work and the neighborhood over almost every weekend. After Harry paid me a couple of dollars for a job, Gert came right behind him and slipped me a little more. I rarely left their house with less than $5.

Another reason I loved going to their house was that I could always look forward to mouthwatering lunches or dinners. Gert was a sensational cook. She made the most tantalizing hamburgers I have ever tasted. She mixed the ground beef with chopped onions, bell peppers, egg, and a little milk. It was more like meatloaf. She cooked the hamburgers in a large cast-iron skillet, using a lid to accelerate the cooking and lock in the juices. She served them on white bread, with lettuce, tomato, cheese, and Miracle Whip. They were enormous and juicy, garnished with fresh corn chips and ice-cold Pepsi.

Dinner with them was like Thanksgiving. Each day Gert prepared supper for Harry, serving several courses: meat and vegetables, usually with freshly baked yeast rolls topped with melted butter, and a choice of beverage. Then she served pie or, best of all, peach or cherry cobbler. During a childhood of sugar water and mayo sandwiches, these meals were like ambrosia.

Some days after school I went there and waited with Gert for Harry to return from work. We would sit on their front porch and talk for hours. She wanted to know about my girlfriends and what type of woman I wanted to marry. I was only ten. She asked what I would name my kids if they were twins. When I didn't answer quickly enough, she made suggestions. We also talked about her life, especially cooking, cleaning, and doing laundry for white people around Columbus. It had been demanding work, keeping her on her feet most of the day. She rarely supplied any details about the people she worked for, only that they were white. Now Harry was taking care of her.

You could set your clock by Harry. Every weekday at 5:45 p.m., he would step off the Whittier Avenue bus. He was always on schedule. He also asked probing questions about my life plans. He told me I should become a leader like Julian Bond, then a Georgia legislator, or a lawyer. When my shoulders slouched or my diction was imprecise, he corrected me. Harry stressed excellence in everything. When I received A's in school, Harry always rewarded me with a gift. Once when I had all A's, he promised to get me whatever I wanted. The result was my first tennis racquet, a wooden Bancroft, similar to Bjorn Borg's.

Gert and Harry also taught me about the meaning of race and color. They told me all the time that being black was not an excuse for not working, for irresponsibility, for appearing dirty, for laziness, for hating whites, or for anything else. Harry told me that with hard work and planning, I could do anything I wanted. He had pictures of Martin Luther King Jr. and John and Bobby Kennedy hanging in his den. He wanted me to go to college and to become a politician or maybe a lawyer.

In these same conversations or lectures, I learned the terms *poor white trash* and *nigger.* Terms like *honky, cracker,* and *redneck* were frequently substituted for *white,* but Harry and Gert were careful to give real-life examples. Not all their white neighbors were honkies or crackers, only those who refused to speak to them after a hearty greeting or those who lived in squalid conditions and made no effort to change. The whites who came to their parties were treated like everyone else, and they had a good time. None of my relatives taught me to hate whites, but they did teach me to be careful around them because many of them discriminated against blacks. No one explained how or why.

Some of my senior relatives cautioned me to find a girlfriend who was light skinned—"not too black." Gert must have told me that a thousand times. She thought it was important that my children be light skinned, preferably with nice hair. My relatives' message was to find a girl who is nearly white—but not white. For reasons I did not understand, lighter was better. I always thought this advice was odd, especially since many of my relatives, including Gert, had dark brown complexions.

Kathe Sandler, a film director, produced an important documentary, *A Question of Color,* on intraracial color biases.[13] In it, blacks from different generations confront the numerous ways in which the intraracial discrimination against many blacks impedes healthy relationships and economic opportunities. Sandler's work reveals the complexity of white supremacy and how blacks themselves have become its agent. The ideal girl/woman is "yellow and long," that is, light skinned with long fine hair. Sandler shows how through everyday conversations and circumstances, blacks learn racist color customs from their families, friends, and the media.

Likewise, each time Gert or Aunt Lilly told me to find a light-skinned girlfriend, they were telling me that complexion mattered. It was the same lesson that early white Ohioans had taught, by limiting economic and political privileges to those most nearly white. My relatives thus were highly color conscious, not color blind. From them I learned race manners.

## CODED SCHOOLS

I started public school in 1965, a decade after the U.S. Supreme Court ruled that segregation in public schools was unconstitutional. Over the next twelve years, I attended four racially identifiable public schools: Deschler (mixed), Fairwood Elementary (black), Johnson Park Junior High (white), and East High School (black). Although during eight of those years, almost all my classmates were black, virtually all my teachers were white. In fact, except for one year at Deschler and three in junior high, most of my daily contact with white people was with my teachers.

All but a few of the teachers at Fairwood were white women. The principal was a white man. Mrs. Whaley had been teaching there forever. She appeared as old as Gert and had taught the parents of some of my classmates. She had a reputation as a strict disciplinarian and would grab any offending student by the earlobe and march him or her to the principal's office, ear in hand. Some kids stood taller than she did, but she was undaunted. She reddened the sides of many heads.

Many of the teachers, however, were unprepared to teach us. For some, teaching was a second, part-time job, and they showed no enthusiasm in their work. They had equally low expectations of their students. The typical class exercise consisted of a fill-in-the-blanks worksheet requiring little interaction or thought. At some point each day, we read from the SRA readers. Some kids read and wrote without a hitch; others pronounced each syllable of each word, sounding their way through the paragraphs. I fell between the extremes but was definitely a poor reader. I don't recall much reading instruction at school or at home. Even though I usually learned by doing, I didn't like to read, especially aloud to the class. I was afraid to mispronounce words or, worse, not to know those that should have been familiar.

At home we sometimes got the newspaper, but our house contained no books or magazines. Instead, I watched hours of television as late as I could stay up. The soaps were ending about the time I arrived home, so I watched *The Edge of Night*. Then Flippo hosted the afternoon movie, followed by the local and national news. Afterward, we watched sitcoms until the evening movie or dramas came on. Some weekends, I watched movies until dawn, my favorites being westerns. I also was a fan of *Police Story*, *The Mod Squad*, *The Fugitive*, and *Perry Mason*. Obviously, none of them helped me with school, but a steady diet of crime and punishment piqued my interest in law.

I had my first black teacher in the fourth grade. Mrs. Ellis was young, in her late twenties. She was stunning, with high cheekbones, golden brown skin, and a radiant, flawless smile. Her thick black hair fell just below her ears. I was nine and in love. I have no memories of that grade, except her.

My best teacher at Fairwood was Mrs. Whitham. What many other teachers lacked—vision and energy—she had in excess. Her charisma and enthusiasm for teaching were infectious, and she made her class feel special. She worked hard and expected us to do so. For every student, Mrs. Whitham kept a posted record of cumulative points earned on assignments. During each six-week grading period, we competed for maximum points. She also gave us prize stars for good behavior and high marks. Through that competitive environment, she taught us that hard work would be rewarded. All of us sought her approval. At the same time, we completed more work than ever. I would try anything for Mrs. Whitham because she never made me feel stupid or afraid to make a mistake. Although I was not Mrs. Whitham's best student, through her I had my first glimmer of my academic potential.

Recess was by far the best part of my elementary school day because that's when I got to play kickball, red rover, or basketball with my friends. Hundreds of kids flooded the asphalt playground. Some played tetherball or jumped rope. We occupied every inch of space, running, screaming, and colliding for thirty minutes.

Almost every day there was at least one fight during recess. Fights seemed to follow me around. I was never tall for my age group, and my weight varied with the date of the last welfare check. Even so, a number of boys and girls regularly wanted to fight me. The battles began with a shove or a punch, which sent me into a frenzy. If someone hit me, no matter how big or tough, I was willing to fight. One boy, Johnny White, and I fought all the time. We didn't need a reason. We fought on the way to and from school, often twice in one day and sometimes on the weekend. During the fury of one protracted skirmish, his lip became pinned onto a jagged edge of the chain-link fence around the playground, opening a wide gash and spraying blood everywhere. I had never seen so much blood. After that, he and I never exchanged another blow.

David Ramseyer and Doug Campbell were my closest friends. I considered David the smartest kid in the school, although Lisa Calley was probably just as smart. The two of them got all the top academic honors at Fairwood, and they also were captains on the school patrol. The Ramseyers lived a long mile from the school in a nice, single-family residential community on Bryden Road. Some days when David went home for lunch, he invited me over. His mom made sandwiches and soup before sending us back.

When my family moved from Livingston Avenue to Cole Avenue, I lived around the corner from Doug, his mother, and his two brothers, Brian and Craig. Doug's parents were divorced, but his dad sometimes came around. Their house was a large two-story brick home with a backyard big enough to play football in. Doug had his own bedroom. The living and dining rooms were spacious, and when Doug's mother was at work, half a dozen boys from the neighborhood piled into those rooms playing games, watching television, or just avoiding the summer heat. Doug and I were inseparable, and his mother treated me like her fourth son. When I was there at dinnertime, she never let me go home without eating.

Neither Doug nor I excelled at Fairwood, channeling our energy instead into sports and girls. Our first love was basketball, then football. We played basketball at all hours, often shooting baskets under the street lights. Anything I could do, Doug believed he could do better, and vice versa. We lifted weights, we wrestled, we danced, we raced, we sang, we swam—always to determine who was better. If I beat him, five minutes later there was another challenge. If he did twenty push-ups, I had to do twenty-one. If I lifted seventy-five pounds, he tried eighty. We compared everything—who was taller, who had the bigger chest, the bigger Afro, and so forth.

We were fierce competitors for girls as well. Doug lived next door to our classmate Sue Lucear. Sue had light skin, long straight hair, and cherubic cheeks. We had watched her grow up since second grade and decided she was one of the cutest girls in the world. We fell over each other trying to impress her, at least until we saw her cousin, Kelly Rhea, who visited mostly in the summer. When both Sue and Kelly were around, Doug and I were delirious. We stopped competing; it was difficult enough just to breathe. One of our rituals was to climb high into the pine tree in Doug's front yard and sing down to them all the latest love songs by Al Green, the Spinners, the Stylistics, or the Dramatics. "Spendin' my days, thinkin' about you baby." We sang off-key every word we could remember of "Let's Stay Together." Kelly and Sue humored us, probably because we were never close enough to touch them. Summers passed like weeks when I was with Doug.

He also was responsible for one of my scariest experiences. It was an unusually hot summer day, and a group of kids were at his house trying to escape the heat. We were playing an electric football game when Doug ventured off unnoticed. When he returned, he had in tow the biggest shotgun I'd ever seen. It was as big as him. He started screaming how he hated us. At first, we just ignored him, thinking he would return the gun immediately. That worked until he leveled the gun at us. Now he had our full attention. When his older brother Brian started toward him, Doug dared any of us to move. I couldn't, I was petrified. Those double barrels looked like cannons. I had heard of kids playing with guns that they thought were unloaded and accidentally shooting someone. That was regular news in black Columbus. Brian, who also was now frozen, pleaded with Doug to put the gun back. He told Doug that the gun might be loaded and that if he pulled the trigger, he might kill someone and have to go to jail. That prospect had no effect. Brian then reminded Doug that if their mother found out about the incident, she would ground him forever. That threat did register, and Doug's joke ended. He laughed heartily, but alone.

During the sixth grade, a few teachers seemed to take greater notice of me. By then, many of them had taught at least one Fair. Except for my sister Theresa, nearly nine years older than me, the Fairs were average students. But Theresa had earned straight A's since grade school and graduated with numerous academic honors at the top of her class. I looked up to her and craved the same praise she had received. That year, Fairwood instituted a new program in which sixth graders would rotate among several teachers each day. Undoubtedly, that innovation was designed to prepare us for junior high, which I was beginning to look forward to. I rotated among Mrs. Whitham, Mrs. French, and Mrs. Thompson. French and Thompson, both black, were as demanding as Mrs. Whitham, and they pushed me in every subject. Even though I worked hard at the assignments, I still had only average skills, however. Reading remained difficult for me, but I progressed through all the SRA levels with A's and B's on most projects.

## BUSING

In the spring, Mrs. Thompson told several of us about a voluntary busing plan that would enable some black children from the east side to attend selected, predominantly white, junior high schools, in our case Johnson Park. She explained that the new school might have better resources and might be more demanding academically than Franklin, the black junior high school in my neighborhood. The plan was one directional—no white kids were bused to the black schools.

Only then did it dawn on me that many of the kids that I had been in school with for five years would scatter in a couple of months. I had not considered the possibility of going anywhere but Franklin, because that's where my siblings went, before going to East High School. David told me he would attend a private school. Doug was simply ready to leave Fairwood. Here was my chance to be different, to participate in an educational experiment. I would have to leave my neighborhood and some of my friends. I wouldn't know many of my new classmates. Uncertain but impressed by Mrs. Thompson's forcefulness, I informed Dee that I would go to Johnson Park. Doug planned to attend as well. My life began to change almost immediately.

Johnson Park had a split schedule: seventh graders attended between 7:30 a.m. and 2:00 p.m. and eighth and ninth graders between 8:30 a.m. and 3:30 p.m. My mornings began at 6:00 a.m., and the school bus left at 7:00. If I missed it, I didn't have any way to travel the four miles other than on the city bus or by foot. Each morning about twenty children from the neighborhood gathered to meet the school bus. Doug and I usually hurried together to meet it.

Some kids riding the bus had not attended Fairwood. One of them, Shawn Allison, started hanging around with me and Doug. He lived with his parents and sister in a brick, two-story house about a block from the bus stop. He was an artist, had a pet alligator, and loved to sing and dance. Shawn was the first black child I had ever met with light green eyes. He looked like a cat. His nice clothes and his muscular frame made him an instant hit with the girls, which to me made him cool.

Johnson Park was a ten-year-old school located in a two-story building just off Livingston Avenue on Waverly. On three sides the school was surrounded by a residential community. On the fourth was a dead-end street about one block long that extended from the back of the school southward to the commercial establishments along Livingston. A Catholic school, Bishop Hartley, was situated across Livingston.

Roger Dumaree was the principal of Johnson Park, and he had two assistants, Mr. Orr and Mr. Bailey. All three were white. Mr. Dumaree looked like a fullback, short, stocky, and formidable, and he seemed immensely popular. Mr. Orr had the persona of a drill sergeant, so I avoided him. But Mr. Bailey was as friendly and easygoing as Mr. Rogers on television. He always had a kind word and a warm smile.

Only about 5 percent of the students at Johnson Park were black, about a third of them from my neighborhood. Our morning trip drew us together, and once at school, we stuck together as much as possible. Usually there were only a handful of blacks in each class, but between classes, during recess, and at lunch we looked for familiar faces in the white sea of new ones. The Johnson Park lunchroom reflected our closeness. An outsider would notice the blacks sitting together and the whites at other tables. But this never bothered me because I knew I was sitting with Doug, Shawn, Effley, and the other black kids because we were close friends. We never excluded white people; we simply ate with friends.

Less than a month after classes began, Doug and I missed the school bus, which meant we had to ride the city bus, which dropped us at the corner of Livingston and Waverly. When we left the bus, we had to walk a long block northward, placing us in back of the school and, as we discovered, isolated. As we walked toward the school, I noticed a group of white kids standing near the end of the road. I didn't think twice about them. We walked hurriedly in their direction, not wanting to be late for school. Neither of us anticipated a threat. They looked like kids from the school, dressed in worn jean jackets and pants. Most were boys, all with long, ungroomed hair.

Suddenly, half a dozen of the boys surrounded us, demanding our money. Startled, we denied having any and tried to walk past them. One of them shoved Doug; another cuffed me. Scared and outnumbered, we quickly surrendered our meager pocket cash, and they ambled off, triumphant but only marginally enriched. We stared at each other, shocked and still trembling, but also increasingly angry. Who the hell were they to take our money? No longer surrounded or off guard, Doug grabbed a large, thick branch, and I found a rock the size of my fist. We raced after them, especially the two who had struck us and the tall, skinny one who had demanded our money.

Now they were the ones to be surprised. Doug and I stood side by side, focused on the tallest kid, who we thought was their leader. With our crude weapons in striking position, we demanded our money back. I could barely talk and tears were forming in my eyes. My anger was rising and my heart was racing. They must have sensed our rage, because they quickly returned our money and backed away.

Word of the incident quickly spread throughout the school. Each time it was told, by us or others, it was exaggerated. Mr. Bailey asked for a conference with each of us. He was easy to talk with, asking about my family, my interests, and why I had chosen to attend Johnson Park. I didn't say much about my family, but I told him about my meeting with Mrs. Thompson. He said he was glad that I had decided to come to Johnson Park. Then he told me that he wished we had reported our mugging to him rather than going after the boys ourselves. He insisted that I should feel safe at the school and said he believed that the kids who had attacked us probably were not students at the school. He told me to take advantage of all that the school had to offer, and he invited me to visit him anytime. I felt some reassurance after talking with him, but I reminded myself to be careful.

This incident made Doug and me celebrities with many of our school-mates, white and black. People quickly learned our names and patted us on the back. We were even more popular among the children on the bus we took to school, and they wanted moment-by-moment recountings. Doug and I never told anyone how afraid and uncertain we really had been.

Being around a lot of whites my age at Johnson Park was an eye-opening experience for me. Before then, I had had no white friends since leaving Deschler. Very few whites ever came to our house, except to collect overdue rent or to turn off the gas. Attending classes with white peers, however, showed me that they were not as different as I had thought. Some seemed smart, some didn't. Some had nice clothes and things, some didn't. Some were friendly, some weren't. Any myth about racial supremacy was shattered during those three years. Like me, my white classmates struggled with school, with puberty, with distractions. Although I didn't understand why their economic status, on average, was much better, it was plain to see every day as I rode through the white neighborhoods surrounding Johnson Park.

The teachers at Johnson Park were tougher, their standards higher, than any I had had before; few of them seemed interested in creating a fun learning environment. For the first time, I had homework in several classes every day. I was expected to keep up and turn in my work on time. If it was late, the penalty was a lower grade. Because I worked after school, this happened frequently.

My French teacher was probably the hardest. He was mysterious looking—not white but not quite as dark as I was—with thick, straight, jet black hair and bushy eyebrows. He hardly ever smiled. I couldn't do anything right for him. He expected us to read and speak in French after the first day. But I had never had foreign language training; English was hard enough. My pronunciation, which never satisfied him, often left him exclaiming "Merde." I never earned better than a C in French at Johnson Park. But even though he was not my favorite teacher, I loved learning about French kings and their palaces. I read everything I could about the

French—their language was my window to a new world of elegance and beauty to which I could transport myself far away from where and how I lived.

My Ohio history class was as dull to me as French was exciting. Mr. Pack's idea of history was to teach us about famous Ohioans and their hometowns. Ohio was the birthplace of a number of American presidents, such as Grant, Harrison, Taft, and Hayes. The city of Lima had produced Thomas Edison, and Steubenville, Dean Martin. For Mr. Pack, Ohio history was a record of the lives and accomplishments of whites. Blacks were invisible, save for a brief mention of Harriet Tubman or Crispus Attucks. We learned nothing about why the cities in Ohio had become so segregated or how whites had accumulated most of the state's wealth, thus giving us the impression that both outcomes were natural or inevitable. The more questions I asked, however, the less friendly Mr. Pack became.

My lack of success in the classroom led me to other activities. Johnson Park had a variety of student clubs and sports teams. When Mr. Bailey announced the student government election, I thought about running for seventh-grade president. At Fairwood I had always taken a back seat to other kids like David, but I decided I wasn't going to do so here. When I told Doug and Shawn about my plan, they encouraged me. Mr. Bailey also thought it was a great idea. My campaign theme was simple: I'm Fair. I won easily, a success that meant a great deal to me. I was now a student leader, helping plan school events and representing my classmates to the principal and teachers. I attended PTA meetings and led recitals of the flag pledge. I also helped the eighth- and ninth-grade council plan the school dances, likely the most important student council function.

Half the boys at the school dreamed of playing on the basketball team. For more than a year, we played salt and pepper games—blacks versus whites—every day during recess and often after school. The white boys played as well as the black ones did. From the time I was six, I had played for hundreds of hours, especially with Doug, morning, noon, and night. When the basketball coach announced tryouts, a buzz engulfed the school. Anticipating his news, Doug and I had been playing even more. More than fifty kids came to the first tryout. I knew some of them from the playground and had gotten to know others in class. The coach explained that only fifteen kids would make the team.

I showed up the next day ready to dazzle them all. Doug and I even wore new Converse All Stars to mark the occasion. I made seven of ten free throws each time but was less accurate from other spots, hitting under 40 percent overall. During scrimmages, I scored on only one shot. When the coach posted the list of those making the first cut, I searched feverishly for my name. It wasn't there, and neither was Doug's. I wouldn't represent the Blue Devils. I felt cheated—surely I was one of the top fifteen players. I went to every home game that season to prove to myself that I should have been selected. That year our team won the city championship, and the coach was right: Every player was demonstrably better than I was.

After my first year at Johnson Park, my family moved from Cole Avenue to Franklin Avenue, two miles north of Livingston, just off Fairwood. The new house was owned by the Ohio Metropolitan Housing Authority. It was a two-story brick structure with a large fenced-in backyard. Off the back door, a patio extended the length of the house. There were four bedrooms upstairs and one downstairs, plus two full bathrooms. We filled all those rooms plus the basement and attic. That house was the nicest we ever lived in, but our stay there didn't last. We had no money to replace the carpet, tile, shower heads, and faucets or for sufficient cleaning supplies. So we used the spaces until they became uninhabitable, and then we moved again.

To avoid changing schools, I had to walk a mile back to the bus stop. When that didn't work out, two of my classmates who lived near Franklin asked their mothers if I could ride to school with them, which I did for the next two years. If I stayed after school, I caught the bus or walked home. I used some of my earnings from St. John's to buy an old bike, which I rode everywhere.

Another consequence of going to Johnson Park was that I spent much less time in my neighborhood. I left early each morning and often didn't return until after nine or ten o'clock. The community surrounding the school housed mostly white, middle-class families, and most of the kids at Johnson Park lived within blocks of their homes. Although their houses were not nearly as large as the ones in my neighborhood, they were much newer and manicured, nicer than any I had ever been in. When I didn't have to work, I spent time at the homes of Vaughn Thomas, Byron Kennedy, Ken Ruffin, and other new friends, many of them blacks who lived in Berwyn. This community was beginning to change color: Recently, a few middle-class blacks had moved in, and some whites were now moving out. As more blacks moved in, many whites posted for-sale signs.

On many evenings, Vaughn, Ken, Shawn, Doug, and others met at the Barnett Recreation Center, one block east of Johnson Park. When we didn't play basketball, we played various games in the multipurpose rooms. At other times, we met at one of the kids' homes for a party. We would pack in twenty or thirty kids—usually in the basement–and practice the latest dances like the Scorpio or Robot. When someone played a slow song, the boys raced to find a girl. At times I danced so close I could feel every muscle on my partner; I also could feel my own body's transformation. Those slow dances led to kissing and touching and the hope for more. It was only a matter of time.

By ninth grade, I thought I was ready. My girlfriend, Debbie Johnson, was planning her birthday party. She was fourteen going on twenty-one. She invited about twenty children, and much to my surprise, she told me she planned to "give me some" at the party. I tried not to let her see my surprise or my fear. I told Doug, and he said I should go for it. The party was on Saturday, and now it was only Wednesday. During the next couple of days, others found out about Debbie's promise and talked about it openly—almost matter of factly. The pressure on me mounted. My first thought was simply to not go; I could say I was sick. But I didn't want my friends to think I was afraid. I had to go. When Debbie learned— probably from Doug—that I was thinking about not coming, she assumed that I was rejecting her. I explained that I really did like her but didn't want to do anything to get into trouble. She assured me we would be careful.

Doug and I arrived at the party just after dark. Debbie's basement was already full, and we greeted friends while I looked for her. She was sitting on the corner of a sofa, talking with another girl. When she noticed me, she got up immediately and began walking toward me. I was trying not to tremble. Debbie had on a pair of slacks and a pullover that exposed her bare midriff. When we hugged, I could smell the fragrance of her lotion. We moved to the dance area. She looked radiant and mature as she pulled me near and whispered her plan: We would slip into the laundry room while others kept an eye out for her mother. We slow danced. My body responded. She led me away. But within seconds, as we kissed and touched, we discovered we had an audience. I had worried for three days about what I would do, and now I had an excuse! Debbie seemed relieved, too. We could rejoin our friends, heads high; we had stopped only because of our lack of privacy. Not even Doug knew how scared I was.

My three years at Johnson Park were rewarding both academically and socially. Although I had to work hard just to get average grades, my skills were much improved; nonetheless, I was still only a C+ student. Indeed, in nearly two-thirds of my classes at Johnson Park I earned C's, which frustrated me, but I always thought I could do better if I had more time for homework.

Doug had not fared even that well. He flunked the ninth grade, a setback that separated us in school for the first time since second grade. I had lost my best friend. Then, a year later, before he was to begin high school, his family moved to Alabama.

**GOING HOME**

During my last year at Johnson Park, when I was in my neighborhood, I usually could be found at Effley and Maurice Brooks's house. They lived with their mother and stepfather behind Doug's house on Fairwood Avenue. Doug had introduced me to them, and I had become friends with Eff while he was at Johnson Park. I introduced him to A Better World, and he once sold more than one hundred boxes of candy. Usually when I went to their house, Eff and Reece were reading or working some kind of mind puzzle. They were the smartest kids I had ever met. They taught me the basics of chess, and we spent hours playing board games, pool, and Ping-Pong. Eff and Reece also liked to dance, which we did as often as we could.

In black Columbus, dancing prowess got one noticed, even respected. Clubs offered prize money for the best dancers. Doug, Shawn, Eff, Reece, and I had been going to local parties and dance clubs for teens every weekend for a couple of years. By ninth grade, we had become regulars at The Right Place, a community center located six blocks from Fairwood that was transformed into a dance club each Friday. Hundreds of teens packed in there, rain or shine, to dance to all the latest R&B recordings. We dressed in nylon shirts, pressed bib overalls, and sparkle socks, with bandannas hanging in our pockets. We danced until they made us leave.

After The Right Place's popularity faded, we went to The 2001, another disco where teens from around black Columbus gathered to perfect the latest moves. We were doing line dances twenty years before anyone had heard of the electric slide. Opening at 6:00 and closing at 10:00 p.m., The 2001 looked like a dance club from the movie *Saturday Night Fever*, with two large dance floors and ample spaces for sitting and talking. We arrived early for maximum dance opportunities. The kids ranged in age from fourteen to eighteen. We always tried to meet the oldest girls, hoping to get at least one slow dance. Those dances were as close to sex as most of my friends came. It was devastating to us when The 2001 closed to kids under eighteen.

Occasionally, I went with Eff and Reece when they visited their grandmother in Plain City, Ohio, about thirty minutes from Columbus. Before then, I had never been to the country. Plain City was a white farming community on whose outskirts a few blacks had purchased several acres and built new homes. Their grandmother lived in a spacious, ranch-style home on a street with only ten houses, where everybody knew everybody else. When one family had a party, the others came. I met all the teenagers in that community in two visits.

When I finished at Johnson Park, I had the choice of attending Eastmoor, which was a high school near Johnson Park, or East, which was near where I lived and where most of my siblings had gone. As with most of the important decisions I had to make, I listened to the advice of my very close friends and any teacher who showed special interest. Many of my Johnson Park friends, including Eff, would be attending Eastmoor. Also, more Eastmoor graduates than East graduates went to college, and I wanted to go to college. On the other hand, going to Eastmoor would mean having to take more early morning buses and continuing to be away from friends in my neighborhood. Two of my brothers and Reece Brooks were seniors at East. East also had a black principal and more black teachers than Eastmoor did. And East had the best high school dances in the city.

Most of the high schools occasionally had dances, on weekends, after football or basketball games, but East sponsored dances that no black student wanted to miss. The prettiest girls in the city came, dressed to impress, in bellbottoms or miniskirts. The gymnasium overflowed with couples swinging to the latest hits from the Jackson Five, the Isley Brothers, or the Silvers. The deejay knew exactly when to play a slow set, always including the long version of "Reasons" by Earth, Wind and Fire—"Longin' to luv you, just for a night, kissin' and huggin' and holdin' you tight, please let me luv you with all my might." Bodies gyrated and blowouts wilted during those slow jams. In short, these dances were a strong incentive to attend East.

My family now lived on Fairwood Avenue, just north of Main Street, about four blocks from East. But I had decided to go to Eastmoor because more of its graduates went to college. I also had a chance to play football there. While I was waiting for Eastmoor to start, East had its new student orientation, and because I had nothing else to do, I went as well. I dressed in a new blue and white dashiki and a pair of navy gabardine slacks. When I arrived at the auditorium, it was packed with friends from Fairwood that I had not seen often during my years at Johnson Park. The biggest surprise of all was that there, seated in the front row, was Kelly Rhea. We greeted each other, and I sat down next to her. Memories flooded back about her, Sue, me, and Doug.

Ed Willis, the principal, a large, handsome black man, stepped up to the podium and started talking about growing up on welfare and how education had enabled him to improve himself. His life story sounded familiar, but I couldn't believe that he had been as poor as I was. Looking at him now, I could detect no outward signs of his past poverty. He spoke about the pride of the East High Tigers and some of its distinguished alumni. Education, Mr. Willis pointed out, was something that could never be taken away, and it was a ticket out of poverty. He exhorted us not to become dropout statistics, and then he introduced his assistants, one of whom was Mr. Bailey from Johnson Park.

Willis's talk was both frustrating and inspiring. I resented his talking about welfare, because I felt as though he were directing it right at me, and I didn't tell people I was on welfare because I was ashamed of it. Moreover, I didn't know whether his comments were intended as derisive. On the other hand, seeing him—his crisp white dress shirt, his gold cuff links, his elegant suit—I began musing that by working hard in school I might be able to become a successful person like him. I left the orientation convinced that I should attend East.

Almost immediately I noticed that East was unlike Eastmoor or Johnson Park, in more ways than its racial composition. East, one of the oldest schools in the city, was located in a large, three-story building on one of the city's busiest streets. The facilities were run down. The classrooms were dilapitated. The heating and plumbing were frequently broken and never seemed to provide heat when it was needed most. Furthermore, East had few modern amenities, for example, only two projectors for more than twelve hundred students. During my visits to some of the white high schools throughout Columbus, I was surprised to find new buildings situated on large, green campuses, with state-of-the-art equipment, some even with carpeting in the bathrooms. Conversely, the bathrooms at East were filthy, usually with several stalls out of order. It was best to avoid using them, but when you had to, you smelled them before you entered.

As had been true at Fairwood, and to some extent at Johnson Park, the teachers at East were faced with huge disparities in the students' ability, and few of the teachers knew how to handle these differences. They didn't dare teach to the top for fear of losing the bulk of the class, whereas some of the students at the bottom read way below grade level. For many of the teachers at East, therefore, the solution was to aim toward the middle, a sort of general studies approach. Accordingly, most of my classmates took general math, general science, and general English. Only a dozen or so students took physics, precalculus, or advanced foreign languages. And even those classes were not comparable to the advanced courses at many white schools.

Fortunately, a few of my teachers at East were outstanding. Mr. Brown was the best math teacher I ever had. He taught algebra in plain English, explaining each formula and each step. Mrs. Preuter taught biology, introducing me to genetics and anatomy. She announced to the class that everyone would start out with an A average and so our job was to keep it. Mr. Gutherie taught physics. Although I never mastered the subject, it wasn't for lack of effort on his part. I simply needed more math. For these teachers and a few others, teaching was an art. They created a learning oasis in the middle of an educational desert.

I will never forget when Tim Ilg, one of my best high school teachers, pulled me aside one day and told me that he thought I had a great personality but that I didn't *know* anything. Personality, he told me, no matter how strong or appealing, would only take me so far. His goal was to challenge me to become a more dedicated student. After the initial shock and hurt feelings, I realized Mr. Ilg was right. I knew little about world history, literature, science, or the arts. It was only then I realized that all the time I had spent working had cut into the time I could have been reading. Mr. Ilg gave me books to read and met with me after school to discuss them. I discovered I knew even less than I thought, but I was lucky that Mr. Ilg wanted to help me. Although I knew that I could learn, I lagged far behind some of the other kids.

Nonetheless, I accepted Mr. Ilg's challenge, enrolling in as many advanced classes as I could. I joined after-school programs, including the debate team and the In The Know team, an interschool academic competition. But I was not ready for the In The Know competition team: These students, three college-bound seniors and one sophomore, were the most widely read kids I had ever met. Aaron Estis was headed to Harvard, Stephanie Ward to Princeton, and Larry King to the Cincinnati Conservatory. They knew answers to questions that I didn't even understand. Each had areas of specialty for which they were responsible. Under Mr. Ilg's direction, our team beat the competition from predominantly white schools and won the 1976 championship. We were proud of them — East had never before advanced this far. Instead, we were known for basketball, football, and dances, not academics.

During my last two years of high school, I was on the In the Know competition team, the debate team, and the student council. When I wasn't at school or working at Battelle, I was usually at the main public library reading everything I could get my hands on. I began to read for pleasure. I read synopses of hundreds of books. Then I read the unabridged texts, loving the exciting places they led me. At night I read English and American poetry, often out loud as if I were reading to an audience. This helped me in debate and when I read aloud in class. I became obsessed with learning. For the first time in my life, it became a priority, and I wanted to excel.

My high school years flew by, and all the work paid off. I had learned to read and had improved my writing skills, earning all A's and one B. Janet Barienbrock, who taught English, should be given the most credit: She taught me more about English in nine months than I had learned in the previous eleven years. She made us diagram entire essays, identifying and labeling every word. Whatever we wrote for her, she returned with extensive comments, often more than what we had written. She tolerated no errors in grammar or spelling. After that, she required us to write research papers. I selected as my subject South Africa's apartheid regime. Mrs. Barienbrock loved it and gave me an A+.

Mrs. Barienbrock also invited recent East graduates attending Harvard, Howard, Princeton, Ohio State, and Cincinnati to speak to our class about their college experiences. She expected some of us to follow them and never treated us as if we could not learn or as if East were the end of the line. As a result, her expectations gradually became ours.

Another significant class during my senior year was P.O.D. — Problems of Democracy. It was primarily a political science, history, and geography class, but during one six-week period, every student had to show that he or she could draw up a budget for a family of three with a child on the way. Each of us earned a hypothetical net salary of $10,000, with which we had to find rental housing, purchase a car, plan and cost out balanced meals for two months, and prepare for the birth of a child. We had to use local services to obtain all our information and to prepare a report of our findings.

I found a two-bedroom house located just off Main Street and Fairwood Avenue for $200 per month. That left $7,600. A three-year-old Cutlass Supreme was available for $125 per month for forty-eight months. Insurance was another $500 per year. That left me with $5,600 for food, utilities, and miscellaneous costs. I allotted $150 per month for utilities, leaving only $3,800 for food. I spent a couple of days in supermarkets pricing foods for balanced menus; food was much more expensive than I had thought. Although I completed the budget within the given parameters, there was no money left for entertainment or emergencies. This project taught me not only about the importance of a budget but also about the education that most of my classmates at East had received. Many were about to graduate never having had a checking account and never having had any experience with financial services, and some were barely even able to complete a job application. P.O.D. was a crash course in general life skills, and after completing it, most of my classmates probably would be able to survive in black Columbus. But their educational disadvantage shackled most of them to lives at the margins of poverty.

I was lucky. The turning point came when I decided to go to Johnson Park, where the students were expected to go to college. I don't know what would have happened if I hadn't gone to Johnson Park. When I arrived at East, I was thinking about college, but I was still far behind. Everything I learned at East and the friends I made there transformed my aspirations into attainable goals. Moreover, I was so busy that I never got distracted by drugs or crime.

My closest friends were either in college or were high school students who participated in academic extracurricular activities. Tony Roseboro had been on the champion In The Know team and was president of the senior class; Jay Tatum had joined the team with me and was on the student council; Virgil Harrell was the vice president of the debate team; and Robert Blackwell was on the student council and head of the year-book staff. All of us were going to college. We rarely found ourselves apart socially. If one had a party, the others showed up. We spent hours playing Monopoly or Risk or card games or discussing world events. We never missed an East dance. And when Chuck Smith, Eff, Larry, Reece, and Aaron were home from college, we hung out with them and longed to join them.

In public school I learned more about why being black mattered. While most of my classmates at East completed a general studies curriculum, many of our counterparts at predominantly white schools took college preparatory courses. At East, only about a dozen students took advanced English, math, or science courses. Very few studied Latin or literature in a foreign language. The opposite was true at a school like Eastmoor. Such differences in course work become differences in test scores, which in turn become the rationalization for determining who is best qualified to attend college. White students, having had better educational opportunities, received offers from the best colleges and, after that, the best jobs, and so on. As long as black schools are inferior to white schools, Americans cannot claim that blacks have equal opportunities, and our racial caste system will remain in place.

In several recent Supreme Court cases, Justice Clarence Thomas complained that some people act as if all black schools are inherently inferior.[14] This is not my point. Clearly, some black schools and colleges are exceptional; even those historically black institutions that lack sufficient resources continue to play a vital role in educating African Americans. But most of them cannot match their white counterparts that consistently receive more funding. That is, these schools are not inferior because blacks attend them, they are inferior because they are overcrowded, with too few effective teachers who can teach kids who have been undereducated for most of their lives. Some schools don't have enough books for all the students; others require students to turn in their books each day. Many do not offer a college preparatory curriculum or prepare their students for standardized tests. Deficiencies like these put black students at an enormous competitive disadvantage for the rest of their lives. Justice Thomas writes as if nothing can be done in accordance with the Constitution to address the inadequacy or inequity of educational opportunity for black children. If he is correct, then equality means nothing.

Although I began to excel in school, I neither understood nor discussed many basic issues. For instance, I did not understand why most black people in Columbus were poor or why most of the middle-class and upper-class residents of Columbus were white. I did not understand why whites and blacks lived in separate communities, why black and white schools were so different, or why a few blacks could afford to own houses in white neighborhoods and send their children to private schools and colleges. My teachers rarely discussed race, white supremacy, or racial caste. When I graduated from high school, I was better prepared to accept racial caste passively than to fight it.

## EQUAL OPPORTUNITY

During my final year of high school, I visited my counselor, Mr. Webb, to discuss colleges. I was interested in four schools: Harvard, Duke, Howard, and Vanderbilt. Harvard was my first choice because, well, because it was Harvard and because Aaron had gone there two years earlier. Howard enjoyed the reputation as the best black college in the country, and each year a number of East High graduates enrolled there. I learned about Duke and Vanderbilt when college recruiters dropped by East after visiting several prestigious private schools in Columbus. When recruiters from around the country made their rounds to Columbus Academy, St. Charles, and Columbus School for Girls, a few also stopped at East. One of our counselors would then round up a few "top" students to meet them.

The Duke recruiter, David Belton, was the most impressive of all of them. Young and dynamic, he represented one of the best private universities in the country. And he looked like me! Reared in Charlotte, North Carolina, by parents who were teachers in mostly black schools, David had attended Duke's rival, the University of North Carolina at Chapel Hill, where he had been the head cheerleader. Despite his Tarheel ties, David's enthusiasm for Duke was contagious, and he also made me feel that I had much to offer the school. You could tell from talking with him that he was interested in more than increasing the numbers of blacks at Duke, that he would be a mentor and friend as well.

Mr. Webb, however, told me that I should prepare to go to one of the local schools, such as Capital University, a private university in Columbus. He didn't think I would do well at a school like Harvard or Duke. I listened politely to his defeatism, trying not to show my disdain. He didn't know how much I hated Columbus, that I wanted more than anything to leave. But he didn't live in black Columbus, so he probably had no idea how I felt. The next time I saw Mr. Webb was to tell him I was leaving Columbus, for Duke.

Like many public and private colleges throughout the country until the early 1960s, Duke did not admit blacks, no matter how smart, how athletic, how wealthy, or how well connected they were. Charles Hamilton Houston and Thurgood Marshall had convinced the Supreme Court that such practices by public schools were unconstitutional. But because it was a private school and thus not affected by the Court's decree, Duke did not abandon this practice until 1963. Since then it has sought to enroll larger numbers of black students. To do so, it has continued to take race into account, but now no applicant is excluded solely on the basis of race.

I was a special admit student at Duke, one of the new students—black as well as white—from around the country that would bring greater diversity to the class of 1982. I had had almost all A's in high school and graduated fifth in a class of more than 250 kids. I had been a member of the honor society and president of the student council and debate team, and I had received numerous awards in high school. Even so, my SAT test scores were far below Duke's median. I had not studied for the test nor been able to take any of the expensive cram courses. Instead, I just signed up and took it one Saturday morning. I scored 850, almost 300 points below the median score for Duke.

David Belton was my champion throughout the Duke admissions process. Despite my scores, he persuaded the committee to take a chance on me: affirmative action at work. But I was not admitted to Duke solely on the basis of my race, and I don't think any white student was excluded solely because of race. Duke did not have a policy that no whites could enroll; it did not engage in "reverse discrimination." Rather, it adopted a diversity admissions policy to ensure that its student body would include some blacks, as well as some whites, from diverse, sometimes underprivileged, backgrounds.

To assist students like me whom it considered at risk, Duke offered a six-week summer transitional program (STP) designed to bridge the gap between high school and college. About fifty students, both black and white, including a number of athletes, were invited to take courses in English and precalculus. This program was another part of Duke's remedial affirmative action strategy, the idea being that by bringing students like me to campus early and allowing us to sample college life, we were less likely to drop out or fail.

The director of STP was Cynthia Hale, a black graduate student in the divinity school. After classes each day, the staff planned other activities to help us adjust to campus life. We had study hall and meetings with counselors regarding study skills. Cynthia was smart and inspiring, with a warm, inviting smile. She believed in all of us and made it clear that she expected us to succeed. She never made any of us feel stigmatized or inferior. We all loved her.

About three weeks into the program, I ran out of money. I had used some of my school savings to help Dee pay a bill. But she hadn't repaid me yet, so I had to explain to Cynthia why I would be late in paying my fees. I was embarrassed, frustrated, and ready to quit. When I awoke the next morning, there was an envelope under my door containing enough money to pay my fee. Since no note was enclosed, I was never certain who had put it there.

STP was helpful in many ways. Some of us formed a support group and together explored the campus and the surrounding community. I also had a glimpse of how hard my college courses would be, but I knew that I could do the work. When STP ended, I returned to Columbus for a few days. These six weeks away from Columbus—only the third time I'd ever been out of Ohio—was the longest I had ever been away from my family and friends, and I had missed them terribly.

Many family and friends wanted to see me before I returned to Duke. In particular, one of my grandfather's sisters, Aunt Faye, asked me to drop by. At age eighty-five, she was my oldest living relative and lived in a retirement home. I had visited her many times with Harry and Gert, and at Christmastime we exchanged small gifts. She told me how proud she was that I was going off to college, the first member of my family to do so. Faye then gave me an envelope containing $200—a fortune! She had been putting it aside for me. Her sacrifice moved me deeply, and her money made an enormous difference during my first days at college. That day I promised myself that I, too, would help my nephews and nieces in some way when they entered college.

One of my East classmates, Jay Tatum, also was going to Duke. We had played pee-wee football together when I was ten. During high school we took most of the same classes and participated in similar extracurricular activities. His parents were divorced. His dad, who had been our football coach, had given us keys to his house, and we came and went at all times of the day and night. Jay's mother, who had been my swimming coach when I was eight, planned to drive us to Duke, which meant that I did not have to spend any of the money that Faye had given me on transportation. Before we left, Jay's stepfather sat me down to explain how hard it was to be successful when one is from a large poor family. He told me that by going away and staying away, I had a great opportunity to leave my past life behind and to help my family later. Much earlier, I had concluded that I had to leave Columbus in order to change my life, and now he confirmed it. Many of my friends' parents lived by the African proverb that "it takes an entire village to raise a child." I could not have escaped black Columbus without them.

I spent my last day at home packing my few belongings in an inexpensive trunk and army surplus duffle bag. The East High School English Department had presented me, as the top student in English, with a new dictionary. Tony gave me a volume of poetry. Theresa and Sheila, my oldest sisters, bought me three new outfits. Dee, who was working at a local bakery, prepared a care package of cookies and pastries. I left at daybreak.

Jay and I moved into Gilbert-Adams Hall on Duke's East Campus two days before classes began. One of the principal benefits of attending Duke was that for only the second time in my life I would be with predominantly white students, this time from throughout the United States and numerous foreign countries. Fewer than 5 percent of the students at Duke were black. I met white kids who came from some of the richest families in the United States. Although very few of the black kids seemed wealthy, many were middle class. I also met a few whites from modest backgrounds whose families worked on small farms or in factories in the South. Some of the white students had never gone to school with blacks and had never had a black friend. And some of the black students had always gone to all-black schools like East.

Duke matched groups of new students with an advanced student counselor to ease the first-year transition. Jay and I were placed in a group with four other guys, including one from England and one from Iran. Merhdad Nemazee's family had fled his country when the shah's government collapsed, and Jay and I became close friends with him. Our group met monthly for meals to talk about academic problems, but because the six of us lived in the same dorm so we saw one another almost every day. Duke was a struggle for all of us.

It was not long before I realized once again that I was not as well trained as many of my classmates. I took calculus, economics, English composition, and history. The classes were much harder than I ever imagined they could be. The pace was swift in every one. I had more homework than I could do and always felt a couple of days behind.

When I received an F on my first history paper, I was devastated. The professor's field was the French Revolution, and he seemed mean and arrogant. He called me to his office and made me read my paper to him. I don't know if he did that because I was black or because I had written such a bad paper. In any case, I was nervous, angry, and humiliated. The more he criticized my organization and writing, the angrier I became. He must have felt sorry for me because before I left his office, he softened and made a few helpful suggestions for better organization and writing. I redoubled my efforts and earned a B in that course.

My experiences in other classes were similar. Everything I had learned from Mrs. Barienbrock seemed inadequate to meet the requirements of my English composition instructor, Jeff Thomas. Because he didn't like my ideas or their presentation, I spent most of his class rewriting assignments. In calculus, L. P. Smith might as well have been speaking Russian; I was lost by the end of the first day. Even though I had earned A's in all my math courses at East and had taken precalculus during STP, neither had prepared me for calculus. Smith taught more to the blackboard than to his students. When someone asked a question, he answered by going through the same steps that had confused us initially. I got a D. My economics course was taught by a Canadian and his graduate assistant. I disagreed with most of their lectures because I didn't see the market as neutral. As far as I was concerned, supply and demand were weighted variables, influenced in part by racial discrimination. Neither Adam Smith nor John Galbraith said enough about America's history of racial bias to change my mind. So after struggling through five economics courses, I changed my major to history.

As a history major, I read about slavery and began to examine the origins of racism in the United States. I studied the Civil War, the promise of the Reconstruction laws, and the failure of Populism. I read about Jim Crow segregation and the subsequent campaign to end it in the public schools and in all public accommodations. Ray Gavins, Larry Goodwyn, and Dick Watson introduced me to the writings of Frederick Douglass, W. E. B. Du Bois, Carter G. Woodson, and John Hope Franklin. As I learned more and more about my own culture and history, I realized how much had been missing from my early education. Most of all, I gained a sense of this country's fixation with racial classifications and its long record of racial privileges for whites and color-based subordination of blacks and other minorities. The more I read, the better I understood the emergence of racial caste in the United States.

Some critics of affirmative action point to decisions by schools like Duke to admit people like me with test scores substantially below the school's standard. They allege such a mismatch is harmful to people like me, presumably meaning that my test scores preclude my competing against other students at Duke and that when students like me fail, we lose the little confidence and self-esteem with which we began.

I disagree. First, Duke gave me a great opportunity, one that did not hurt me in any way. Indeed, all the harm that I suffered came well before Duke, during my years of educational deprivation in ghetto schools that lacked rigor and were run by teachers who had no idea how to improve their students' skills. Even though I went to school every day, I was educated as if high school were the end of the line. Then Duke gave me a chance for more. I learned that its high standards were not beyond my capacity but, rather, only beyond my training.

Second, the white students at Duke displayed a wide range of achievement as well. Not all of them had high test scores, and some of them seemed no better off than me. Some had been admitted to Duke under different special admissions programs—for athletes, children of alumni, large donors, or economically disadvantaged whites. Others had been sponsored by the Methodist Church. Those using the mismatch argument should therefore include these other admits in their attack, but they don't.

Third, the mismatch idea turns history on its head and, if pursued to its logical end, would lead to an even more harmful educational caste system. That is, critics of educational affirmative action should ask why blacks and other minorities frequently lag behind whites on standardized tests. Could it be the result of past educational deprivation? Is the only possible explanation genetic inferiority? Given that most African Americans in this country are barely a generation from illiteracy—a condition in most cases imposed on them—we should be shocked when we do not see a gap.

Beyond education and a degree, Duke gave me a chance to form adult friendships with whites. At Johnson Park, few of my close friends were white. We lived in different places; interracial dating was discouraged; and I rarely spent time away from school with whites. But at Duke, blacks and whites lived in the same dorm, used the same showers, and ate their meals in the same cafeteria. We studied together, sat in class together, and socialized together. The only time I was not with mostly white students was when the Black Student Alliance had a meeting or a party.

I lived in the same room for three years, next to the resident adviser's. Every dorm had upper-division students who worked as counselors in exchange for room and board. One of them was Tom Jeffries. Tom was the son of a Methodist minister, and his mother was a local activist for autistic persons—one of Tom's brothers was a high-functioning autistic adult.

I first met Tom when he applied for the student trustee position on Duke's board of trustees. I chaired the selection committee, and he impressed me more than any other candidate. All his comments were about service—to the students, the university, and the larger Durham community. He wasn't arrogant or self-absorbed, as were many of the other applicants. Unfortunately, Tom seemed very shy, and many on the committee thought he would never be heard. Nonetheless, he was my first choice. After another student was selected, I called Tom to tell him how much I appreciated his ideas and that I hoped he would stay involved in campus life.

Within a year, he was my resident adviser and neighbor. Tom's boyish looks left many parents wondering how someone so young looking could have so much responsibility. But once he spoke, his graceful ways disarmed even the most skeptical. His door was always open, literally and metaphorically, inviting us in. At least once a month, Tom's parents dropped by for a visit and to bring him snack foods. When I met them, I saw how Tom had learned his care for others. His parents were almost like missionaries. They not only served a church but also worked to improve race relations in the state.

Tom was a diligent student, studying every day late into the night. Sometimes we worked together and talked about world issues, about the death penalty, abortion, school desegregation, and affirmative action. Tom had a keen sense of fairness and a deep concern for the poor. He wanted to become a doctor in order to provide medical services for those who could not obtain quality care, but his MCAT scores were too low for the best medical schools. Several schools advised him that he should take more science courses and then take the test again. Although Tom was disappointed, he never wavered in his goal. Before he finished this additional work, he applied to the Peace Corps and was accepted for work in Zaire. I shared his elation with some ambivalence, however, as I was not ready for one of my closest friends to graduate. During my final year, after he had gone, I missed him.

Through a few friends like Tom, I learned while at Duke that not all whites despised blacks, that some wanted to live in integrated communities, and that some abhorred racial discrimination. Tom was one of the few people that I met at Duke with whom I could talk about racial discrimination without making either of us feel guilty or under attack. At Duke, I learned that some whites were committed to racial justice, and coming from black Columbus, that was an important lesson.

During my last year at Duke, I served as a resident adviser in an all-freshmen, three-hundred-person dorm. Two of the seven RAs were black, and more than 90 percent of the students were white. Within a few days, I had students at my door complaining about their courses, especially English composition and Jeff Thomas. I spent long nights talking with these new students about self-confidence and self-esteem. Most of them were uncertain, insecure, and traumatized by bad teaching. They appreciated that I was a Thomas survivor.

When some students rushed fraternities and sororities, I saw how important those groups were to the social opportunities at Duke. Part of my job was to counsel those students who were rejected, which was hardest when one roommate was accepted and the other was not. I explained to the students why I had never pledged a fraternity, how exclusive and arbitrary many of them were, and why they shouldn't participate in such divisive groups. I encouraged them to join other clubs that were open to all, without discrimination. But my advice helped comfort only a small number of students.

None of my students failed to notice I was black. For some it meant a new experience, the first time in their lives that they had had a black person supervising them. For others it was no big deal, as they had gone to schools with a few blacks. For some of the black students, I was someone to talk to about racism at Duke. Like Tom Jeffries, I tried to keep my door open to all my students.

**THE CHARACTER OF COLOR**

My college experiences also showed me that white students "belonged" at Duke in ways that blacks did not. I don't know whether the white students at Duke were aware of the racial privileges they enjoyed there. Most of them probably never heard anyone say that they were at Duke only because of their race, had anyone ask if they were athletes or comment on how well they spoke. I suspect that few were stopped by the campus police and asked to produce identification or explain what they were doing on campus or that few were followed when they shopped in local stores. In the classroom, few white students were treated as authorities on race or spokespersons for all whites. Few had to worry that they would be rejected from social activities or clubs because of their race. Indeed, a significant privilege of whiteness is not having to think about being white.[15]

Nobody at Duke was color blind. My classmates always noted my race, as did my professors and the administrators. I noted theirs, too. The black workers at Duke served the food and manicured the grounds, and the white workers held virtually all the administrative jobs. In each job I held on campus, I was the only one or one of very few blacks working in a similar capacity. Duke had both black clubs and white clubs. I was a member of the Black Student Alliance and one of a handful of black students elected to the student government.

After intimate—though mostly clandestine—associations with white women at Duke, most made it clear to me that their parents would not approve of our relationship. The content of my character was beside the point; my color had its own character, which was not based on my integrity or my acts but, rather, on the belief that my color made me less. Just like my ancestors in Ohio, I was still not white enough.

In addition to everything else I learned at Duke, I became even more aware of how being black made me different—still American, but black. I discovered that my racial classification had given me a different history of cumulative disadvantage in obtaining social, political, and economic opportunities in the United States, based in great part on racial privileges for whites. Blacks could not live among whites, vote on the same basis as whites did, or attend elite schools as whites did. They could not play in the same public parks, swim in the same pools, or obtain service in the same public accommodations. No matter where I went or what I accomplished in the United States, I would always be black: a black Duke student, a black law student, a black lawyer, a black law professor, perhaps even a black law dean or a black university president. Being black was fine. But I learned that despite my racial and cultural pride, when many whites and even some blacks used the term *black*, it was as a negative modifier of my personhood and all my achievements. All my accomplishments stood to be diminished by the taint of my race.

I both loved Duke and hated it. I loved the educational opportunity I had there, and I made lifelong friends during those years. But I hated the feeling that some people on and off campus despised me before I even uttered a word. Some acted as though I had violated a sacred custom: I had not kept my place. I wanted so much to be American and black, and I hoped that whites would learn to celebrate my blackness and not see it as a blemish. I desperately sought signs from whites that they were committed to integration and racial equality. I hated that I saw so few.

Every African American must struggle through what Du Bois described as his or her "twoness" — "an American, a black; two souls, two thoughts, two unreconciled strivings; two warring ideals in one dark body, whose dogged strength alone keeps it from being torn asunder." [16] How can I love a country that denies me equal citizenship? How can I live among people whose wealth was derived in part from my exclusion? How can I help whites understand that I am not a problem and that my blood is not tainted? The challenge for whites is to accept that America has never had a race problem; rather, it has had a white supremacy problem. White supremacy has made color-blind relationships among Americans impossible.

## DIVERSITY AS ONE FACTOR

Ever since I realized I would not be a running back for the Dallas Cowboys, I have wanted to become a lawyer. I did not know many lawyers in Columbus, but several were active in local politics and were often in the news. Dee had a friend who was a lawyer who sometimes gave her money. Lawyers all appeared comfortable economically. Also, many of the people in Congress were lawyers, and I wanted to be a national leader. So I thought that going to law school would enable me to help others. I had grown up with *Perry Mason*, *The Fugitive*, and similar dramas about law. Books like Harper Lee's *To Kill a Mockingbird*, John Howard Griffin's *Black Like Me*, and Ann Fairbairn's *Five Smooth Stones* made me want to fight racial discrimination, and what I learned at Duke made me even more determined to study law. How, I wondered, could a nation supposedly founded on principles of freedom, equality, and fairness have our history of discrimination?

I applied to ten law schools during my final year at Duke, long shots like Stanford, Georgetown, UCLA, and Berkeley, but also to Ohio State, Washington at St. Louis, USC, Oregon, Howard, and UC Davis. All the schools had special admissions programs, and all were interested in enrolling some black students. Every application requested data about race. The process was decidedly not color blind.

My first choice was Stanford, in part because my second Duke roommate, Ken Barrett, had gone there. I had earned good grades at Duke, especially in history. My senior thesis received an honorable mention from the department; I had been student body president, served as a dormitory resident adviser, and had worked throughout college. My LSAT score was high, but not spectacularly so. Although I took the test twice and raised my score, I still fell below the median at Stanford, which rejected me. Fortunately, I was admitted to half a dozen schools, including UCLA.

I was accepted at UCLA through an affirmative action program in which 40 percent of the entering class were admitted as "diversity" students. The admissions committee examined those files looking for special factors or characteristics beyond grades and test scores, such as determination, life experience, economic or cultural disadvantage, language difficulty, community service, advanced degrees, race, gender, and disability. Many, but not all, the minority students in the UCLA law school are admitted as diversity students, and some whites are as well.

UCLA started its diversity program in response to the *Bakke* decision, in which the Supreme Court held that even though fixed racial quotas were unconstitutional, race could be one of several factors that schools could use in admissions decisions. The Court referred to the undergraduate admissions program at Harvard as an example of a constitutional program. Harvard admitted a farm boy from Idaho, a poor child from West Virginia, a Latina from East Los Angeles, and a black kid from the Chicago projects. Although it did not ignore grades and test scores, they were only two factors among many others. The Court emphasized that under the Harvard plan, every applicant was treated the same; no one— including me—was excluded solely on the basis of race. After *Bakke*, schools throughout the country instituted modified diversity programs.

The manner in which UCLA administered its diversity program created an unintended hierarchy among students, with some nondiversity admits and some diversity admits clashing over who belonged at the school. Most diversity students had a compelling personal story of hardships overcome. The more tragic the story, the more likely it was that a diversity applicant would be admitted. The admissions staff did not take time to ask nondiversity admits about their stories: if his or her scores were high enough, a nondiversity applicant's life story was irrelevant. Some white students were so insensitive as to tell minority students they didn't belong at UCLA, that they had taken the place of a better-qualified white student. Some professors and administrators pointed to the high attrition rates of some minority students or the lower bar passage rates as evidence that diversity was a bad policy.

The result was predictable: some minority students felt insecure and stigmatized. But those feelings were not created by the diversity policy; rather, they were caused by the many whites who did not support the policy, whites who really believed that diversity admits did not deserve a scarce resource like a law degree. Most of the minority students, however, bided their time, graduated, and passed the California bar examination. But many of them remember how some whites at UCLA treated them, and they don't have much goodwill for the school now.

It would have been better if UCLA had reviewed all its applications under the diversity standard that Justice Lewis Powell championed in *Bakke*, with every applicant having to demonstrate not only academic achievement and promise but also unusual human experiences and qualities. I know that some of the nondiversity students had compelling stories, too, but they were not made part of the admissions decision. Every student at UCLA should have been a diversity admit, for then there would have been no labels dividing the students; all would have been only UCLA law students.

With the 1995 vote by the University of California's board of regents to end racial considerations in admissions, UCLA's diversity program has been jeopardized. It is not surprising that the regents didn't mention the university's preferences for veterans and children of alumni or donors or influential people like the regents themselves. Why has the discussion of preferential admissions in California and elsewhere focused primarily on race? The simple answer is power. The regents' vote symbolizes the subordinate status of many racial minorities, who do not have the political or economic power to prevent their being excluded from schools they help finance through taxes. Ironically, at the same time that regents were voting to end affirmative action for students of color, some of them were making telephone calls on behalf of the children of their friends to help them be admitted.

The vote to end race as a factor in admission constituted a major setback for race relations in this country, portending a return to a time when very few minority students were enrolled at any of the University of California campuses. In fact, this decision will take California back to educational tracking, with even more minorities attending California's second- or third-tier colleges. Everyone in California knows that the public colleges of choice are the UC campuses, not the community colleges or the California State universities, the reason being that the UC campuses have the state's best educational resources. How unfair to reserve those campuses for an elite segment of California's or the nation's population.

Pete Wilson, the current governor of California and former presidential candidate, can stand before the television cameras and use words like *fairness* and *equal opportunity*, but he should know that if test scores become the only criterion for admission at a UC campus, only Asians, a smaller number of whites, and a still smaller number of Latinos and other minorities will qualify. There is nothing fair about educational caste in a country with our history of educational discrimination, and there is nothing fair about telling most blacks and other minorities they cannot attend the best public colleges in the state. If blacks, Latinos, and Native Americans cannot attend the UC schools, they will not have the same employment opportunities as those who can. They will not be able to live in decent housing, and most will remain in America's racial caste system. And that is a recipe for disaster.

I benefited tremendously from attending law school at UCLA. Up to that time, my world had been significantly bipolar—black and white. But while I was at UCLA, I met for the first time substantial numbers of Latinos, Mexicans, Asian Pacific Islanders, Japanese, Chinese, and Koreans. Race matters for other nonwhites as well. When I served as chair of the Black Law Students Association (BLSA), it sponsored programs for the law school and served as an advocacy group for black students. Other minority student groups had similar organizations. We acknowledged our different racial identities and talked about racial subordination and the law as an instrument of that subordination. We also shared food, music, religion, and other cultural traditions. Some of us tried to celebrate our diversity; we did not pretend to be color blind.

Within that diversity throughout Los Angeles, I lived first as a black student, then as a black associate at a corporate law firm, and later as one of six black members of the UCLA law faculty. At the law school and in my law practice, my colleagues did not subscribe to color-blind rhetoric. I knew that some of my professors had reputations for helping minority students succeed in school and get jobs, whereas others vehemently opposed remedial affirmative action. Some of the lawyers I worked with at my firm reached out to me and taught me how to serve clients effectively; others seemed to hold me to a higher standard of performance than they did the other new associates. For them, my mistakes only confirmed their belief that I was not competent. None of my professional colleagues was color blind.

## THE DECEPTION OF COLOR BLINDNESS

Suppose there was a national vote in the United States in which you were asked to honor the following pledge: "I shall never tolerate in my life or in the life or practices of my government the differential treatment of other human beings by race. I shall never treat any person less well than another or favor any person more than another on the basis of the person's race." [17] Would you vote for and live by such a pledge? How would it change the way you live? Are you color blind?

At first glance, a color-blind society seems ideal. Can you imagine a future in America without second-class citizenship based on race? [18] If each American adopted the color blindness pledge, they would gain much. There would be no more educational and occupational tracking by race; no more residential apartheid; no more racial gerrymandering of legislative or judicial districts; no more opposition to interracial dating, marriage, or adoption; no more funding white schools better than black schools; and no more affiliating with social clubs and churches on the basis of the other members' race. Sunday morning at eleven o'clock would cease to be the most segregated hour in America. Indeed, embracing the pledge would mean a personal and public repudiation of racial prejudice and theories of white superiority.

Yet many Americans interpret the principle underlying the color blindness pledge as prohibiting policies that advance white supremacy and black caste and also invalidating remedial policies designed to reverse the present effects of this nation's long history of racial preferences for whites. They contend that such remedial policies—whether in education, employment, voting, or elsewhere—constitute reverse discrimination and are constitutionally equivalent to prior forms of discrimination against blacks. For them, remedial affirmative action policies are illegal, immoral, racist, and antithetical to the achievement of racial equality. [19] This is twisted. So might be the pledge.

Remedial affirmative action has none of the attributes of this country's earlier whites-only policies. For blacks, more than thirty decades of preferences for whites has translated into debasement, into a status as America's perennial outsiders, historically and systemically excluded from all the means of acquiring economic and political power. Blacks thereby became a subject race in the United States, their lives defined by racial caste.

Whites, by contrast, are not a subject race in this country. The past three decades of remedial affirmative action—which has benefited not only some blacks but also many other minorities, white women, and socially or economically disadvantaged white men—have not meant the debasement of whites, nor have they made whites into outsiders in America or excluded them from all means of acquiring economic or political power. Remedial affirmative action does not promote white caste. It is not invidious discrimination. Surely, this important distinction is relevant to our assessment of its constitutionality. Our amended Constitution prohibits the establishment of racial supremacy, but it does not preclude policies designed to eliminate white supremacy or black caste.

Color blindness is a fiction that could apply only to a utopian world. But in the United States it is a trap that prevents Americans from eliminating white supremacy and racial caste. Americans live, play, work, worship, and even die in institutions that have enshrined racial caste as normal. In my schooling, I frequently learned about the accomplishments of outstanding whites, but seldom about those of outstanding blacks. At home and in my neighborhood, I experienced the cruelty of racial poverty and observed some of the manifestations of self-hate and desperation, such as widespread violence, teenage parenting, and drug trafficking, that are commonplace in poor black communities. I saw black people abused by whites and by one another and heard blacks talk about their hatred for whites. I lived by race and was aware of my color every day.

Gregory Williams, dean of the Ohio State University College of Law, writes in his book *Life on the Color-Line: The True Story of a White Boy Who Discovered He Was Black* how his racial appearance placed him in "racial limbo." Williams grew up as a white child in Virginia, attending all-white schools and living in all-white neighborhoods, only to learn at age nine that his father had been passing as white but was in fact black. When his parents divorced, Greg moved with his father and younger brother to Muncie, Indiana, where they lived in a black neighborhood and considered themselves black. Williams explains why his new racial classification so significantly changed his family. For example, many activities he had once taken for granted were no longer open to him or other blacks in Muncie. One cannot read Williams's book and still believe that Americans are color blind.

Only thirty years ago, Americans finally made state-sponsored discrimination against blacks illegal. Nonetheless, the attitudes that fostered centuries of racial discrimination have apparently withstood changes in the law. Some whites still refuse to treat blacks as full citizens, not wanting to give them the same opportunities that they have. When blacks make great strides in achievement, they cry "reverse discrimination." As far as these whites are concerned, blacks have already gotten too good a deal.

Some poor whites, with almost as few opportunities as blacks, continue to act as if blacks are responsible for their low status. They complain about modern remedial affirmative action policies that also have benefited some of them. Thus, the chorus against affirmative action is growing louder, with some whites and a few blacks charging that it is wrong or unfair. Blacks are now told by Supreme Court Justice Antonin Scalia and others that there is just one race in America[20] and so blacks should forget about being black. But that is impossible and, furthermore, assumes that blackness is the problem. It also makes whiteness and white supremacy invisible.

I reject color blindness as either a potential theory of constitutional analysis or a utopian goal because despite my best efforts to fight it, I am an agent of racism. We live in a country pervaded with racism. Some of my friends and colleagues tell me they are not racists and they don't believe that I am a racist. However, it is a mistake to use that label only for overt bigots who espouse the doctrine of white supremacy. One need not wear a Klan robe to be a racist.

Racism has been defined as "a conscious or unconscious attitude, action, or institutional structure which subordinates a person or group because of his, her, or their color."[21] We don't seem to apply that definition anymore. I am an agent of racism, a racist, because I live in a society whose fundamental values, actions, and institutions reflect an indifference to racial caste. Racism is so pervasive that all Americans have become its agents.

The myth of color blindness, however, permits many Americans to pretend that they are not agents of racism, to ignore or treat as normal all the symptoms of racial caste that they encounter each day. Racism—both overt and subtle—and institutional subordination remain entrenched in the United States. Blacks and other racial minorities still are treated as inferiors, are given inferior jobs and legal rights, are compelled to accept inferior schooling, are forced to live in inferior housing and neighborhoods, are made to use inferior public facilities, and are constantly told that they are inferior human beings and have only limited chances to be otherwise.[22]

Racial caste is a product of past deliberate racial choices. The conditions in the lives of blacks today were derived from slavery and official and customary segregation. Where blacks live, their aggregate income, their self-image and degree of self-confidence, the nature and stability of their families, their attitudes toward authority, and their levels of educational and cultural attainment have been significantly affected by their historical treatment in the United States. A racial caste continues to exist because of our failure to eradicate it. Americans are agents of racism, then, because their country has been racist since its colonial beginnings. Americans' collective historical experience is littered with racist images, practices, and institutional structures that place whites over blacks. Americans were not created equal; at best they only pretend to aspire to nominal equality.

For most of my adult life, I have tried to understand racism in the United States and to identify ways to eliminate it. Charles Lawrence was correct when he wrote

> Racism in America is much more complex than either the conscious conspiracy of a power elite or the simple delusion of a few ignorant bigots. It is a part of our common historical experience and, therefore, a part of our culture. It arises from the assumptions we have learned to make about the world, ourselves, and others as well as from the patterns of our fundamental social activities.[23]

Racism has a universality that extends to everyone who lives in the United States. Just because someone doesn't want to be a racist doesn't mean that person automatically is not. We may no longer say *nigger* or *whitey,* but many Americans still judge others, if only to themselves, solely on the basis of their skin color. Thus, to assert that I am an agent of racism, a racist without self-recrimination, is an essential step toward identifying the ways in which my attitudes, conduct, and institutional memberships promote racial caste. The color blindness model undermines the identification of the racial caste's infrastructure.

Many Americans have tried to eliminate overt racism from their lives, by avoiding any conduct that they deem overtly racist. As a result, many become indignant at the claim that they are racists. However, when we examine more closely the most routine affairs of Americans, we see that racial subordination and overt racism still abound. We bank with institutions that actively discriminate against blacks. We shop at stores that hire virtually no blacks. We send our children to schools that we know are better than those available to most blacks and other racial minorities. Fighting racial subordination requires us to identify it and to protest it in all its manifestations. But the doctrine of color blindness hinders such an attack.

Occasionally I meet Americans who suggest that they do not think of me as black. To them, I want to shout, "Why?! Why don't you see me as black?! I am. I always will be. I want to be black. So, see me as I am!" In the United States, race is almost always an issue between blacks and whites—if not between the individuals themselves, then between them and their families or their peers. Reactions of family and friends are often especially problematic when an intimate, interracial relationship develops. To prove my hypothesis, I ask them how they would respond if their son or daughter chose to marry a person from a different racial group. Usually, after some statement about how hard it is for the offspring of such relationships, they concede my point.

My racial identity is an important link to Dee, her parents, and so on back into history. The color blindness myth permits us to continue to ignore contributions of African Americans, blacks, Negroes, coloreds, and Africans to the creation of the United States' wealth; the myth is antithetical to eliminating racial caste.

If my narrative can be generalized—as I believe it can be—the color blindness myth is harmful, as it permits Americans to continue to live as if they were in a fairy tale. It allows us to act as if our history never happened. It absolves us of any responsibility for racial caste, and it permits us to pretend that modern remedial affirmative action is the same as past policies promoting white supremacy.

I, for one, cannot live those fairy tales. I am not and do not wish to be color blind. No one in America is. To the contrary, Americans from birth to death are intensely color conscious, and we all are implicated in the persistence of racial caste.

This book is intended to promote racial understanding, to describe how we have come to such a horrible racial predicament in America, and to suggest how we can move beyond it. As I will explain, blacks have not chosen to be America's underclass; instead, they have been assigned that place, with little power to do much about it. Indeed, because blacks are a numerical minority in America, they have had to depend on the goodwill of whites to halt the most egregious racial discrimination against them. White goodwill toward blacks has been limited and episodic, and the lack of goodwill explains why racial discrimination and caste appear so intractable.

# PART TWO

## WHITE PRIVILEGE AND BLACK DESPAIR: THE ORIGINS OF RACIAL CASTE IN AMERICA

Justice Oliver Wendell Holmes's aphorism that "a page of history is worth a volume of logic"[1] has particular relevance to an examination of racial caste in the United States. American history provides a variety of reasons for repudiating tales of equality, myths about a color-blind tradition, and charges that remedial affirmative action is unfair. Many persons in the United States have convinced themselves that it has been the most just, equal nation in history, that all men are created equal, that everyone has the same opportunities to achieve success, and that those who fail are inferior. But if we actually hold up American history to the country's supposed ideals, we will see that they are true for only a small segment of the population. America has simply not been America for everybody.

Since the seventeenth century, racial preferences favoring whites, especially males, served as virtual tenets of American law, relegating most people of color and most white women to an underclass. The image of the self-made, individualistic American is in fact a mask hiding America's true record of race, gender, and class privilege and concealing the struggle of racial minorities, white women, and even poor white men, to gain equality.

When the mask is removed, however, we can see in America's unadulterated history how in the absence of federal antidiscrimination laws, some whites made their whiteness a basis for privilege and blackness a badge of infamy. After the Civil War and again in the 1960s, new constitutional amendments and the accompanying federal statutes were intended to undo white privilege and black caste. Today, as Americans reevaluate the meaning of those laws, they must do so contextually; otherwise, America's past will be its future.

To begin this discussion of white privilege, I shall briefly review the racial attitudes of whites toward blacks that made possible the codification of slavery. The records of our Constitutional Convention in 1787 reveal that under America's new Constitution, whiteness meant privilege. Later, such events as the *Dred Scott* decision confirmed that persons of African ancestry were not citizens according to the Constitution. The effect of that case was extended when the Court declared that separate was equal, leading us up to the 1960s and America's second civil war and reconstruction.

## THE DECLARATION OF INFERIORITY

Americans rarely talk candidly about their racial attitudes. In fact, whiteness is almost never examined and evaluated in the way that blackness has been. A person from another planet who read America's papers, watched its television programs, or attended its schools might well believe that Americans were color blind. But at the end of nearly three and a half centuries of existence, America cannot suddenly declare itself to be what it has never committed to being.

Nearly two centuries before Thomas Jefferson wrote that all men are created equal, his English predecessors claimed their superiority over people of color in the New World. They made Native Americans, Mexicans, mulattoes, and blacks into outsiders, colonies within colonies. Thus, when the white colonials adopted traditional English legal and cultural standards, they embraced white supremacy, among other inequities.

Black slavery in colonial America was a declaration of war against all persons who appeared to be black. It was the ultimate assertion of white supremacy and black debasement. For the slaves, it was not relevant that the Englishmen who came to America had the Greeks and Romans or the Spanish and Portuguese as models for their form of human enslavement. What was important was that they believed in white superiority and black inferiority. Such ideas were prevalent in English literature,

travel journals and diaries, and other writing even before whites established black slavery.

In his landmark work on racial attitudes of white Englishmen toward
blacks, Winthrop Jordan wrote:

> In England perhaps more than in southern Europe, the concept of black-
> ness was loaded with intense meaning. Long before they found that some
> men were black, Englishmen found in the idea of blackness a way of
> expressing some of their most ingrained values. No other color except
> white conveyed so much emotional impact. As described in the *Oxford
> English Dictionary*, the meaning of *black* before the sixteenth century in-
> cluded, "Deeply stained with dirt; soiled, dirty, foul. . . . Having dark or
> deadly purposes, malignant; pertaining to or involving death, deadly; bane-
> ful, disastrous, sinister. . . . Foul, iniquitous, atrocious, horrible, wicked. . . .
> Indicating disgrace, censure, liability to punishment, etc." Black was an
> emotionally partisan color, the handmaid and symbol of baseness and evil,
> a sign of danger and repulsion.
>
> Embedded in the concept of blackness was its direct opposite—white-
> ness. No other colors so clearly implied opposition, "beinge coloures ut-
> terlye contrary"; no others were so frequently used to denote polarization:
>
> > *Everye white will have its blacke,*
> > *And everye sweete its sowre.*
>
> White and black meant purity and filthiness, virginity and sin, virtue and
> baseness, beauty and ugliness, beneficence and evil, God and the devil.[2]

Englishmen reacted with distaste and repulsion to the color and other
physical characteristics of blacks in Africa. Some Englishmen tried to
explain the cause of blackness. Was it a biblical curse? Was it permanent?
Did blacks evolve from a different species than whites? Blackness was
perplexing, especially to those who believed in one God, and blacks in
Africa seemed especially strange because they had a different religious
tradition; they were not Christians, which made them heathens or savages
to many of their white observers and captors. Whites described blacks as
uncivilized and savage-like, and they compared them, physically and
sexually, with "libidinous" African apes. Nearly a century before the
American Declaration of Independence, the terms *Negro* and *slave* were
used interchangeably and, likewise, *Christian, English, white*, and *free* were
synonymous.[3]

Long before *coon, boy, tom*, or *nigger* became common perjorative labels
in the United States, public images of blacks consisted of vulgar caricatures: swollen, protruding lips, unkempt hair, bulging eyes, and a disposi-

tion that was alternately happy, docile, lazy, stupid, childlike, uncivilized, violent, and oversexed, the last attribute particularly in respect to white women. Such labels help explain why America's color line has continued to prevail. Why not integrate schools? Why not permit interracial marriages? Why not live in integrated neighborhoods? Why not let blacks vote or enjoy public accommodations on the same basis as whites did? The most obvious answer: the black image in the contemporary white mind.[4] Through the popular culture, whites in America created Sambo, Aunt Jemima, pickaninny, and Uncle Tom—brute caricatures of blacks in song, dance, film, and literature.[5] Commentators who claim that remedial affirmative action causes stigma don't stop to think how long blackness itself has been a basis for stigma and exclusion.

Racial attitudes translate into actions and laws, the legacies of which are responsible for the current racial crisis in the United States. Many whites acted in accordance with their racial attitudes to exclude blacks from white schools in Massachusetts and from graduate and professional schools in Alabama, Texas, Missouri, Oklahoma, Florida, and elsewhere, and to keep black families out of white neighborhoods in Michigan, Missouri, and elsewhere. In addition, to prevent blacks from voting in Texas, South Carolina, and Mississippi, among other states, whites used so-called white primaries, elections in which only whites could vote, and they limited some jobs, such as those of police officer and firefighter, bus driver, and conductor, to whites only. It is this venal combination of racist attitudes and actions that has poisoned America's soul.

Writing in 1960, Justice William O. Douglas summarized one state's actions:

> Louisiana requires that all circuses, shows, and tent exhibitions to which the public is invited have one entrance for Whites and one for Negroes. No dancing, social functions, entertainment, athletic training, games, sports, contests "and other such activities involving personal and social contacts" may be open to both races. Any public entertainment or athletic contest must provide separate seating arrangements and separate sanitary drinking water and any other facilities for the two races. Marriage between the two races is banned. Segregation by race is required in prisons. The blind must be segregated. Teachers in public schools are barred from advocating desegregation of the races in the public school system. So are other state employees. Segregation on trains is required. Common carriers of passengers must provide separate waiting rooms and reception room facilities for the two races and separate toilets and separate facilities for drinking water as well. Employers must provide separate sanitary facilities for the two

races. Employers must also provide eating places in separate rooms and separate eating and drinking utensils for members of the two races. Persons of one race may not establish their residence in a community of another race without approval of the majority of the other race. Court dockets must reveal the race of the parties in divorce actions. All public parks, recreation centers, playgrounds, community centers and "other such facilities at which swimming, dancing, golfing, skating or other recreational activities are conducted" must be segregated.[6]

As we approach the end of the millennium, many whites deny both America's record of white privilege and that their routine actions are influenced by stereotypes of blacks, rooted in the past, that cause them to avoid blacks whenever possible. But the evidence is compelling. Such stereotypes explain why, for example, when a certain number of black families move into all-white communities, many whites immediately move away. Some insist that they move for economic reasons, not racial ones. But, then, why is it that when blacks move into a neighborhood the housing prices fall? This phenomenon only reinforces residential segregation and racial caste, and it continues despite federal laws prohibiting racial discrimination in housing.

It is unclear whether white Americans truly believe that blacks are different or whether they only pretend to believe this in order to rationalize their treatment and avoidance of blacks. Whichever the case, the beliefs and actions of many whites invariably translate into widespread discrimination against blacks—against me.

## MARGINAL AMERICANS

American history texts have traditionally treated the early status of blacks and the establishment of slavery as historical asides. Such books rush through the British colonies and the new settlements at Roanoke, Jamestown, or Plymouth, describing the early white settlers, their hardships, and their perilous encounters with the Native Americans. They rarely describe the new settlements as imperialistic land grabs. The reader is never told that the American Indians were legitimate landowners with concomitant legal rights. Rather, they are portrayed as "tawny heathens or savages," obstacles to English progress and profit.

These texts similarly give short shrift to the treatment of blacks. Few note the centrality of slavery to the economic emergence of colonial America or the relationship between the attitudes that fostered the development of black slavery and contemporary racial caste. Because Americans misunderstand the history and persistence of white supremacist beliefs, as well as America's history of white privilege, many also do not understand the historical legitimacy of remedial affirmative action.

Perhaps the most popular text of its time was Ulrich B. Phillips's *American Negro Slavery*, published in 1918, which portrayed blacks as "lusty, cheerful and submissive." Although some of Phillips's "darkies" were intelligent and esteemed for domestic service, they were not destined for hard work. Others were gentle but prone to theft. Still others were rebels, known for running away, instigating insurrections, or committing suicide. Phillips presented such disparaging traits as regionally fixed, depending on where in Africa the slave had been captured. To Phillips, Africa was primitive, and the slave trade left its victims "quite possibly better off on the American plantations than the slave captors who remained in the African jungle."[7]

The most obvious weakness of Phillips's book was his inability to analyze slavery from the economic or political perspective of the slave. Rather, he wrote as if blacks were voiceless objects, without will or ambition, desire or ability, to "self-make it" in America. He ignored the fact that slavery, Jim Crow segregation codes, and de facto segregation practices were, in effect, affirmative action for whites. Likewise, he was indifferent to how white privilege caused black caste. Indeed, it was this longstanding racial favoritism that eventually forced the federal government to adopt antidiscrimination laws. For these reasons, a book about contemporary remedial affirmative action must begin with slavery in colonial America, not with the policies initiated during the last few decades.

A historian like Phillips—who refers to blacks as "darkies"—is obviously unlikely to describe slavery as a system of white racial privilege. Fortunately, however, in this century we have reassessed the supposed "nature" of blacks. John Hope Franklin's *From Slavery to Freedom*[8] is the modern standard for readers seeking a comprehensive examination of the black experience in the United States. Franklin's triumphs are his treatment of blacks as complex human beings rather than mere objects and his portrayal of whites as conflicted, alternately revealing and concealing their racial hostility toward blacks. But Franklin does not ignore the efforts of some whites to repudiate white supremacy. Only through such nuanced understandings can we begin to discern the connection between America's history of white privilege and its current black caste.

Some critics of remedial affirmative action might accuse me of "running the slavery argument into the ground" for bringing it up in this context. Others might argue that slavery is too remote from and thus irrelevant to our current racial situation. But they are deluded by the belief that when slavery ended, whites stopped discriminating against blacks. Too many white Americans accept a romantic recounting of our history that goes something like the following:

> Early in our history there was slavery, which was a terrible thing. Blacks were brought to this country from Africa in chains and made to work in the fields. Some were viciously mistreated, which was, of course, an unforgivable wrong; others were treated kindly. Slavery ended with the Civil War, although many blacks remained poor, uneducated, and outside the cultural mainstream. As the country's racial sensitivity to blacks' plight increased, the vestiges of slavery were gradually eliminated by federal statutes and case law. Today, blacks have many civil rights and are protected from discrimination in such areas as housing, public education, employment, and voting. The gap between blacks and whites is steadily closing, although it may take some time for it to close completely. At the same time, it is important not to go too far in providing special benefits for blacks. Doing so induces dependency and a welfare mentality. It can also cause a backlash among innocent white victims of reverse discrimination. Most Americans are fair-minded individuals who harbor little racial prejudice. The few who do can be punished when they act on those beliefs.[9]

This tale, or metanarrative, is extremely harmful, in part because it offers false solace to Americans who don't know history and also because its interpretation of history is inaccurate. This version of the events overlooks America's centuries-old practice of race-conscious privilege for whites and simultaneous color-based subordination of blacks. It states that blacks are no longer victims of widespread discrimination, that their lives in racial caste are the product of past practices for which no one— especially no one living—is responsible, that most whites do not now practice racial discrimination, and that over time, the few remaining racists will be isolated and ostracized and racism will be eliminated. Finally, the story implies that Americans have already done what they can and should do about racial caste, and it assumes that to act affirmatively against racial discrimination with remedial policies is "reverse discrimination," which will provoke a dangerous white backlash. Blacks thus are counseled to wait for equality. As recent retreats in civil rights make clear, "wait" means "never."[10]

Our slave legacy is highly relevant to our assessment of remedial affirmative action. To assert the contrary is akin to asserting that free wage labor is irrelevant to an analysis of how certain early Americans accumulated wealth. Slaves accumulated nothing, being property with no rights to property. Slavery made all blacks—whether classified as slave, mulatto, or "free"—the subjects of whites, no matter what their economic status. By law or custom, the poorest white was superior to any black. Furthermore, the policies that replaced formal slavery continued to reinforce blacks' caste position.

## INVENTING AMERICAN SLAVERY

The racial history of blacks and whites in what is now the United States includes so many shocking episodes that it is little wonder that some historians have tried to gloss over it. It is beyond the scope of this book to describe the capture of each slave, the conditions on the slave ships, the breakup of slave families, slave life on the plantations, slave rebellions, or the emergence of domestic slave breeding. That has already been done. However, a look at Virginia, the home of George Washington and Thomas Jefferson, reveals how white privilege and black caste were established during the colonial period. To be sure, there were many variations, depending on the region[11] as well as the number of slaves, mulattoes, or free blacks in the area compared with that of whites: Virginia "pioneered a legal process that assured blacks a uniquely degraded status—one in which cruelties of slavery and pervasive racial injustice were guaranteed by its law. Just as [other colonies] emulated other aspects of Virginia's policies, many colonies would also follow Virginia's leadership in slavery law."[12] For our purposes, the Virginia experience provides an ample illustration of the emergence of "the peculiar institution" of slavery and what was, in essence, the most extreme form imaginable of affirmative action for whites.[13]

In 1619, John Rolfe (of Pocohantas fame), the secretary and recorder of Virginia, wrote that "there came to Virginia a Dutchman of Warre that sold us twenty Negers."[14] It is unclear whether those first twenty blacks were slaves or indentured servants, but most historians agree that their status was that of indentured servants.[15] The first African Americans "were listed as servants in the census counts of 1623 and 1624, and as late as 1651 some blacks whose period of service had expired were being assigned land in much the same way that it was being assigned to whites who had completed their indenture."[16]

More important, if these first blacks were not slaves, then for at least a brief period during the seventeenth century, a less hegemonic, less cruel relationship was possible among blacks and whites.[17] And if blacks initially were indentured servants, then slavery was not inevitable "but rather a deliberate choice (among many alternatives) made by [white] men who sought greater returns than they could obtain from their own labor alone, and who found other types of labor more expensive."[18]

Slavery was, in sum, a means for many whites in the business of tobacco, sugar, rice, cotton, tar, or shipping to get rich. Black slaves were the ultimate form of cheap labor. Because of their color and language, blacks could not easily escape. If one looked to Africa or the Caribbean, their supply seemed inexhaustible, and whites already believed that blacks were inferior.[19]

Even before Virginia adopted its first slave statutes, judicial decisions, similar to those in Ohio, resolved the rights and liabilities of blacks in relation to whites. The cases show the variety of issues that arose from the practice of slavery in America, including the legal significance of mixed blood; the impact of Christian baptism on a person's status; litigation in regard to the domestic slave trade, or the movement of slaves or free blacks from one state to Virginia; the regulation of marital relationships between slaves owned by different masters, or voluntary or involuntary sexual relations between slaves and whites; the procedures for freeing slaves, as well as the sale, price, and marketing of slaves; how whites disposed of their slaves through their wills; cases concerning rebel slaves; and those charged with crimes and their punishment.[20]

Early judicial opinions from Virginia observed the following hierarchy in cases adjudicating the rights of American Indians, poor whites, and blacks. It shows that slavery had already assigned most blacks to the bottom of the working class, a position that few have escaped even today:

White indentured servants
White servants without indentures
Christian black servants
Indian servants
Mulatto servants
Indian slaves
Black slaves[21]

One of the earliest judicial decisions in Virginia to refer to blacks was *Re Davis* (1630). The case report reads: "Hugh Davis to be soundly whipt before an assembly of Negroes & others for abusing himself to the dishonor of God and shame of Christianity by defiling his body in lying with a Negro, which fault he is to actk. next Sabbath day." [22] Presumably, Davis was white, since he was charged with having sex with a black woman. Assuming that fact, the report rests on a perception of white supremacy and black inferiority grounded in religion. Notice that the same attitudes served as the basis for many states' ban on interracial marriages until the late 1960s. [23]

This theory of racial supremacy is even more apparent in other cases. For example, in *Re Sweat* (1640), Sweat was charged with impregnating a Negro woman servant belonging to a third party. The court ruled that "the said Negro woman shall be whipt at the whipping post and the said Sweat shall tomorrow in the forenoon do public penance for his offense at James city church in the time of devine service according to the laws of England in that the case provided." [24] Note not only the public shaming required of Sweat but also the differential punishment. That is, assuming that Sweat was white, his punishment appears much less severe than that of the black woman.

This difference between the punishment of blacks and whites for similar offenses became commonplace, and it remains a hotly contested issue today, especially in the comparative sentencing disparities in drug trafficking and capital murder cases. In drug cases there are at least two concerns moving through the courts: whether prosecutors disproportionately prosecute blacks for possession of crack and whether the sentencing disparities between crack and other forms of cocaine are a legally sanctioned form of racial discrimination. The preliminary data show that 88 percent of the federal crack defendants are black and that in 1995, the United States Sentencing Commission recommended the elimination of harsher sentences for the possession of crack versus powder cocaine. The president and Congress, however, rejected the recommendation. [25]

Justice William Brennan squarely addressed racial disparities in *McCleskey v. Kemp.* Warren McCleskey, a black man, was convicted of killing a white police officer during a robbery. The jury recommended that McCleskey be sentenced to death, the trial court agreed, and the Supreme Court of Georgia affirmed. [26] Ultimately, McCleskey filed a petition for a writ of habeas corpus in federal court, claiming that Georgia's death-sentencing process was administered in a racially discriminatory manner in violation of the Eighth and Fourteenth Amendments. In support of his claims, McCleskey presented a statistical study of more than two thousand murder cases from Georgia during the 1970s, indicating that defendants charged with killing white persons received the death penalty in 11 percent of the cases but that defendants charged with killing black persons received the death penalty in only 1 percent of the cases.[27]

This study found that the death penalty was assessed in 22 percent of the cases involving black defendants and white victims, 8 percent of the cases involving white defendants and white victims, 3 percent of the cases involving white defendants and black victims, and only 1 percent of the cases involving black defendants and black victims. Similarly, prosecutors sought the death penalty in 70 percent of the cases involving black defendants and white victims, 32 percent of those involving white defendants and white victims, 19 percent of the cases involving white defendants and black victims, and only 15 percent of the cases involving black defendants and black victims.[28] The lower federal courts rejected McCleskey's petition, and the U.S. Supreme Court affirmed by a vote of five to four.

In regard to McCleskey's Fourteenth Amendment challenge, the Court wrote that a defendant has the burden of proving the existence of purposeful discrimination and that it had a discriminatory effect in McCleskey's case. The Court found that by relying on the study, McCleskey offered no evidence specific to his own case that would support an inference that racial considerations played a part in his sentence. The Court thus concluded that "because discretion is essential to the criminal justice process, we would demand exceptionally clear proof before we would infer that the discretion has been abused." To prove discriminatory purpose, the Court wrote, McCleskey would have to demonstrate that agents of the state had followed a course of action in his case "because of, not merely in spite of, its adverse effects upon an identifiable group." Moreover, the Court concluded that the study did not demonstrate a constitutionally significant risk that racial bias would affect Georgia's capital sentencing process. Finally, the Court declared that it was beyond its province to determine the appropriate punishment for particular crimes and thus McCleskey's claims and statistical studies should have been presented to legislative bodies.[29]

The four dissenting justices accepted the study's validity and stated that it proved that Georgia's death-sentencing process created an intolerable risk that McCleskey's sentence would be influenced by impermissible racial considerations. Justice Brennan recalled that Georgia and other states had had dual systems of criminal justice as far back as the colonial period, which differentiated between crimes by and against whites and blacks, and also the Georgia Penal Code, which contained separate sections for slaves and free persons of color and all other persons. So, for example, the rape of a free white female by a black was punishable by death, but the rape of a white female by anyone else was punishable by a prison term of two to twenty years. The rape of blacks was punishable by a fine or imprisonment at the discretion of the Court. Justice Brennan concluded that Georgia's history of racially biased criminal justice and its continuing legacy buttressed the probative value of the Baldus study and McCleskey's constitutional claims:

> Considering the race of a defendant or victim in deciding if the death penalty should be imposed is completely at odds with this concern that an individual be evaluated as a unique human being. Decisions influenced by race rest in part on a categorical assessment of the worth of human beings according to color, insensitive to whatever qualities the individuals in question may possess. *Enhanced willingness to impose the death sentence on black defendants, or diminished willingness to render such a sentence when blacks are victims, reflects a devaluation of the lives of black persons.*[30]

Brennan rightly revealed that the American criminal justice system has long been infected with racial animus against blacks.

To assert that blacks were relegated to caste does not prove, as some people have argued, that blacks had no rights. Historical evidence confirms that some blacks in seventeenth-century Virginia did have rights and that others were ordered freed after their terms of indenture. For example, early colonial court records tell us that John Graweere, "a negro servant to William Evans," petitioned the court for permission to purchase the freedom of his young son. The court granted Graweere's petition and ordered "that the child shall be free from the said Evans or his assigns and to be and remain at the disposing and education of said Graweere and the child's godfather—who undertaketh to see it brought up in the Christian religion as aforesaid."[31] Graweere was able to exercise other rights as well, including keeping hogs, purchasing his child's freedom, and petitioning the court. In both *Negro Mozingo v. Stone* (1672) and *Moore v. Light* (1673), the Virginia courts ordered that blacks "Remayne free" and receive "Corne and Clothes According to the custome of the Country," suggesting, again, that some blacks were indentured servants rather than slaves.[32]

The same legal system that gave privileges to some black servants simultaneously sanctioned perpetual servitude for others. In several commercial transactions in the 1640s, blacks were sold by contract for life. In one case, Francis Potts sold a black woman and child to Stephen Carlton, "to the use of him forever." In another, William Whittington sold a ten-year-old girl, "along with any issue she might produce for her and her children's 'lifetime and their successors forever.' "[33]

Once the practice of selling blacks for life became common, it was not long before the courts began to impose perpetual servitude on blacks as punishment for their crimes. In *Re Negro John Punch* (1640), three runaway servants were captured in Maryland and sentenced to be whipped. The court then imposed different sentences on them on the basis of color:

> One called Victor, a Dutchman, the other a Scotchman called James Gregory, shall first serve out their times with their master according to their Indentures, and one whole year apiece after the time of their service is Expired . . . and after that service . . . to serve the colony for three whole years apiece, and that the third being a negro named John Punch shall serve his said master or his assigns for the time of his natural life here or elsewhere.[34]

The *Punch* decision demonstrates that from the earliest days of colonial life, colonial courts were willing to exercise extreme partiality in favor of whites and against blacks.

A similar conclusion can be made from the one-sentence-long opinion in *Re Warwick* (1669): "Hannah Warwick's case extenuated because she was overseen by a negro overseer." Assuming that Warwick was a white servant, the opinion suggests that the testimony of a black overseer was doubtful or impermissible. Thus, *Warwick* implies that the function of blacks in Virginia was to be ordered by whites and never to order whites.[35]

Although prior statutes restricted blacks, it was not until 1659 that Virginia legislation referred to them as slaves.[36] The statute in this case provided a tax credit for merchants bringing slaves into the country, which led directly to an increased supply of slave labor.[37] During the 1660s, blacks in lifetime bondage had become the primary labor force in colonial Virginia. By then, the Virginia legislature had enacted statutes punishing whites who conspired in the company of Negroes to escape service and exempting slave owners from criminal prosecution for the casual killing of slaves. In addition, the legislature enacted a statute declaring that baptism did not alter the bondage of blacks or Native Americans. In 1670, Virginia enacted a law dividing non-Christian servants into two categories: those who are imported into the colony by shipping, "who shall be slaves for their lives," and those "who shall come by land, who shall serve until age 30."[38]

By 1680, Virginia developed a statutory scheme that denied most blacks even the limited rights enjoyed by poor whites.[39] One statute illustrates the extent of the debasement of blacks in Virginia:

> Whereas the frequent meetings of considerable numbers of Negro slaves under pretense of feasts and burials is judged of dangerous consequence, [it is] enacted that no Negro or slave may carry arms, such as any club, staff, gun, sword, or other weapon, nor go from his owner's plantation without a certificate and then only on necessary occasions; the punishment of twenty lashes on the bare back, well laid on. And further, if any Negro lift up his hand against any Christian he shall receive thirty lashes, and if he absent himself or lie out from his master's service and resist lawful apprehension, he may be killed and this law shall be published every six months.[40]

Such acts became the model of black control and repression throughout the South for much of the next two centuries. Blacks, whether slave or free, were restricted and defenseless.

After eliminating blacks' basic civil rights, the Virginia legislature codified the status of slaves as a form of property. Consider the following law, which Virginia enacted in 1705:

> All Negro, mulatto, and Indian slaves within this dominion shall be held to be real estate and not chattels and shall descend unto heirs and widows according to the custom of land inheritance, and be held in "fee simple." Provided that any merchant bringing slaves into this dominion shall hold such slaves whilst they remain unsold as personal estate. All such slaves may be taken on execution as other chattels; slaves shall not be escheatable.
>
> No person selling any slave shall be obliged to have the sale recorded as upon the alienation of other real estate. Nothing in this act shall be construed to give the owner of a slave not seized of other real estate the right to vote as a freeholder.[41]

Although the legislature revised the 1705 act every several years until 1792, its provisions remained essentially the same.

The Virginia experience with the codification of slavery is representative of other colonial experiences. State slave codes show that most blacks in the United States—whether slave, mulatto, or free—did not enjoy equal rights with most whites. Instead, the codes contained various combinations of the following provisions:[42]

- Restricting certain occupations to whites.
- Prohibiting slave manumission or ordering manumitted persons to leave the state within a fixed period.
- Denying most blacks the right to freely assemble.
- Preventing most blacks from entering some states.
- Preventing free blacks from engaging in trade or commerce with slaves.
- Regulating the sale or return of slaves.
- Prohibiting blacks from obtaining education, voting, or testifying in court against a white person.
- Prohibiting blacks from keeping any weapons or certain animals, such as dogs, horses, or some livestock.
- Authorizing more severe punishment (often death) for blacks, especially slaves, in most criminal convictions.
- Prohibiting blacks from traveling without passes or certificates.
- Prohibiting sexual and marital relationships between whites and blacks.

By the time the U.S. Constitution was drafted, Virginia had sanctioned black slavery for nearly 120 years. The slave codes were America's first affirmative action policies, but unlike current remedial affirmative action, these earlier preferences promoted white supremacy and black caste. During the ensuing period while the Constitution was being drawn up, whites chose to expand their racial privileges, and our current racial predicament is a result of those choices.

## THE ROAD TO CONSTITUTIONAL CASTE

Probably most Americans do not know the story of Crispus Attucks or why his life and death exemplified one of the great ironies of our constitutional history. Attucks, a runaway slave, had worked for twenty years as a seaman in Boston. In March 1770, British soldiers fired on several colonists protesting British colonial legislation and the presence of the British military in Boston. Five people, including Attucks, died in the Boston Massacre. Attucks's sacrifice was poignant: why would a fugitive slave give his life for a country that denied him equality?[43] Indeed, Attucks's death for America was in vain, for by the time the Virginia statesmen prepared their bill of rights in 1776, slavery had been sanctioned in all thirteen colonies.[44]

The Declaration of Independence was the United States' freedom manifesto. It announced the union of the colonies as independent states and listed the reasons that they had severed their ties to the British Crown. The colonies' representatives complained about King George's tyranny and despotism, writing that "all MEN are created equal, that they are endowed by their Creator with certain unalienable Rights, that among these are Life, Liberty and the Pursuit of Happiness." [45] Yet even Thomas Jefferson, who wrote those stirring words, also stated that he thought blacks were inferior to whites:

> The improvement of the blacks in body and mind, in the first instance of their mixture with the whites, has been observed by everyone, and proves that their inferiority is not the effect merely of their condition of life. . . . This unfortunate difference of color, and perhaps faculty, is a powerful obstacle to the emancipation of these people. [46]

Despite its references to equality and unalienable rights, the final draft of the Declaration of Independence said nothing about slavery in the colonies. Quite the contrary: in order to promote the interests of whites, our Founding Fathers, including a majority of those who wrote the Constitution, sacrificed the rights of blacks by providing for—in no fewer than eight clauses—the continuation of this vile practice while delicately declining to name the practice *slavery*. [47]

In the end, the society described by Jefferson, James Madison, and others in America's foundational legal documents excluded the half-million blacks held in slavery. As did the first slaveholders, white American revolutionaries chose to exclude blacks from their new equality. Thus, when Speaker of the House Newt Gingrich and others talk about renewing America through Jeffersonian principles, millions of Americans would be well advised to question their status under this vision.

Our tradition of racial privileges for whites was incorporated into the U.S. Constitution in Pennsylvania during the summer of 1787. Accordingly, to understand why our government initiated contemporary remedial affirmative action policies in the mid-twentieth century, we must know what happened that hot summer when the drafters of the Constitution embraced race-conscious preferences for whites, thereby continuing a course charted more than a century earlier in the British colonies.

Between May 14 and September 17, 1787, fifty-five white men met in Philadelphia to revise the Articles of Confederation. Among those delegates were leading citizens and property holders from twelve of the thirteen new states, including lawyers, politicians, judges, philosophers, merchants, and war heroes. The absence of blacks, white women, Native Americans, and poor whites raises questions about what the framers meant by the term *the People.*[48]

The delegates' immediate task was to revise those Articles most consistent with their competing economic and political interests, constructing a plan that would survive scrutiny in state conventions. But those conventions, too, excluded meaningful participation by persons of color, white women, and most poor whites. And it is through this lack of representation that the delegates compromised our freedom to be blind to race, gender, or class.

Although the Constitutional Convention did not begin when scheduled, by May 25 seven of the state delegations had selected George Washington as president of the Convention. On May 29, with nine states represented, Edmund Randolph of Virginia took the floor to explain the significance of the delegates' task. Randolph enumerated the defects in the Articles of Confederation and then presented a series of remedial resolutions, which became known as the Virginia plan. For the next two weeks, delegates meeting in the Committee of the Whole discussed the Virginia plan.[49]

On June 15, William Patterson of New Jersey proposed replacing the Virginia plan with the New Jersey plan. The principal difference between the two was that the Virginia plan proposed a strong national government composed of legislative, executive, and judicial branches, whereas the New Jersey plan recommended enhancing only the federal legislative power.[50] The delegates rejected the proposal to replace the Virginia plan.

During the remaining three months of the Convention, the delegates met collectively and in subcommittees to debate and draft provisions of the Constitution. These deliberations finally resulted in a Constitution consisting of a bundle of compromises. Not having a constitutional model from which to borrow, the delegates used their own experiences from their respective states and lessons from abroad, which had made them aware of domestic and foreign economic and political rivalries, compacts between states and foreign governments, and the dangers of national aristocracies and monarchies. The government that emerged was a delicate balance of power between large and small states with competing economic and political interests.

Among the compromises agreed to in Philadelphia, none has proved more significant to our nation's history than those regarding the rights and legal status of persons of African descent, whether slave or free. In 1787, most of the blacks in the thirteen states were slaves; as property, like cows or horses, they were subject to the dominion of their owner. Accordingly, when the delegates met in Philadelphia, one of the central questions before them was whether the Constitution would contain compromises sanctioning slavery.[51]

The original Constitution does not use terms like *slave* or *slavery*. However, in the Convention records, many delegates frequently—and apparently interchangeably—use the terms *slaves*, *blacks*, and *negroes*, as well as linking the terms *whites* and *free Citizens*.[52] Thus, looking white and having no known African ancestry presumably meant that one was a free citizen, and looking black meant that one was neither free nor a citizen.

The most difficult race-conscious compromise for the delegates was apportioning the state's representation in and taxes to the House of Representatives.[53] The delegates had to determine whether the ruling criterion should be wealth, population, property, or tax contributions. So they decided to count the whole number of free persons, including indentured servants but excluding Indians not taxed, and three-fifths of all other persons.[54] This provision was interpreted to mean that slaves (most blacks) were to be counted in a three-to-five ratio, with five slaves equaling three free persons.

Yet when reading what became article I, section 2, clause 3, it is difficult to discern whether the delegates intended free blacks to count as whole persons or as three-fifths persons. For example, on July 9, when the delegates took up the apportionment clause again, it became clear that many were concerned about including persons of African descent in their calculations for House seats. Patterson "could regard Negroe slaves in no light other than property . . . and if Negroes are not represented in the States to which they belong, why should they be represented in the General Government?"[55] Did Patterson have in mind just the slaves in the South or all blacks who were excluded from representation in any state?

Similarly, Rufus King of Massachusetts noted that eleven of thirteen states had agreed to consider slaves in the apportionment of taxes, believing that taxation and apportionment should go together. The next day

King reminded the delegates that blacks in the southern states would be counted in a ratio of five to three; that is, five slaves would count as three whole persons.[56] Again, did King mean that all blacks in the South were slaves and thus the terms were interchangeable?

On July 11, delegates Pierce Butler and General Charles Cotesworth Pinckney, both of South Carolina, "insisted that blacks be included in the rule of Representation, equally with the whites" and thereafter moved to strike out the words *three-fifths*.[57] They did not, however, use the term *slave*, again indicating that in their minds, the words *black* and *slave* had the same meaning.

To apportion taxes, the delegates from the southern states did not want to count slaves as whole persons because that would have required those states to pay more taxes. On the other hand, the delegates from outside the South understandably did want to count slaves when calculating taxes.[58] Their compromise is a good example of how the Constitution embraced race-conscious privileges for whites: White southerners would increase their representation in the House but decrease the amount of direct taxes; white northerners would lower the amount of direct taxes paid by the southern states but limit southern representation; and both groups would benefit at the expense of blacks, who would neither gain the protection of the federal government or receive its resources.

After rejecting the motion to count black slaves on an equal basis with whites, the delegates tentatively accepted the three-fifths clause but continued their criticism of it and other provisions relating to slavery. Rufus King reported that he was opposed to using numbers as the rule of representation "and was particularly so on account of the blacks ... admission of them along with Whites at all, would excite great discontents among the States having no slaves." Both James Wilson and Gouverneur Morris of Pennsylvania expressed their opposition as well, before the delegations voted six to four to reject the inclusion of three-fifths of the blacks.[59]

On the following day, some delegates expressed their concern about the plan to count blacks in the apportionment calculations. Pinckney was alarmed that South Carolina would not be represented in Congress based on its total number of blacks and argued that his state should therefore not be taxed on that same basis. "Property in slaves," he believed, "should not be exposed to danger under a government instituted for the protection of property." The ensuing discussion among delegates Oliver

Ellsworth of Connecticut, Randolph, Wilson, King, and General Pinckney and the younger Charles Pinckney shows yet again how they used the terms *blacks*, *slaves*, and *Negroes* interchangeably.[60]

On July 13, Butler reminded his colleagues that the "security the Southern States want is that their Negroes may not be taken from them." He had little reason to fear. Not only did the delegates agree to protect slave property, but within a few days they also agreed to suppress "dangerous commotions, insurrections and rebellions,"[61] another indirect, yet unmistakable, racial privilege for white slave owners, ensuring the suppression of slave revolts by the power of the federal government.

By July 23, the delegates were ready to turn over their proposed resolutions to the Committee of Detail, which included delegates John Rutledge of South Carolina, Randolph of Virginia, Nathaniel Gorham of Massachusetts, Ellsworth of Connecticut, and Wilson of Pennsylvania.[62] Then the delegates adjourned between July 27 and August 5, during which time the Committee of Detail wrote the first draft of the U.S. Constitution.

On August 6, the delegates received the Committee of Detail report, which included reiterations of the three-fifths clause and the insurrections clause, along with a prohibition on taxing exports or the importation of slaves, as well as a ban on the congressional prohibition of the slave trade. In response to these provisions, King repeated that to his mind, the admission of slaves was a most grating circumstance, and he thought it would also be so to many of the people of America. He argued that permitting slavery would weaken the South and require the other states to come to its aid, and therefore, "either slaves should not be represented, or exports should be taxable" to help the government raise revenues to defend the southern states.[63]

Gouverneur Morris's exhortation to the delegates reveals how troubling the slave compromises were to the Convention's participants, and he moved to insert *free* before the word *inhabitants* in the draft of article VII, section 3. He

> never would concur in upholding domestic slavery. It was a nefarious institution. It was the curse of heaven on the states where it prevailed. . . . Upon what principle is it that slaves shall be computed in the representation? Are they men? Then make them Citizens and let them vote. Are they property? Why then is no other property included? . . . The admission of slaves into the Representation comes to this: that the inhabitant of Georgia and South Carolina who goes to the Coast of Africa, and in defiance of the

most sacred laws of humanity tears away his fellow creatures from their dearest connections & damns them to the most cruel bondages, shall have more votes in a Government instituted for the protection of the rights of mankind, than the Citizen of Pennsylvania or New Jersey who views with laudable horror, so nefarious a practice.[64]

Morris's motion failed, ten to one. Nonetheless, his objections captured the difficulties that he and other delegates had in debating the slave compromises. His concerns were not so much with the "wretched Africans" but, rather, with slavery's exacerbation of the economic and political inequality between northern and southern whites.

On August 21, Luther Martin of Maryland proposed altering the draft of article VII, section 4, to allow a prohibition or tax on the importation of slaves. He argued that the section as written would "leave an encouragement to the traffic" and that "it was inconsistent with the principles of the revolution and dishonorable to the American character to have such a feature in the Constitution." Rutledge responded that he "would readily exempt the other states from the obligation to protect the Southern States against [slaves]." He warned that if the northern states "consult their interest, they will not oppose the increase of Slaves which will increase the commodities [of which] they will become the carriers." Ellsworth added, "The morality or wisdom of slavery are considerations belonging to the States themselves. What enriches a part enriches the whole, and the States are the best judges of their particular interest." Charles Pinckney was firmer: "South Carolina can never receive the plan if it prohibits the slave trade." [65]

The following day, in perhaps the most significant display of anguish over the competing economic and political interests of whites, a dozen delegates weighed in regarding the slave compromises. Roger Sherman of Connecticut favored leaving the matter to the states, some of which had already begun to abolish slavery. Colonel George Mason of Virginia had several concerns, including the westward expansion of slavery and the competition of slave labor with that of poor whites: slaves "prevent the immigration of whites, who really enrich & strengthen a Country." On the other hand, Ellsworth contended that "[s]lavery in time will not be a speck in our Country." Charles Pinckney said again that "[a]n attempt to take away the right [to import slaves] as proposed will produce serious objections to the Constitution which he wished to see adopted." The senior Pinckney stated flatly, "South Carolina & Georgia cannot do without slaves." Abraham Baldwin of Georgia argued that the Convention should not be considering local issues like slavery. Wilson observed "that if South Carolina & Georgia were themselves disposed to get rid of their importation of slaves in a short time as had been suggested, they would never refuse to Unite because the importation might be prohibited." In his view, the exemption on taxing slaves was a bounty. Elbridge Gerry of Massachusetts thought that the delegates "had nothing to do with the conduct of the States as to Slaves, but ought to be careful not to give any sanction to it." [66]

In contrast, John Dickinson of Delaware "considered it as inadmissible on every principle of honor & safety that the importation of slaves should be authorised to the States by the Constitution." For him, the real question was "whether the national happiness would be promoted or impeded by the importation, and this question ought to be left to the National Government not to the States particularly interested." After stating the pertinent law of North Carolina, Hugh Williamson "thought the Southern States could not become members of the Union if the clause should be rejected, and that it was wrong to force any thing down, not absolutely necessary, and which any State must disagree to." King "remarked on the exemption of the slaves from duty whilst every other import was subjected to it, as an inequality that could not fail to strike the commercial sagacity of the Northern and middle States." [67]

John Langdon of New Hampshire argued strenuously that he "could not with good conscience leave [slavery] with the States who could then go on with the traffic, without being restrained by the opinions given here that they will themselves cease to import slaves." General Pinckney noted candidly that "he did not think South Carolina would stop her importations of slaves in any short time, but only stop them occasionally as she does now." Rutledge was even more frank, declaring that "[i]f the Convention thinks that North Carolina, South Carolina & Georgia will ever agree to the plan, unless their right to import slaves be untouched, the expectation is vain." [68]

A few delegates, noting the strain of the debate, called for a commitment to the subcommittee of all the related clauses, with one noting, "These things may form a bargain among the Northern & Southern States." In the spirit of such a deal, Sherman remarked that "it was better to let the Southern States import slaves than to part with them, if they made that a sine qua non." By a vote of seven to three, with one abstention, the issues were submitted to the Committee of Eleven for further consideration.[69]

On August 24, the Committee of Eleven recommended:

> The migration or importation of such persons as the several States now existing shall think proper to admit, shall not be prohibited by the Legislature prior to the year 1800, but a tax or duty may be imposed on such migration or importation at a rate not exceeding the average of the duties laid on imports.[70]

In response, General Pinckney moved to change to 1808 the year limiting the importation of slaves, and his motion passed. Gouverneur Morris wanted the clause to name the states that had insisted on protecting slavery. But this was not acceptable to many delegates, who did not want to offend the people in those states and who preferred using a description other than slaves. It was then agreed to amend the importation clause to read "1808, but a tax or duty may be imposed on such importation not exceeding ten dollars for each person."[71]

On August 28, the delegates briefly discussed the fugitive slave clause and agreed to the following:

> If any person bound to service or labor in any of the United States shall escape into another State, he or she shall not be discharged from such service or labor, in consequence of any regulations subsisting in the State to which they escape, but shall be delivered up to the person justly claiming their service or labor.[72]

On September 9, the delegates appointed a Committee of Style, consisting of Dr. William Samuel Johnson of Connecticut, Alexander Hamilton of New York, Morris, Madison, and King, to revise and arrange the articles. Accordingly, on September 12, Johnson submitted to the delegates a draft constitution and accompanying letter for Congress.[73]

In the final days of the Convention, several delegates spoke of the difficulty they had in signing the proposed constitution, their main objection being the scope of the executive and judicial powers. Gerry stated that he would withhold his name for several reasons, including "3/5 of the blacks are to be represented as if they were freemen."[74]

To understand the predicament created by the framers' compromises on race, we should assume that they had rejected broad constitutional inequality. What would have happened if none of the Constitution's provisions protected slavery? If it had provided that blacks and women be able to vote, attend school, hold and convey property, obtain employment, and otherwise participate in the economic and political life of America on the same basis as white men could? What would have happened if the Constitution had prohibited racial discrimination? If being classified as black had not been made a badge of inferiority, and white, one of privilege? It is difficult to imagine how different America might be. Unfortunately, and not surprisingly, given their worldview, the drafters set the United States on a course of racial inequality and disunity from which it still has not recovered. Through the explicit protection of slavery, the framers wrote white privilege and black caste into the Constitution.

The Constitution of the United States is thus a series of compromises reached by white male property holders—southern planters and northern merchants. At the heart of their agreements was the race-conscious intention to place the interests of whites above those of blacks. Thus, America's modern racial predicament concerning the constitutional legitimacy of remedial affirmative action policies can be traced to the debacle at Philadelphia and to the slave codes and racial attitudes preceding it.

The Declaration of Independence and the Constitution of the United States were proslavery documents that protected slavery by omission or commission and assumed the debasement and disenfranchisement of blacks, whether slave or free. Frederick Douglass clearly understood his outsider position when he stated in an 1852 Fourth of July oration:

> What to the American slave is your Fourth of July? I answer, a day that reveals to him, more than all other days of the year, the gross injustice and cruelty to which he is the constant victim. To him your celebration is a sham; your boasted liberty an unholy license; your national greatness, swelling vanity; your sounds of rejoicing are empty and heartless; your denunciations of tyrants, brass-fronted impudence; your shouts of liberty and equality, hollow mockery; your prayers and hymns, your sermons and thanksgivings, with all your religious parade and solemnity, are to him mere bombast, fraud, deception, impiety, and hypocrisy—a thin veil to cover up crimes which would disgrace a nation of savages.[75]

In a similar spirit on the occasion of the bicentennial of the Constitution, Justice Thurgood Marshall wrote about his reluctance in joining the celebrations:

> I cannot accept this invitation, for I do not believe that the meaning of the Constitution was forever "fixed" at the Philadelphia Convention. Nor do I find the wisdom, foresight, and sense of justice exhibited by the framers particularly profound. To the contrary, the government they devised was defective from the start, requiring several amendments, a civil war, and momentous social transformation to attain the system of constitutional government, and its respect for the individual freedoms and human rights, that we hold as fundamental today.[76]

In sum, the revolution that occurred in the United States between 1776 and 1791 did not liberate blacks in the same way that it did many whites. Most blacks remained enslaved or, if free, circumscribed by state laws that limited and, in some cases, prohibited their exercise of basic civil rights.

## LOSING SECOND-CLASS CITIZENSHIP

After the ratification of the Constitution in 1791, overt, government-sponsored or -sanctioned racial discrimination was the rule for most blacks living in the United States. Then, in the mid-1960s, the civil rights movement forced the federal government to address institutionalized racism and enact antidiscrimination laws. Unfortunately, the federal government's commitment to enforce those laws was weak and short-lived. Even though governmental discrimination is now illegal, functional white supremacy has not been eliminated, and racial caste is worsening.

If we could fast-forward from the late eighteenth to the mid-twentieth century, we would see dozens of events demonstrating state and federal governmental advancement of white supremacy and black caste that explain why racial caste is so pervasive in America today. Consider, for example, the expansion of slavery across the western frontier. Contrary to what the champions of slavery at the Constitutional Convention asserted about its demise, slavery did not die out. When Congress prohibited the importation of slaves in 1808, the practice went underground until it was supplanted by slave breeding and a vigorous domestic slave trade. Blacks were bred like cattle. So even in the absence of legal importation, the slave population swelled to nearly four million by 1865.

Even among those whites who opposed slavery, few envisioned the United States as a place where blacks and whites could live together with equal rights. Instead, some abolitionists—including members of the American Colonization Society and the American Anti-Slavery Society—tried to colonize blacks outside the United States. Furthermore, when slavery ended, few whites embraced ex-slaves as their equals; some even took it upon themselves to remove blacks from their towns. After the Civil War and during Reconstruction, Congress appeared ready to end white supremacy policies. But the political branches of the federal government were divided, and the Supreme Court interpreted the three Civil War amendments narrowly, leaving it to the states to determine the civil rights of former slaves. The result was another century of official, government-sponsored policies of white supremacy and judicially approved separate and unequal rights for blacks.

One of the more important national debates of the early nineteenth century took place between those who wanted slavery to expand into the new states and territories and those who did not. The contest included slave traders, slave breeders, and slave owners who wished to hire their slaves out to third parties, all of whom could earn additional wealth by supplying slaves to new parts of the country, as well as free persons engaged in manufacturing or agriculture who had to compete against goods produced by slave labor. The sectional fight over the existence and expansion of slavery thus continued for the next half-century, with the Civil War its ultimate result.

The backdrop to that war included the shift of a majority of the slave population from the Atlantic and Upper South to the Lower South where a new cotton kingdom was emerging, the enactment of more extensive slave codes covering every aspect of slave life, passage of the Missouri Compromise of 1820,[77] the Fugitive Slave Act of 1850,[78] the Kansas–Nebraska Act of 1854,[79] and the announcement by the Supreme Court of its decision in *Dred Scott v. Sandford*.[80]

During the first half of the nineteenth century, slavery—now prohibited in Vermont, Connecticut, Rhode Island, Delaware, and Massachusetts—became largely a Southern institution. The Missouri Compromise provided that the northern section of the Louisiana Purchase would be nonslave territory and that the southern portion, including Missouri, would be proslavery. The Fugitive Slave Act gave slave owners protection under federal law for the recapture of runaway slaves. Under the Kansas–Nebraska Act, Congress held that the residents of these territories could decide locally whether to organize as slave or free states, in accordance with the doctrine of popular sovereignty. These new laws therefore confounded the disputes between slave and nonslave states.

Consider the early history of the *Dred Scott* case. Scott, born into slavery in Virginia around 1800, became the property of Peter Blow, with whom he moved from Virginia to Alabama in the 1820s and then to St. Louis, Missouri, around 1830. There can be no doubt that Blow's control over Scott had the sanction of Virginia, Alabama, and Missouri slave law, as well as the relevant federal law. Once in St. Louis, Blow, who might be described as slave poor, sold several of his slaves.[81]

Dr. John Emerson, an army surgeon, purchased Scott and later permitted him to marry another slave. The Scotts had two children, who by law also became slaves of Emerson. In this way, slavery continued from generation to generation. When Emerson traveled to various army assignments, he frequently took Scott with him. The Dred Scott litigation arose out of Scott's travels with Emerson into free states and territories, with Scott claiming that under the law, those travels made him a free person.

With the financial and legal help of whites who opposed slavery, Dred Scott sued for his family's freedom on the grounds that he had been taken to Fort Armstrong, Illinois, which, according to the Missouri Compromise, was in a nonslave state and to Fort Snelling in the Wisconsin Territory, which, according to the Ordinance of 1787, was a nonslave territory. Several states, including Missouri, had adopted the common law policy that if a slave were taken into a free state or territory for an indefinite period, the slave on his or her return to the slave state could sue for freedom.[82]

When Scott filed his first complaint in the trial court at St. Louis in 1846, the legal precedents in Missouri appeared favorable. The most significant Missouri case, which had been decided almost ten years earlier, was *Rachel v. Walker*.[83] Rachel, a slave, had accompanied her master, an army officer, to Fort Snelling where they remained for several years. On their return to St. Louis, Rachel sued for her freedom. The Missouri Supreme Court upheld Rachel's claim for freedom, declaring that an officer of the U.S. Army who takes his slave to a military post within a territory where slavery is prohibited and keeps her there for several years forfeits his property in such a slave by virtue of the Ordinance of 1787. Because of that precedent, Scott must have been fairly confident he would prevail.

However, between 1846 and 1857, two events occurred that foreshadowed the now infamous *Dred Scott* opinion. First, in *Strader v. Graham*,[84] the U.S. Supreme Court held that it would follow the state supreme court's interpretation of state slave laws. Thus, the Court held that it would not negotiate the conflicts of law that emerged between slave and nonslave states. Second, in 1852 the Missouri Supreme Court disregarded its precedent (*Rachel v. Walker*), holding that Missouri was not obliged to observe the laws of nonslave states or territories.[85] Thus by 1852, the law of slavery in Missouri had been construed to protect property interests in slaves, notwithstanding laws such as the Ordinance of 1787 or the Missouri Compromise.

After eleven years of litigation in state and federal courts and two arguments before the Supreme Court, *Dred Scott*,[86] a case that had begun as a simple trespass dispute, became an important constitutional case regarding "(1) Negro citizenship; (2) the status of slaves who had been held on free soil; and (3) the constitutionality of federal legislation prohibiting slavery in the territories."[87] On all three questions, the Court ruled against blacks: Scott was not a citizen; under the law of Missouri, he was still a slave; and Congress did not have the power to prohibit slavery in the territories of the United States.

Although the Court might have decided the case on narrow, technical grounds, Chief Justice Roger Taney wrote the proslavery, prowhite supremacy opinion that has become his legacy and that hastened the beginning of the Civil War:[88]

> The question is simply this: Can a Negro, whose ancestors were imported into this country, and sold as slaves, become a member of the political community formed and brought into existence by the Constitution of the United States, and as such become entitled to all rights, and privileges, and immunities, guaranteed by that instrument to the citizen?
>
> The question before us is, whether the class of persons described in the plea in abatement comprise a portion of this people and are constituent members of this sovereignty?
>
> We think they are not, and that they are not included, and were not intended to be included under the word "citizens" in the Constitution. . . . On the contrary, they were at the time considered as a *subordinate and inferior class of beings, who had been subjugated by the dominant race*, and, whether emancipated or not, yet remained subject to their authority, and had no rights or privileges but such as those who held the power the Government might choose to grant them.[89]

Taney insisted that blacks, whether slave or free, were subjugated by the dominant race. He was correct. However, his error was to conclude that such racial domination meant that blacks were not citizens according to the Constitution. That is, there is no place in the Constitution to which Taney could point that distinguished between free blacks and whites. Nor could Taney maintain that there were no free blacks living in America. Thus, the only conclusion that Taney was justified in making was that many whites had violated the letter and spirit of the Constitution by subjugating free blacks. If equal treatment were the test for establishing citizenship, many Americans today could be classified as noncitizens.

Taney next wrote that no state could confer national citizenship, according to the Constitution, on a person or class of persons whom the framers did not intend to be embraced as citizens. This meant that Missouri, for example, could not confer U.S. citizenship on freed slaves by making them citizens of Missouri. He surmised that persons of African ancestry, whether slave or free, were not considered citizens by the framers and thus were not entitled to sue in the federal courts.[90] Again, Taney was wrong about the framers' intent, for they did not limit status as a free person to whites. In fact, this idea was specifically rejected during their deliberations at the Constitutional Convention. But Taney simply ignored that evidence.

He then recounted in detail what he described as the "universal" characterization of persons of African descent during the eighteenth and nineteenth centuries:[91]

> They had for more than a century been regarded as beings of an inferior order, and altogether unfit to associate with the white race, either in social or political relations; and so far inferior, *that they had no rights which the white man was bound to respect*; and that the Negro might justly and lawfully be reduced to slavery for his benefit. He was bought and sold and treated as an ordinary article of merchandise and traffic, whenever a profit could be made by it. The opinion was at the time fixed and *universal* in the civilized portion of the white race.[92]

Taney's opinion in *Dred Scott* was one of the most decisive moments in the nationalization of white supremacy in America, as his opinion gave judicial sanction to the commodification and subordination of all blacks, whether slave or free, to exclude them from the federal courts. This decision shows that the malign racial attitudes of whites toward blacks changed very little between the seventeenth and nineteenth centuries. Even today, one sees evidence of Taney's beliefs. For example, many whites still live away from blacks as if blacks were unfit to associate with. Many whites continue to enroll their children at schools and universities with virtually no black students or teachers. Many whites refuse to support black political candidates, especially in statewide or national elections. Thus, it is no surprise that when whites were polled about the performance of the 1996 Republican nominees at the debates before the Iowa caucuses, many of them thought that Alan Keyes was the most effective. Nonetheless, he finished near the bottom of the field in the actual voting. Although they may choose their words more carefully, many whites betray by their behavior the belief that blacks have rights that they must respect.

Only two members of the Court ruling on the *Dred Scott* case dissented. Justice Benjamin Curtis of Massachusetts wrote a long, careful dissent that challenged each of Taney's conclusions regarding the citizenship of blacks and showed that in numerous states before and after the ratification of the Constitution, some blacks did in fact exercise some of the rights of free citizens.[93] Justice Curtis's dissent—all but lost in constitutional history—warrants a close examination for readers searching for a contemporaneous critique of Taney's analysis.

Taney's racial attitudes also found voice in other political circles. At a 1858 campaign rally during his campaign for the presidency, Abraham Lincoln expressed views consistent with Taney's:

> I will say then that I am not, nor ever have been in favor of bringing about in any way the social and political equality of the white and black races [applause]—that I am not nor ever have been in favor of making voters or jurors of Negroes, nor of qualifying them to hold office, nor to intermarry with white people, and I will say in addition to this that there is a physical difference between the black and white races which I believe will forever forbid the two races living together on terms of social and political equality. And inasmuch as they cannot so live, while they do remain together there must be the position of superior and inferior, and I as much as any other man am in favor of having the superior position assigned to the white race.[94]

Was this simply nineteenth-century political expediency? Did the Great Emancipator pander to white supremacy when it suited his interests? The same man who wrote the Gettysburg Address evidently could not envision social and political equality between blacks and whites in America. If Lincoln could subscribe to racial supremacy, why couldn't politicians today do the same? And wouldn't political expediency be just as likely when discussing welfare reform or affirmative action?

### RECONSTRUCTION AND SACRIFICE

After the war over slavery, the United States again had an opportunity to reject racial preferences for whites and to promote racial equality. For a time it appeared that the postwar government, led by a number of powerful whites such as Thaddeus Stevens and Charles Sumner[95] and a cadre of new black lawmakers such as Senators Hiram Revels and Blanche Bruce and Representatives Joseph Rainey, Benjamin Turner, Josiah Walls, Robert Brown Elliot, Robert DeLarge, and Jefferson F. Long[96] would give to blacks the same basic civil rights enjoyed by whites, as well as property confiscated during the war. Indeed, in the decade of "Reconstruction," between 1865 and 1875, Congress enacted three new constitutional amendments and four federal civil rights statutes designed to give former slaves the same rights as whites had.

The first was the Thirteenth Amendment:

> Section 1. Neither slavery nor involuntary servitude, except as a punishment for crime whereof the party shall have been duly convicted, shall exist within the United States, or any place subject to their jurisdiction.
>    Section 2. Congress shall have power to enforce this article by appropriate legislation.

Under this amendment, Congress enacted a series of federal statutes that were both race conscious and remedial. For example, the Freedmen's Bureau Act established the Bureau of Refugees, Freedmen, and Abandoned Lands, an agency to assist former slaves and white refugees who after the war lacked shelter, food, or other necessities of life.[97] The bureau also established schools, supervised employment contracts between former slaves and their employers, and managed abandoned and confiscated lands, including leasing some of them to former slaves.[98] The Freedmen's Bureau Act was an early form of remedial affirmative action that Congress enacted over the veto of President Andrew Johnson.

Congress also enacted federal laws prohibiting white supremacy. The Civil Rights Act of 1866[99] provided

> That all persons born in the United States . . . of every race and color, without regard to any previous condition of slavery or involuntary servitude . . . shall have the same right, in every state and Territory in the United States, to make and enforce contracts, to sue, be parties, and give evidence, to inherit, purchase, lease, sell, hold, and convey real and personal property, and to full and equal benefit of all laws and proceedings for the security of person and property, as is enjoyed by white citizens . . . any law, statute, ordinance, regulation, or custom, to the contrary notwithstanding.

For the first time, federal law mandated for blacks the same rights that whites had.

But the hopes of blacks were not to be realized. Most of the southern states responded to the new amendment and federal laws with predictable defiance:

> Most Southern whites, although willing to concede the end of slavery even to the point of voting for the adoption of the Thirteenth Amendment, were convinced that laws should be speedily enacted to curb blacks and to insure their role as a laboring force in the South. These laws, called Black Codes, bore a remarkable resemblance to the ante-bellum Slave Codes and can hardly be described as measures which respected the rights of blacks

as free individuals. Several of them undertook to limit the areas in which blacks could purchase or rent property. Vagrancy laws imposed heavy penalties that were designed to force all blacks to work whether they wanted to or not. Numerous fines were imposed for seditious speeches, insulting gestures or acts, absence from work, violating curfew, and the possession of firearms.[100]

Congress responded to such state practices with the Fourteenth Amendment:

> Section 1. All persons born or naturalized in the United States and subject to the jurisdiction thereof, are citizens of the United States and of the State wherein they reside. No State shall make or enforce any law which shall abridge the privileges or immunities of citizens of the United States; nor shall any State deprive any person of life, liberty, or property, without due process of law; nor deny to any person within its jurisdiction the equal protection of the laws. . . .
>
>   Section 5. The Congress shall have power to enforce, by appropriate legislation, the provisions of this article.

Like the Thirteenth, the Fourteenth Amendment fundamentally altered the relationship between federal and state government. Its provisions expressly restricted the states' powers, prohibiting them from treating black citizens differently from whites. Section 2 threatened to reduce the number of a state's delegates to the House of Representatives if it discriminated against male inhabitants in voting.

When more congressional investigations found ongoing discrimination against blacks in voting, Congress enacted the Fifteenth Amendment:

> Section 1. The right of citizens of the United States to vote shall not be denied or abridged by the United States or by any State on account of race, color, or previous condition of servitude.
>
>   Section 2. The Congress shall have power to enforce this article by appropriate legislation.

This amendment made it illegal for the government to deny anyone the right to vote on account of race, but it did not prohibit discrimination on other bases such as sex, class, or education. And it was through such loopholes that many states found ways to continue to deny blacks their right to vote until the enactment of the Voting Rights Act of 1965.

This is how some white Texans, for example, were able to eliminate black voters. First, the state's Democratic Party excluded black participation in the primaries. When that practice was struck down by the Supreme Court,[101] the party started the Jaybird Democratic Association, a "private" club, in which membership was limited to white people. Furthermore, only members could vote in its primary, and only the winners of that primary got their names on the general election ballot. Finally, in 1953, the Court invalidated all white primary schemes.[102]

Such evasions also explain why in the early 1960s, thousands of blacks and whites went to Mississippi, Alabama, and elsewhere to demand that blacks be allowed to register and vote. When blacks in Mississippi were denied their voting rights in the selection of state delegates to the Democratic Convention in 1964, they organized their own party, the Mississippi Freedom Democratic Party, and sent their own delegation. And when the convention organizers refused to acknowledge the only democratically elected delegates, Fannie Lou Hamer—who had already lost her home and her job and had been permanently disabled from a jailhouse beating—demanded before a national audience an end to political apartheid in the South. But it was the death of two white Freedom Summer volunteers, Andrew Goodman and Michael Schwerner, alongside a black volunteer, James Chaney, that galvanized thousands of others to go to the South to fight voter discrimination in cities like Philadelphia, Mississippi, and Selma, Alabama.

Much as the Fifteenth Amendment was sidestepped, other Reconstruction legislation suffered a similar end. The Civil Rights Acts of 1875[103] provided

> That all persons within the jurisdiction of the United States shall be entitled to the full and equal enjoyment of the accommodations, advantages, facilities, and privileges of inns, public conveyances on land or water, theaters, and other places of public amusement; subject only to the conditions and limitations established by law, and applicable alike to citizens of every race and color, regardless of any previous condition of servitude.

Since Congress enacted an equal accommodations bill in 1875, why in 1960 were Joseph McNeill, Ezelle Blair Jr., Franklin McCain, and David Richmond, then freshmen at A & T College in Greensboro, North Carolina, refused service at a local Woolworth lunch counter? Why were blacks refused lodging at the Heart of Atlanta Motel in downtown Atlanta, Georgia, or equal accommodations at Ollie's Bar-b-que in Birmingham, Alabama?

The answer is simple: laws don't always govern a society resistant to them. Many whites did not demand that these new constitutional and federal statutory provisions be enforced; in fact, they often blatantly defied them. Also, a majority of the Supreme Court did not share Congress's view of its new powers under the Civil War amendments. For example, in the *Slaughter-House Cases*[104] the Court ruled that the protections of the privileges and immunities clause of the Fourteenth Amendment did not include violations of basic civil rights such as the right to contract, buy or lease property, sue, or give evidence in court. Justice Samuel F. Miller's opinion never once mentioned the federal statutes that had recently been enacted. Instead, the Court read narrowly the citizenship and privileges and immunities clauses as if they were meaningless. Three years later in *United States v. Cruikshank*,[105] the Court applied the principle of *Slaughter-House Cases* to rule that the Civil Rights Act of 1870 provided no relief to two blacks who alleged that their right to assemble had been violated, because the right to assemble was not one of the privileges and immunities of national citizenship.

Reconstruction ended abruptly with the Hayes–Tilden Compromise. In the presidential election of 1876, Democrat Sam Tilden appeared to be the early winner. However, after Rutherford Hayes and the Republicans challenged the election returns in Florida, South Carolina, and Louisiana, Hayes claimed a one-vote victory. Tilden and the Democrats challenged the vote. As was its duty under the Constitution,[106] Congress took up the election dispute, and when it was unable to resolve it, Congress adopted a special resolution establishing a committee to decide who should become president. The committee consisted of fifteen white men, eight Republicans and seven Democrats. Not surprisingly, they voted by party, so Hayes became president. As the quid pro quo for the presidency, Hayes and the Republicans agreed to withdraw the remaining federal troops from the state houses in Louisiana and South Carolina and to restore home rule, which meant that blacks would again lose their rights, because of a compromise among whites.[107]

Six years later, the Supreme Court delivered its greatest blow to the Reconstruction laws in the *Civil Rights Cases*,[108] by invalidating the first two sections of the Civil Rights Act of 1875, which outlawed discrimination in public accommodations. The Court held that because the provisions were directed at private individuals and not the state or its agents, they were unconstitutional. The Court, as though in a deep fog, insisted that private discrimination was beyond the reach of the Fourteenth Amendment and specifically beyond the powers of Congress under section 5.[109] In light of similar cases, the Court made it virtually impossible to use the Reconstruction acts to proscribe discriminatory conduct by private individuals. Nearly a century elapsed before those laws were reenacted.

## SEPARATE AND UNEQUAL

As bad as these developments were, worse was yet to come. In 1896 in *Plessy v. Ferguson*, the Supreme Court upheld the constitutionality of state laws mandating racial separation. Homer Plessy had challenged the constitutionality of a Louisiana statute requiring separate railway cars for whites and blacks, on the grounds that it violated his rights under the Thirteenth and Fourteenth Amendments. Plessy alleged that because he was seven-eighths Caucasian and only one-eighth Negro, he was entitled to every right, privilege, and immunity that applied to white citizens of the United States. His claim echoed those of early Ohioans claiming a proportion of whiteness entitling them to all consequent privileges.[110]

The Court rejected both constitutional challenges. Justice Henry B. Brown wrote, in words filled with disdain, that the Thirteenth Amendment prohibited only slavery and involuntary servitude:

> A statute which implies merely a legal distinction between the white and colored races—a distinction which is founded in the color of the two races, and which must always exist so long as white men are distinguished from the other race by color—has no tendency to destroy the legal equality of the two races, or re-establish a state of involuntary servitude.[111]

As for the Fourteenth Amendment challenge, Brown concluded, noting as evidence of his separate but equal philosophy the existence of separate schools for blacks and whites in the District of Columbia and in various states, as well as state laws forbidding interracial marriage:

> The object of the amendment was undoubtedly to enforce the absolute equality of the two races before the law, but in the nature of things it could not have been intended to abolish distinctions based upon color, or to enforce social, as distinguished from political, equality or a commingling of the two races upon terms unsatisfactory to either.[112]

Notice also how Justice Brown echoed the views of Taney and others when he conceded Plessy's claim that one's reputation of belonging to the white race is a kind of property:

> Conceding this to be so . . . we are unable to see how this statute deprives [Plessy] of, or in any way affects his right to such property. *If he be a white man and assigned to a colored coach, he may have his action for damages against*

*the company. . . . Upon the other hand, if he be a colored man and be so assigned,*
*he has been deprived of no property, since he is not lawfully entitled to the reputation*
*of being a white man.* [113]

Justice John Marshall Harlan was the lone dissenter in *Plessy*, arguing
that the Thirteenth Amendment not only struck down slavery but also
prohibited any burden or disability that constituted a badge of slavery or
servitude. He contended that when joined with the Fourteenth Amendment's protection of citizenship, "the two amendments, if enforced according to their true intent and meaning, will protect all the civil rights
that pertain to freedom and citizenship." [114]

Although the language of the Fourteenth Amendment was prohibitory,
Harlan believed it also contained

> a necessary implication of a positive immunity, or right, most valuable to
> the colored race—the right to exemption from unfriendly legislation
> against them distinctively as colored—exemptions from legal discrimina-
> tions, implying inferiority in civil society, lessening the security of their
> enjoyment of the rights which others enjoy, and discriminations which are
> steps toward reducing them to the condition of a subject race . . . [115]the
> Constitution of the United States, in its present form, forbids, so far as civil
> and political rights are concerned, discrimination by the general govern-
> ment or the states against any citizen because of his race. All citizens are
> equal before the law. . . . [116]
>
> The sure guaranty of the peace and security of each race is the clear,
> distinct, unconditional recognition by our governments, national and state,
> of every right that inheres in civil freedom, and of the equality before the
> law of all citizens of the United States without regard to race. [117]

What did Harlan mean by his dissent in *Plessy?* What was the context for
his insistence that the American Constitution is color blind? Harlan's
primary concern in *Plessy* was undoing black caste. He understood the
implicit message behind segregation statutes: that blacks are inferior,
unfit to associate with whites. Harlan did not pronounce his color blindness principle in an equal society but, rather, in one in which race was a
benchmark for status. He considered the Louisiana law unconstitutional
because it implied the inferiority of blacks and the superiority of whites.
However, some commentators have made elaborate arguments that Harlan intended that the government never be able to use race as a criterion
in its decision making, including when the government sought to remedy
past discrimination or eliminate current caste. [118] But these arguments
take Harlan's statements out of context and turn his color blindness

principle on its head.[119] Justice William Brennan observed how Justice Brown's opinion in *Plessy* turned the equal protection clause "against those whom it was intended to set free, condemning them to a 'separate but equal' status before the law, a status always separate but seldom equal."[120] And now some people want to recast Harlan's dissent *against* blacks, condemning them to racial caste.

In 1954 the Court repudiated the *Plessy* opinion in *Brown v. Board of Education*.[121] *Plessy* still is important, however, for its validation of white superiority and the idea that being white has a value akin to that of property. Surely, this is what Martin Luther King Jr. had in mind when he expressed his hope that his four children would one day live in a nation in which they were not judged by the color of their skin but by the content of their character.[122] He understood that in the United States, being black has not been treated as a form of currency but, rather, as a disqualifier. Dr. King might also have hoped that Americans might one day live in a nation in which whites were not selected by the color of their skin but by the content of their character. Only then can America end its tradition of white racial privilege and race consciousness.

## THE COLOR LINE

In 1903, W. E. B. Du Bois, correctly prophesying the rigid segregation that arose in the United States after *Plessy*, wrote that "the problem of the twentieth century is the problem of the color-line—the relation of the darker to the lighter races of men in Asia and Africa, in America and the islands of the sea."[123] Like their predecessors from the late eighteenth and throughout the nineteenth century, state and local lawmakers at the start of the twentieth century continued to advance race-conscious policies and customs favoring whites and restricting blacks. Under the mantra of "Jim Crow," segregation was required as never before:

> That code lent the sanction of law to a racial ostracism that extended to churches and schools, to housing and jobs, to eating and drinking. Whether by law or by custom, that ostracism extended to virtually all forms of public transportation, to sports and recreations, to hospitals, orphanages, prisons, and asylums, and ultimately to funeral homes, morgues, and cemeteries.[124]

In the face of such discrimination, black leadership fell into several ideological camps. One, led by Booker T. Washington, maintained that blacks should "cast down their buckets" and accept the crumbs provided by whites for their industrial training and support at places like Tuskegee Institute. Washington believed blacks should not insist on political and social equality: "In all things that are purely social we can be as separate as the five fingers, yet one as the hand in all things essential to mutual progress." [125] To his credit, Washington understood a century ago what some black leaders today fail to teach, that the plight of African Americans is linked to their relationship to whites. But Washington's Atlanta Compromise, though appealing to many whites, produced opposition among other black intellectuals. Foremost among this group was Du Bois, who castigated Washington for accepting the separate but equal philosophy of *Plessy* and compromising on demanding equal political rights, including suffrage. Du Bois's *The Souls of Black Folk* spelled out why Washington's philosophy was harmful to the masses of blacks, relegating them to civil inferiority.

Conditions remained so poor for blacks early in the twentieth century that Marcus Garvey and his Universal Negro Improvement Association (UNIA) gained wide popularity, promoting black pride and self-determination. Long before Stokely Carmichael and others proclaimed "Black Power" in the 1960s, Garvey, a Jamaican by birth, insisted that blackness was a symbol of beauty and strength and that Africans had a noble past of which blacks in America should be proud. He tapped their feelings of oppression and exhorted blacks that their only hope was to flee America and build their own country in Africa. Hundreds of thousands of African Americans hailed Garvey as a hero and their leader, but in the end, very few signed up to leave the United States. Indeed, there is no evidence that at any time since Emancipation, masses of African Americans have abandoned America. Why would they leave their country, which they helped build?

Garvey's meteoric rise did not precede without criticism from other black leaders, who thought his relocation scheme was wrongheaded and shortsighted and who viewed him as a pompous self-promoter. Yet his broad appeal shows how some react to a charismatic messenger who stands up to white domination. Indeed, this same phenomenon may explain the popularity among some blacks of Louis Farrakhan, despite his virulent anti-Semitism. Many white Americans fail to note the life conditions that lead to calls for black nationalism. Instead, they focus on the messengers rather than the Americans with darker skin who simply want full citizenship. Until whites throughout America eliminate racial caste, Farrakhan or others will attract sympathetic audiences. Even if many African Americans find his anti-Semitism repulsive and indefensible, they still agree with him that white supremacy is a disease.

Whites rarely are aware of the extent of the color line in twentieth-century in America or what it took from overworked and underpaid lawyers to end "Jim Crow" laws. One of them, Justice Thurgood Marshall, was born into America's racial caste in July 1908 in Baltimore, Maryland, approximately one year before a group of blacks, whites, and Jews founded the National Association for the Advancement of Colored People (NAACP).[126] As a lawyer, jurist, and public servant, Marshall helped lead the attack on America's system of apartheid. But his life also demonstrated how racial discrimination foreclosed opportunities to all blacks, regardless of class.

Marshall's great-grandfather was brought to this country as a slave, and his grandfather, a free person of color, was a soldier in the Union Army. Marshall's father was a Pullman porter and then a steward at an exclusive all-white yacht club; his mother was an elementary school teacher. He described his childhood as comfortable but limited by a rigid color line.[127] Like Marshall, many blacks in this country can look back four or five generations and find a slave relative. Moreover, many blacks have parents or grandparents whose employment choices were limited to teacher, domestic, porter, agricultural worker, and the like.

For Marshall and millions of other blacks, post-*Plessy* America was a cruel paradox: despite the nation's written principles of fairness, equality, and due process, the reality of white racial privilege continued to prevail. Equal opportunity was a myth. Instead, blacks like Marshall came of age in the face of political and economic discrimination, including grandfather clauses; poll taxes; discriminatory educational or property qualifications; literacy tests; all-white primaries, juries, schools, and occupations; segregated public accommodations; and racially restrictive residential covenants, all supported legally by local rule or extralegally by race riots, intimidation, or lynchings.

Marshall's public education took place in one-race schools; because of his color, he was presumed unfit to attend schools with white children in Baltimore. Little four-year-old Sarah Roberts had suffered this same humiliation in Boston in 1850,[128] as would Linda Brown one hundred years later in Topeka.[129] Both children were forced to go to inferior, overcrowded, and underfunded schools, even though both lived within walking distance of less crowded, better-funded white schools. The two girls' character and economic status were irrelevant to their exclusion.

Marshall graduated with honors in 1930 from Lincoln University, a prestigious all-male, all-black college near Chester, Pennsylvania. In the fall of that year, he was denied admission to the University of Maryland's law school, his first choice, solely because of his race: Maryland did not admit any blacks. Numerous blacks who had any hope of going to college had to go to historically black colleges or not go. Today, those same black colleges are under attack as separatist, a mischaracterization possible only when critics ignore the historical exclusion of all blacks from many state-supported schools for whites only.

With the door closed at Maryland, Marshall attended the Howard University School of Law, where he graduated first in his class in 1933. After graduating, he joined the Maryland Bar Association and opened a small law office in Baltimore. He became a counsel for the local NAACP in 1934, and in that capacity he and his mentor, Charles Hamilton Houston, a distinguished lawyer and educator who directed the NAACP's earliest attacks on Jim Crow laws, convinced a Maryland appellate court that the University of Maryland's exclusion of Donald Murray from its law school was unconstitutional.[130]

In 1936, Houston recruited Marshall to join the NAACP's legal staff in New York. Two years later Marshall succeeded him as chief counsel. For a quarter century, between 1938 and 1961, Marshall was the principal architect of the legal strategy to end official, state-sponsored segregation in the United States.[131] Under his leadership, the NAACP and, after 1940, the NAACP Legal Defense and Educational Fund (LDF), the nonprofit agency created by Marshall to finance desegregation litigation, attacked every form of segregation in the United States. In *Smith v. Allright*,[132] he won in a case concerning the all-white Democratic primaries in Texas and throughout the South which effectively denied blacks their right to vote by prohibiting them from participating in the primary that selected the Democratic nominee. In *Shelley v. Kraemer*,[133] he convinced the Supreme Court that the judicial enforcement of racially restrictive covenants in real estate transactions that prevented blacks from living in certain communities was unconstitutional. He also won the cases before the Court that segregation in interstate transportation and in public graduate and professional schools violated the Constitution.[134] Lloyd Gaines, Ada Sipuel, and Heman Sweatt all were aided by Marshall and the LDF when

Missouri, Oklahoma, and Texas denied them admission to universities. Marshall also served as one of Autherine Lucy's lawyers in her challenge against the University of Alabama's policy of segregation.[135]

Perhaps Marshall's greatest legal victory came in 1954 when the U.S. Supreme Court agreed that segregated public schools were unconstitutional, notwithstanding the separate-but-equal doctrine of *Plessy v. Ferguson*. In *Brown v. Board of Education*,[136] Marshall convinced the Court that segregated schools were inherently unequal. He reiterated arguments from earlier cases that in segregated schools neither the tangibles nor the intangibles were equal and added that it caused substantial harm to all children, especially black children, who were thereby stamped with a badge of inferiority. Marshall thus linked state-sponsored segregation with racial caste in the way that Justice Harlan had done in his dissent in *Plessy*.

In a unanimous opinion written by Chief Justice Earl Warren, the Court gave notice that segregation in public affairs would end:

> Does segregation of children in public schools solely on the basis of race, even though the physical facilities and other "tangible" factors may be equal, deprive the children of the minority group of equal educational opportunities? We believe that it does. . . .
> . . . To separate [children] from others of similar age and qualifications solely because of their race generates a feeling of inferiority as to their status in the community that may affect their hearts and minds in a way unlikely ever to be undone. . . .
> . . . Separate education facilities are inherently unequal. Therefore, we hold that the plaintiffs [have been] deprived of the equal protection of the laws guaranteed by the Fourteenth Amendment.[137]

Unlike the Court, the nation was divided over *Brown*. In the South, where schools were segregated by law, critics read it as federal excess and interference.

*Brown* had many critics in part because the Court accepted sociological data as proof of the harm of segregation to black children. The essence of the objection was that the ruling was not decided on neutral principles of reason or law, principles transcending the immediate result.[138] But *Brown* clearly states that segregation in public education violates the equal protection clause of the Fourteenth Amendment. Conversely, the opinion might have read that white school officials have no rights, associational or otherwise, to arrange schools in a manner that denies black children equal educational opportunity or that places them in a caste position.

Ultimately, however, the *Brown* opinion did not go far enough to expose and denounce an obvious racial privilege to whites (segregated schools) for what it was. By couching its decision in terms of racial harm to black children, the Court failed to explain to white Americans that white supremacy was unconstitutional. Was this too much to expect from an all-white Court? Were members of the Court blind to white privilege? The opinion could have declared that segregated schools place black children in a caste position, in much the same way that Harlan had criticized the separate railway car statute in *Plessy*. Even though *Brown* was the most important race case decided by the Court in the twentieth century, the Court missed an opportunity to openly repudiate white privilege. Its failure has consequently made it much easier for proponents of color blindness to misappropriate *Brown*, just as some did with Harlan's dissent in *Plessy*.

After *Brown*, between 1955 and 1968, America again faced a constitutional crisis. At its center was racial discrimination. Numerous state and local authorities, from Arkansas to Virginia, pronounced *Brown* unconstitutional and pledged to close their schools before they would desegregate them. Newspapers ran editorial after editorial deriding the Court's decision. When the governor and the legislature of Arkansas insisted they were not bound by the Court's holding, the Supreme Court answered decisively that its interpretation of the Fourteenth Amendment was the supreme law of the land and that such defiance of a constitutional decision was in direct conflict with the supremacy clause of the Constitution.[139] President Dwight D. Eisenhower thereupon ordered federal troops to Little Rock, Arkansas, to halt interference with school desegregation at its Central High School.[140]

The civil rights crisis extended beyond the schools to virtually every aspect of life in America. For example, 1955 saw the mutilation and murder of fourteen-year-old Emmett Till in Money, Mississippi, for speaking freshly to a white woman. Pictures of Till's grotesque corpse were shown throughout the country as more evidence of racial violence.[141] In a farcical trial, an all-white, all-male jury acquitted Till's killers. In 1963, Medgar Evers, the NAACP's field secretary for Mississippi, was shot in the back in front of his home in Jackson. Two all-white juries deadlocked over whether Evers's alleged killer, Byron de la Beckwith, was guilty, showing yet again that American criminal justice was not color blind. (In 1995, a mixed-race jury finally convicted de la Beckwith.) In the fall of 1963, only weeks after 250,000 Americans marched on Washington, demanding an end to job and housing discrimination, race riots erupted in Birmingham, Alabama, after a bomb ripped through the Sixteenth Street Baptist Church, killing four young black girls.[142] In 1964, after a painstaking search, federal authorities found the bodies of three civil rights workers, Andrew Goodman, James Chaney, and Michael Schwerner, in Philadelphia, Mississippi.[143] The following year in Selma, Alabama, Jimmy Lee Jackson, Violla Liuzzo, and Rev. James Reeb were killed for participating in voting rights demonstrations or for daring to defend themselves from racial violence. As the body count, black and white, increased, the nation began to take notice. Americans were anything but color blind.

## CRITIQUING COLOR BLINDNESS

Numerous others have set forth competing critiques of the color blindness principle. Indeed, in the late 1960s and early 1970s, the issue split leading legal scholars.[144] Since then, each side has tried to explain why color blindness is or is not good policy. Some people insist that color blindness is essential to advancing equality,[145] whereas others find its opposite—color awareness or race consciousness—more consistent with constitutional guarantees of equality.[146] For example, Andrew Kull argued forcefully that race is an improper criterion for classifying or assigning government benefits or burdens under the law and that in nearly all settings, the government should act without reference to the race of any party. Kull might, albeit cautiously, make an exception for blacks. On the other side, Neil Gotanda contended that the color blindness principle was inconsistent with the meaning of equality in the Constitution and that government could use racial classifications when eradicating past and continuing racial caste.[147]

Color blindness is a confusing metaphor. Rhetorically, the argument is that if individuals and government stopped using race to disadvantage others, the United States could advance beyond its history of racial subordination. But Americans have shown that they will not stop discriminating unless forced to do so. Others insist that the government cannot achieve its educative role of teaching that racial discrimination is wrong while simultaneously permitting the use of racial classifications to benefit a small racial minority. This contention rests on the premise that every racial classification is the same; that remedial affirmative action is the same as whites-only quotas. This is simply wrong.[148]

American history does not teach that racial discrimination is "illegal, immoral, unconstitutional, inherently wrong, and destructive to a democratic society." [149] American history is instead taught more as a tribute to prominent white men in business and government than as an analysis of human relationships. Indeed, throughout my formative education, I learned almost nothing about racial discrimination by whites against blacks.

The champions of color blindness ignore the clearest lessons of America's racial history, which teach that (1) since its inception, the United States has had a policy of racial supremacy that continues to subordinate blacks and other minorities while privileging whites; (2) efforts by Congress and later by the Supreme Court to eradicate the policy of racial supremacy have been sidetracked by members of those institutions and by noncompliance throughout the nation; (3) Americans are intensely aware of color and regularly use it to privilege some and disadvantage others; (4) most of the Supreme Court's landmark race cases reflect color awareness, not color blindness; and (5) the Court's application of the color blindness principle will extend the nation's legacy of white supremacy into the next century.

Another aspect of the confusion surrounding the color blindness principle concerns its original meaning. As I pointed out earlier, Justice Harlan's dissent in *Plessy* can reasonably be interpreted as prohibiting racial subordination and requiring its affirmative eradication. David Strauss took a similar position with regard to *Brown*, contending that the prohibition against discrimination established in that case was not rooted in color blindness but "is, like affirmative action, deeply race-conscious; like affirmative action, the prohibition against discrimination reflects a deliberate decision to treat blacks differently from other groups, even at the expense of innocent whites." [150] When the Court banned segregation in *Brown*, blacks cheered triumphantly, optimistic that equality was nearer than ever. Yet now some argue that both Harlan's *Plessy* dissent and *Brown* repudiate remedial affirmative action rather than white supremacy. Because of this confusion and its damaging effect on black racial hopes, the color blindness doctrine should be abandoned.

The color blindness model preserves "white" rule in the United States, extending racial caste from one generation of blacks to yet another [151] and maintaining America as a " 'white' country: in character, in structure, in culture." [152] America's Founding Fathers gave themselves an original advantage that subsequent generations of whites have inherited.

But many whites ignore this history, believing that white racial hegemony is normative. "Color-blind constitutionalists live in an ideological world where racial subordination is ubiquitous yet disregarded—unless it takes the form of individual, intended, and irrational prejudice."[153] The color blindness doctrine today enshrines the very racial subordination that Justice Harlan insisted was unconstitutional.

Given how race operates in the United States, color blindness rhetoric seems pretentious and counterintuitive. Americans are trained throughout life to think in terms of racial categories, to believe that those categories are natural, pure, and immutable. Consider that government statistics and records regarding any significant fact—education, income, accumulated wealth, birth, marriage, voting, type of employment, crime, unemployment, or disease—are often organized and reported by racial groupings. Oddly enough, despite all this racial training and information, Americans today are not supposed to act on the basis of race. Thus, they learn to choose carefully the race of their life partners and neighbors. Americans learn that people who challenge racial lines frequently suffer reprisals, such as loss of employment, social ostracism, or anonymous threats of intimidation, such as the burning of black churches.[154]

In the United States, almost anyone can see that there still are black neighborhoods, schools, parks, swimming pools, restaurants, churches, social clubs, funeral homes, and even cemeteries. And usually not very far away, but beyond the economic or political reach of most blacks, are white neighborhoods, schools, parks, swimming pools, restaurants, churches, social clubs, funeral homes, and cemeteries. How can people living and thinking in such a world apply a color blindness model when they have been trained to think and live in those very terms? They cannot.

Color blindness is counterintuitive in other ways. Americans not only recognize race and divide by race; they also assign moral worth and culpability on that basis. There is a generally unstated assumption that black people are poor and unlettered because they lack the capacity and ambition of whites, that "they" have what "they" deserve. This argument was recently used in books by Shelby Steele, Thomas Sowell, and Dinesh D'Souza. Each contends that blacks make excessive claims to victimization and have not learned an ethic of individual responsibility.[155] The corollary assumption also is obvious, yet unstated: white people are not poor and are lettered because they are more capable and have more ambition and better values than blacks do; thus "they" have what "they" deserve. It is no wonder that when possible, some minorities prefer to be classified or to pass as white.[156]

In the United States, being classified as white has a distinct value. Whites continue to earn higher wages than blacks do for comparable work, and life expectancy for blacks remains lower than for whites, by several years. Also, whites can obtain commercial loans on more favorable terms than blacks can, and they can obtain housing with fewer obstacles than blacks can. These racial realities were presented to millions of Americans in the fall of 1991 when the staff of ABC television's *Primetime Live* went undercover in St. Louis, Missouri. The news agency followed two twenty-eight-year-old men, one black and the other white, in search of employment, housing, a new car, and services at local stores. Jobs that had been filled when the black applicant inquired were still available when the white applicant arrived ten minutes later. The apartment that was available for lease to the white applicant was not available a few minutes later to the black applicant. The white applicant was given better terms for a car loan and immediately obtained service at local stores. When the two men were locked out of their cars forty feet apart, several whites assisted the white person, but none of them helped the black man.[157] Color blindness masks racial privileges.

The St. Louis experiment reveals that it still is a privilege to be white in the United States. A significant source of this racial privilege is the racial affinity or sympathy that whites show to other whites, in contrast to the racial indifference, or often hostility, that many whites show to blacks.[158] The doctrine of color blindness ignores the roles of racial affinity and indifference in routine decision making.

Moreover, color blindness is counterintuitive because the labels *black* and *white* have symbolism beyond color. When we encounter members of a race, we also meet a complex set of common racial generalizations and experiences. We even assign points of view based on racial generalizations. Therefore, color blindness discounts the significance of racial generalizations in the United States.[159]

Color blindness also presupposes Americans' equal status by race, even though blacks and whites have never had equal status in the United States. The Declaration of Independence may have proclaimed equality among men, but this declaration was limited to a ruling class of white men. Moreover, our Constitution did not contain an explicit provision regarding equality until the Fourteenth Amendment was passed, almost a century later, in 1868. But after more than a dozen decades, we are still debating what that provision of equality means in relation to racial subordination. If racial equality is to have any rational meaning, its nature and scope must encompass the comparative status of blacks and whites. Therefore, the color blindness model prematurely forecloses a full explication of the principle of racial equality.[160]

The color blindness doctrine—viscerally appealing as it is to many whites—essentially restates the doctrine of separate but equal. It ignores the reality that America remains a divided and unequal nation, that racial enmity is again on the rise, and that whites continue to hold economic and political advantages, in large part by virtue of their historical control over blacks.[161] We must never forget that the *Plessy* Court gave us both the separate-but-equal doctrine and the color blindness doctrine. The former, however, was articulated by the majority in defense of white supremacy, and the latter appeared in the dissent. Nonetheless, some people continue to insist that the color blindness principle means that remedial affirmative action policies designed to eliminate racial caste are constitutionally equivalent to those that promoted racial supremacy.

This is not what Justice Harlan intended, and it is an interpretation that is perverse, ahistorical, and unjust—and should be abandoned for the fraud that it is.

ᘐ

**PART THREE**

# THE CONSTITUTIONALITY OF REMEDIAL AFFIRMATIVE ACTION

**N**ow that I have explained, using both personal and historical reasons, why remedial affirmative action is effective and justifiable and why color blindness will extend white privilege into the next century, I want to show why remedial affirmative action does not violate people's constitutional rights. The Supreme Court has claimed on numerous occasions that the Constitution prohibits invidious racial discrimination, that is, policies intentionally designed to discriminate and enacted because of their discriminatory effects.

The Court has distinguished between governmental policies that promote racial supremacy and those that rest on a remedial purpose, such as eliminating racial (or gender) caste. Thus, whereas the Court struck down school segregation, it upheld a school board policy to require schools to provide remedial reading and to use race as a factor in faculty and student assignments.[1] Since the remedial context of modern affirmative action has made a difference in the Court's analysis, I shall begin there.

### THE ORIGINS OF REMEDIAL AFFIRMATIVE ACTION

Modern remedial affirmative action began in response to widespread racial discrimination in employment.[2] In the 1930s and 1940s, when my

**115**

mother Dee was a child, there were white jobs and black jobs, just as there were white schools, churches, and communities and black schools, churches, and communities. Black job classifications in the South were, by long tradition, principally in agriculture and domestic service, with a few blacks working as ministers or teachers at black churches and black schools. In those days, merit was not the basis for employment. No matter how well educated or accomplished a black worker was, he or she could not obtain a job explicitly reserved for whites, mostly men. Blacks worked as railroad firemen and brakemen before the advent of steam engines, in coal and iron ore mines, in lumber and steel plants, and in construction jobs. Then, as more whites joined unions, they evicted black workers from various occupations.

When blacks migrated north and west, away from the legal color line of the South, they encountered an equally inflexible custom restricting them to a only few black job classifications. In large urban centers like Philadelphia, Chicago, Washington, D.C., and Los Angeles, with growing black and minority populations, many trades and crafts were open only to whites, in accordance with union policy or local custom. The typical union membership statement was similar to the following from the Order of Sleeping Car Conductors: "The applicant for membership shall be a white male, sober and industrious, and must join of his own free will." [3] In numerous industries, unions covering shipbuilding, machinists, maritime, construction, transit, and trucking excluded blacks from membership or relegated them to the hardest, dirtiest, most dangerous, lowest-paying work.

When blacks challenged whites-only practices to compel occupational desegregation, they met with vehement opposition. For example, in 1944 the "City of Brotherly Love," Philadelphia, narrowly avoided a race war when white transit workers struck to protest the desegregation of job classifications and the promotion of blacks in the Philadelphia Transportation Company (PTC). [4] Some whites claimed then—as many do now— that blacks were unfairly taking their jobs. Union leaders posted handbills that read:

> Your Sons and Buddies that are away Fighting for the Country, are being stabbed in the back on the Home Front by The National Association For the Advancement of Negroes, and the [Fair Employment Practice Committee,] which is a 100% Negro Lobby. . . . During the last War the Prohibitionists Raided the Country While The Boys were away fighting and During this War The Negroes are Raiding the country while the White

Mens [*sic*] backs are turned. The Negroes in this War are Reaping A War Loot Harvest. The Negroes are taking Every Advantage to Gain Control of All the Jobs and Everything Else that belongs to the White People, while they are away fighting. . . . The P.T.C. trolley Men are the Latest Victims of these Active Negro Lobbies.[5]

The handbill implies that blacks were not fighting and dying in the war and that certain jobs belonged to whites, plain and simple. In fact, of course, many black men went to war for this country and died on the battlefield. Others came home only to find that little had changed for them in America, that employment remained colorized. A crisis was averted in Philadelphia only when President Franklin D. Roosevelt ordered the seizure of the company and called on National Guardsmen to restore order.

In Philadelphia and elsewhere, transit companies had designated certain jobs, including that of bus driver and the conductor and motorman on streetcars, as "white men's jobs." Blacks, on the other hand, could work as car cleaners or porters. There was no system of merit. No black—no matter how capable—could work as a conductor or bus driver. But such policies were on a collision course with an increasingly impatient public and a federal government that could not reconcile whites-only jobs with the rhetoric of equality that was at the center of the American war effort. Indeed, America's apartheid made it vulnerable to criticism comparable to that of Nazi Germany.[6] How could America condemn Hitler when its own backyard was so rife with racial supremacy?

One can trace contemporary remedial affirmative action policies from early references in the New Deal legislation of the 1930s, through efforts to eliminate racial discrimination in the war industries, to the executive orders and civil rights acts of the 1960s.[7] Some of the New Deal legislation explicitly provided that "in employing citizens . . . no discrimination shall be made on account of race, color, or creed."[8] This meant that white men could not continue to discriminate against people of color.

In 1941, when President Roosevelt was threatened by A. Phillip Randolph, head of the Brotherhood of Sleeping Car Porters, with a national march on Washington to protest employment discrimination, he declared, in Executive Order 8802, that it was "the policy of the U.S. that there shall be no discrimination in employment . . . because of race, creed, color or national origin."[9] Roosevelt's order required employers and labor organizations to provide for the full and equitable participation of all workers in the defense industry—without discrimination.[10] It was not a declaration that Americans were color blind; it was exactly the opposite: a mandate to end employment quotas for white men throughout the defense industries.

This antidiscrimination clause was widely disregarded during the Truman and Eisenhower presidencies. In 1960, Vice President Richard M. Nixon reported to President Eisenhower that overt discrimination was not as prevalent as believed but that employers were not greatly interested in establishing a positive policy of nondiscrimination that kept qualified minority and female applicants from being hired and promoted on the basis of equality.[11]

The Nixon report influenced the scope of President John F. Kennedy's Executive Order 10,925, which not only outlawed overt discrimination but also required that contractors pledge to take affirmative action to ensure that applicants would be employed and treated without regard to race, color, religion, or national origin. This order also gave the President's Committee on Equal Employment Opportunity the power to adopt appropriate rules and regulations to achieve its goals.[12]

Michael Sovern compared the work of the Kennedy and Eisenhower administrations and found that Kennedy's committee was far more effective in investigating and resolving discrimination complaints.[13] One such complaint is illustrative: The NAACP charged that a federal agency had made a mockery of Executive Order 10,925 by awarding the Lockheed Aircraft Corporation a $1 billion jet plane contract despite its discriminatory employment practices. According to the complaint, Lockheed was to manufacture the planes at its Marietta, Georgia, plant, whose discriminatory conditions included the limitation of blacks to unskilled or semi-skilled jobs, with the blanket exclusion of blacks from the company's apprenticeship program; segregated cafeterias, drinking fountains, and restrooms; and a segregated union. Within seven weeks of the complaint, the president of Lockheed signed a statement promising far-reaching reforms regarding the recruitment, employment, and training of qualified minority candidates.

Following the NAACP's success with this complaint, a "Plans for Progress" campaign emerged, with federal contractors committing their companies to antidiscrimination, including the affirmative recruitment of minorities for employment, training, and promotion. Mobil Oil, in Beaumont, Texas, agreed to eliminate its separate seniority lines for blacks and whites and its separate facilities. Avco Corporation, in Richmond, Indiana, abandoned its policy of not hiring blacks. National Aniline, in Chesterfield, Virginia, agreed to implement a program of equal opportunity and to desegregate its plants. For those companies such as Comet Rice Mills, in Arkansas, Louisiana, and Texas, and Danly Machine Specialties, in Cicero, Illinois, that did not hire blacks or limited them to low-wage, unskilled jobs, the committee declared that they could not obtain new government contracts until they submitted to the committee full reports on their employment practices. Within two to four weeks of the ban, both companies, fearing the loss of lucrative contracts, moved to correct their practices.[14]

In addition, Congress's enactment of titles II, VI, and VII of the 1964 Civil Rights Act—legislation designed to prohibit discrimination in public accommodations and race and gender discrimination by private employers and agencies or educational institutions receiving federal monies—enhanced the strength of prior antidiscrimination policies and remedial affirmative action directives.[15] Section 706(g) of title VII gave courts the authority to enjoin unlawful employment practices (race and gender discrimination) and to order such affirmative action as might be appropriate. It also created the Equal Employment Opportunity Commission.[16]

In 1965, President Lyndon B. Johnson issued additional orders, including Executive Order 11,246, which was the most comprehensive and has come under the greatest attack:

> It is the policy of the United States to provide equal opportunity in Federal employment for all qualified persons, to prohibit discrimination in employment because of race, creed, color, or national origin, and to promote the full realization of equal employment opportunity through a positive, continuing program in each executive department and agency.[17]

This order talks about the realization of equal opportunity for all qualified persons, but despite claims to the contrary, none of its provisions mandates the hiring of unqualified employees. Rather, it restructures federal affirmative action law from being voluntary (under Executive Order 10,925) to being obligatory.

Section 201 of the order gives authority to the secretary of labor to administer its provisions regarding nondiscrimination, and section 209 gives the secretary a choice of sanctions for noncompliers, including the power to cancel or terminate contracts. Section 202 contains the provisions required in each contractor's agreement, including a statement that "the contractor will take affirmative action to ensure that applicants are employed, and employees are treated during employment, without regard to their race, creed, color, or national origin." Section 203 requires each contractor to file compliance reports containing data on the contractor's employment statistics, policies, practices, and programs that the labor secretary may prescribe.[18]

During President Nixon's first term, when federal agencies tried to enforce affirmative action regulations, requiring contractors to establish hiring goals and timetables for the employment of minority workers and evidence of good-faith efforts to achieve these goals, the policies were challenged as illegal quotas.[19] Typical of such challenges was the 1971 attack on the Philadelphia Plan, promulgated under the authority of Executive Order 11,246, which required bidders on any federal or federally assisted construction contracts for projects in the five-county area around Philadelphia to submit an acceptable affirmative action plan, including specific goals for the inclusion of minority manpower in six skilled crafts: ironworkers, plumbers and pipe fitters, steamfitters, sheet metal workers, electrical workers, and elevator construction workers. The plan also required bidders to make good-faith efforts to meet targeted minority hiring goals within timetables established by Assistant Labor Secretary Arthur Fletcher, who, by the way, remains a proponent of remedial affirmative action.[20]

The plan was illegal, insisted the plaintiffs, because it was beyond the scope of executive power under the Constitution and was inconsistent with titles VI and VII, among other laws. The federal circuit court rejected all the plaintiffs' constitutional and statutory challenges,[21] making it clear that it viewed the Philadelphia Plan as race conscious: "Indeed the only meaning which can be attributed to the affirmative action language which since March of 1961 has been included in successive Executive Orders is that Government contractors must be color-conscious."[22] That is, in 1971, this court did not think that color-conscious remedial affirmative action was illegal. Quite the contrary, the court believed that Congress and the president intended that employers working under federal or federally assisted projects hire minority and female workers. But as the affirmative action programs expanded, so did the public debate over them.

## THE COURT OF LAST RESORT

As remedial affirmative action policies were extended within employment and to other areas, including education, political participation, and housing programs, the opposition also grew, scholarly criticism mounted, and judicial opinions split, requiring the Supreme Court to step in. As the ultimate voice on constitutional interpretation, it is the Supreme Court's duty to determine whether governmental policies violate constitutional rights.

*Regents of the University of California v. Bakke*[23] was the first decision of the Supreme Court to analyze the constitutionality of race-conscious affirmative action. The medical school of the University of California at Davis opened in 1968 with an entering class of fifty: forty-seven whites, three Asians, no blacks, no Mexican Americans, and no Native Americans. The Davis faculty saw this lack of diversity as a problem and so devised a special admissions policy to increase diversity in future classes.

The new policy consisted of both a regular admissions process and a special admissions process. Under the regular policy, candidates whose overall undergraduate grade point averages fell below 2.5 on a scale of 4.0 were summarily rejected. Following a personal interview, each of the remaining candidates was rated on a scale of 1 to 100. This rating combined the interviewers' summaries, overall grade point average, grade point average in science courses, scores on the Medical College Admissions Test (MCAT), letters of recommendation, extracurricular activities, and other biographical data, to arrive at each candidate's "benchmark" score. In 1973, a perfect score was 500, and in 1974, it was 600. The full committee then reviewed each applicant's file and scores. The chair was responsible for placing names on the waiting list. But they were not placed in strict numerical order; instead, the chair could include persons with "special skills." Despite his scores of 468 out of 500 and 549 out of 600, Allan Bakke, a white male, was rejected in 1973 and 1974 and was not placed on the waiting list in either year.

The special admissions program operated with a separate committee, a majority of whom were members of minority groups. On the 1973 application form, candidates were asked to indicate whether they wished to be considered as "economically and/or educationally disadvantaged" applicants; on the 1974 form, the question was whether they wished to be considered as members of a "minority group," which included blacks, Latinos, Asians, and Native Americans. If this question was answered affirmatively, the application was forwarded to the special admissions committee. Such applicants were rated by the special committee in a process similar to that used by the general admissions committee, except that special candidates did not have to meet the 2.5 grade point average cutoff applied to regular applicants. Following each interview, the special committee assigned to each special applicant a benchmark score. The special committee then presented its top choices to the general admissions committee. The general committee did not rate or compare the special applicants against the regular applicants but could reject special candidates for failing to meet course requirements or other specific deficiencies. The special admissions committee continued to recommend special applicants until the number prescribed by faculty vote had been admitted. Bakke was never considered under the special admissions program.

Bakke challenged the Davis medical school's special admissions policy, which at that time set aside sixteen of its one hundred places in the entering class for members of designated racial minorities. The Superior Court of California sustained Bakke's challenge, holding that Davis's program violated state and federal constitutional and statutory provisions. The court thereupon enjoined Davis from considering the race of applicants in making admissions decisions. It refused, however, to order Bakke's admission to medical school, holding that he had not carried his burden of proving that he would have been admitted but for the constitutional and statutory violations. The Supreme Court of California affirmed those portions of the trial court's judgment, declaring the special admissions program to be unlawful and enjoining Davis from considering the race of any applicant. The California Supreme Court also directed the trial court to order Bakke's admission, an order that was stayed pending review by the U.S. Supreme Court.

The Supreme Court split into two camps, with Justice Lewis Powell serving as the critical swing vote for each. Justices William Brennan, Byron White, Thurgood Marshall, and Harry Blackmun were on one side, holding with Powell that race could be considered along with other "diversity" factors in making admissions decisions but that, according to Justice Powell, it could not be the sole factor. On the other side were Chief Justice Warren Burger and Justices Potter Stewart, John Paul Stevens, and William Rehnquist agreeing with Powell that the Davis admissions policy was constitutionally invalid and that Bakke should be admitted.

Justice Powell's opinion remains very important to determining how the government can use race in making decisions without running afoul of the Constitution. Powell first addressed the scope of section 601 of title VI of the 1964 Civil Rights Act: "No person in the United States shall, on the ground of race, color, or national origin, be excluded from participation in, be denied benefits of, or be subjected to discrimination under any program or activity receiving Federal financial assistance." [24]

To determine the meaning of this statute, Powell reviewed its voluminous legislative history:

> Although isolated statements of various legislators, taken out of context, can be marshaled in support of the proposition that Section 601 enacted a purely color-blind scheme, without regard to the reach of the Equal Protection Clause, these comments must be read against the background of both the problem that Congress was addressing and the broader view of the statute that emerges from a full examination of the legislative debates.

According to the statute's floor manager in the House, the problem confronting Congress was discrimination against blacks at the hands of recipients of federal funds and how to guarantee them equal treatment:

> The bill would offer assurance that hospitals financed by Federal money would not deny adequate care to Negroes. It would prevent abuse of food distribution programs whereby Negroes have been known to be denied food surplus supplies when white persons were given such food. It would assure Negroes the benefits now accorded white students in programs of higher education financed by Federal funds. It would, in short, assure the existing right to equal treatment in the enjoyment of federal funds.[25]

When people refer to the Civil Rights Act of 1964, they often ignore or forget its historical context. But Powell did not, holding that title VI prohibited only those racial classifications that would violate the Constitution.[26]

Powell next turned to the question of whether the special admissions policy was a goal or a quota:

> It is settled beyond question that the rights created by the first section of the Fourteenth Amendment are, by its terms, guaranteed to the individual. The rights are personal rights. The guarantee of equal protection cannot mean one thing when applied to one individual and something else when applied to a person of another color. If both are not accorded the same protection, then it is not equal.

Powell continued, "[A]ll legal restrictions which curtail the civil rights of a single racial group are immediately suspect. That is not to say that all such restrictions are unconstitutional. It is to say that courts must subject them to the most rigid scrutiny."²⁷ As I will show later, this is the same standard of review the Supreme Court used in its 1995 affirmative action cases. Therefore, it can be argued that the diversity model endorsed by Justice Powell in 1978, which survived strict scrutiny review, does not violate the Constitution.

Powell explained that the reach of the equal protection clause had been expanded beyond the protection of former slaves to all ethnic groups seeking protection from state-sponsored discrimination:

> During the dormancy of the Equal Protection Clause, the United States had become a Nation of minorities. Each had to struggle—and to some extent struggles still—to overcome the prejudices not of a monolithic majority, but of a "majority" composed of various minority groups of whom it was said—perhaps unfairly in many cases—that a shared characteristic was a willingness to disadvantage other groups. As the Nation filled with the stock of many lands, the reach of the Clause was gradually extended to all ethnic groups seeking protection from official discrimination.²⁸

To support his argument, Justice Powell cited language from cases between 1880 and 1954 in which the Court applied the equal protection clause to Irish, Chinese, Austrian, Japanese, and Mexican Americans. He thereby introduced the concept of ethnic fungibility into equal protection jurisprudence. For him, blacks were simply one of many minorities in the United States struggling against discrimination.

Powell's view trivializes the causes and effects of current racial caste and, furthermore, is inconsistent with the specific history of racial subordination of blacks by whites outlined in Part 2. His reference to immigration in the United States seems especially curious in a case such as *Bakke*: it is as if Justice Powell believed that white males like Allan Bakke had experienced a history of racial discrimination similar to that of blacks, Native Americans, Asians, or Mexican Americans. But neither he nor anyone else, then or now, can point to an American tradition of discrimination against whites on the basis of race.

Powell did not stop with his ethnic fungibility theory:

> Because the landmark decisions in this area arose in response to the continued exclusion of Negroes from the mainstream of American society, they could be characterized as involving discrimination by the "majority" white race against the Negro minority. But they need not be read as depending upon that characterization for their results. It suffices to say that "[o]ver the years, this Court has consistently repudiated '[d]istinctions between citi-

zens solely because of their ancestry' as being 'odious to a free people whose institutions are founded upon the doctrine of equality.' " [29]

This argument, too, is misleading. The landmark decisions to which Powell alludes are the same ones that Charles Houston, Thurgood Marshall, and other lawyers litigated on behalf of blacks who were denied their constitutional rights by whites in and out of government. In addition, in Powell's discussion of title VI, he pointed to the purpose of its enactment, to ensure blacks the rights enjoyed by whites. Powell's equal protection discussion implies some sort of reciprocal discrimination by black "majorities," in or out of government, thereby denying whites their constitutional rights. Yet he does not give a single example.

Justice Powell ignored the fact that Bakke was not excluded from Davis solely on the basis of race. Between 1971 and 1974, the regular admits included only 1 black, 6 Mexican Americans, and 37 Asians out of the 336 new students. During that same period, the special program admitted 21 blacks, 30 Mexicans, and 12 Asians. Bakke was not admitted because during the subjectively objective admissions process, he apparently annoyed the chair of the committee—perhaps because of his views about Davis's affirmative action plan—and he gave Bakke his lowest benchmark score. Thus, even if Davis had not set aside sixteen places for minorities, it is unlikely that Bakke would have been admitted. Therefore, to compare the Davis policy with one that excludes all members of a racial group from a campus misconceives apartheid-era cases.

Powell also ignored the historical backdrop of the enactment of remedial affirmative action policies. He wrote that the equal protection clause would no longer permit the recognition of "special wards," intimating that in light of affirmative action, blacks were somehow special wards of the government. Powell's language is similar to that used by Justice Joseph Bradley one hundred years earlier in the *Civil Rights Cases:*

> When a man has emerged from slavery, and by the aid of beneficent legislation has shaken off the inseparable concomitants of that state, there must be some stage in the progress of his elevation when he takes the rank of a mere citizen, and ceases to be the special favorite of the laws, and when his rights as a citizen, or a man, are to be protected in the ordinary modes by which other men's rights are protected.[30]

Powell's return to Bradley's language is chilling, especially because he made no effort to examine the historical justifications for remedial affirmative action and because for nearly a century after the 1880s, blacks' rights were not protected.

Powell also undervalued the constitutional significance of racial subordination in the Court's prior equal protection decisions:

> The Equal Protection Clause is not framed in terms of "stigma." Certainly the word has no clearly defined constitutional meaning. It reflects a subjective judgment that is standardless. All state-imposed classifications that rearrange burdens and benefits on the basis of race are likely to be viewed with deep resentment by the individuals burdened. The denial to innocent persons of equal rights and opportunities may outrage those so deprived and therefore may be perceived as invidious. . . . One should not lightly dismiss the inherent unfairness of, and the perception of mistreatment that accompanies, a system of allocating benefits and privileges on the basis of skin color and ethnic origin.[31]

Again, Powell wrote as though he were ignorant of the long tradition of whites-only policies that led to the issuance of numerous executive orders and the enactment of the 1957, 1960, 1964, 1965, and 1968 federal voting and civil rights legislation. These laws were not passed to subordinate whites; they were enacted to mandate that whites, especially white men, discontinue their unfair monopolies. Powell could not have meant that it was unfair to eliminate those quotas for whites, could he?

For Powell, there were serious problems of justice connected with the idea of a preference itself:

> First, it may not always be clear that a so-called preference is in fact benign. . . . Second, preferential programs may only reinforce common stereotypes holding that certain groups are unable to achieve success without special protection based on a factor having no relationship to individual worth. Third, there is a measure of inequity in forcing innocent persons in respondent's position to bear the burdens of redressing grievances not of their making.[32]

Here Powell presents one of the most often-stated rationales for opposing affirmative action: Bakke was innocent and could not individually be made to sacrifice his deserved slot in medical school.

But Powell's words reveal a hidden bias, implying that in America one's claim to whiteness is not a source of privilege. Moreover, Powell failed to address why Bakke's claim to innocence was stronger than those of minorities who were not admitted under Davis's race-neutral policies. Those minorities who were routinely rejected had no moral culpability, either; they had not established ghetto schools for themselves. Since they, too, were innocent, why would Powell strike the balance in favor of Bakke? Why was he more deserving than Patrick Chavis, the black applicant who supposedly took his place? The answer apparently was that Bakke had higher test scores and grades than all of the special admits. But isn't there a bias in the use of test scores and grades? If minorities in America have not had equal educational opportunities in underfunded and overcrowded schools, is it fair to exclude them from higher education on the basis of their lower scores? And aren't there other benchmarks of achievement that predict diligence, desire, potential, and character? The debate over affirmative action is partly about who among those qualified will be trained. Americans should not, therefore, define qualifications in a way that presumptively excludes large segments of their population.

Nowhere in his opinion did Powell insist that all racial classifications were invalid. To the contrary, he simply held that racial classifications were subject to strict review, requiring the government to articulate a "substantial" interest for using them, and proof that the policy was "narrowly tailored" to achieve the government's goal. Davis's medical school had four goals:

- Reducing the historic deficit of traditionally disfavored minorities in medical schools and in the profession.
- Countering the effects of societal discrimination.
- Increasing the number of physicians who will practice in communities currently underserved.
- Obtaining the educational benefits that flow from an ethnically diverse student body.[33]

Only the last goal—educational diversity—was significant enough to meet the substantial (compelling) interest requirement of strict scrutiny.

Ultimately, Justice Powell concluded that race "may be deemed a 'plus' in a particular applicant's file." He supported diversity admissions programs like Harvard's that consider all applicants—based on all their qualifications—for all available places:

> Such [diversity] qualities could include exceptional personal talents, unique work or service experience, leadership potential, maturity, demonstrated compassion, a history of overcoming disadvantage, ability to communicate with the poor, or other qualifications deemed important. In short, an admissions program operated in this way is flexible enough to consider

all pertinent elements of diversity in light of the particular qualifications of each applicant, and to place them on the same footing for consideration, although not necessarily according them the same weight.[34]

For Powell, diversity admissions programs were constitutional because they treated every applicant as an individual with fungible subjective qualities. The diversity policy did not rest on the candidate's membership in a group but, rather, focused on each applicant's individual qualities. Therefore, a candidate would never be rejected under such a plan solely because of race. And, Powell wrote, good faith by the admissions committees would be presumed, absent a showing to the contrary.[35]

Although Powell's logic is often problematic to the extreme, he was correct here to endorse the use of diversity factors. Indeed, such a policy does no more than acknowledge what is a reality in America: In numerous ways, whiteness has been a plus factor in public and private decision making, and it is impossible to prevent all but the most egregious cases of white privilege. To balance the scales, therefore, it is necessary to make other racial classifications a plus as well.

There is no reason that a diversity model could not be used outside education as well. It does not promote racial caste for whites, and it ensures an end to educational and occupational segregation. Any plan short of that would freeze out minorities and white women, who have only recently gained limited access to the means of advancement in this society. In recent cases, the Supreme Court has failed to indicate whether a diversity model would survive its latest rulings.

### THE INVENTION OF REVERSE DISCRIMINATION

If Bakke was a victim, it was not of racial discrimination, but of a history of racial privilege for white males who still disproportionately fill American medical schools. To Bakke and others like him, I say, don't blame contemporary African Americans; instead, blame whites from previous generations whose privileges have produced a new system in which whiteness is no more a plus than another person's race.

Since *Bakke*, the Court has decided several similar cases in which a white plaintiff has challenged affirmative action programs sponsored or mandated by a governmental or private entity. Perhaps the clearest conclusion that one can draw from these cases is that the Court remains substantially divided regarding the meaning and requirements of the equal protection clause and title VII in cases involving remedial racial classifications. I shall review these landmark cases in some detail because they illustrate both why affirmative action programs were adopted and why we must continue to use them.

## United Steelworkers of America v. Weber

In 1974, the United Steelworkers of America (USWA) and Kaiser Aluminum (Kaiser) entered into a collective bargaining agreement that included an affirmative action plan. This plan was designed to eliminate conspicuous racial imbalances in Kaiser's almost exclusively white craft forces. A case like *Weber* reveals a union and a company coming to terms with its policies of racial privilege, in this case a policy reserving craft jobs for whites. The company agreed to discontinue its all-white quota for craft jobs. In its place, black craft-hiring goals were set for each plant, equal to the percentage of blacks in the local labor forces. To enable the plants to meet these goals, on-the-job training programs were established to teach unskilled production workers, black and white, the skills necessary to become craftworkers. The plan reserved half of all openings in the newly created training programs for black employees.

During the plan's first year of operation at Kaiser's Gramercy, Louisiana, plant, thirteen craft trainees were selected to participate in the in-plant training program, seven blacks and six whites. The most senior black trainee had less seniority than several white employees whose applications were turned down. Consequently, one of them, Brian Weber, instituted a class action against USWA and Kaiser.[36]

Five members of the Supreme Court held that title VII does not prohibit private employers and unions from bargaining collectively for a remedial affirmative action plan. The Court rejected Weber's claim that Congress, by means of title VII, intended to prohibit all race-conscious affirmative action, holding that the statute must be read against the background of its legislative history and the historical context from which the act arose. The Court underscored, for example, that "in 1947 the nonwhite unemployment rate was 64% higher than the white rate; by 1962 it was 124% higher." Thus, Congress knew that "the crux of the problem was to open employment opportunities for Negroes in occupations which had been traditionally closed to them," and so it enacted title VII to address that discrimination against black workers.[37]

The Court concluded that the Kaiser–USWA affirmative action plan was permissible because its purposes mirrored those of title VII and the plan did not unnecessarily trammel the interests of the white employees, require the discharge of white workers and their replacement with new black hires, or create an absolute barrier to the advancement of white employees. Finally, the plan was only a temporary measure.[38]

Two members of the Court, Chief Justice Burger and Justice Rehnquist, dissented, believing that the quota in the collective bargaining agreement discriminated on the basis of race in flagrant violation of title VII. To them, Congress's intent for title VII was unequivocal: to ban all race discrimination, including so-called benign discrimination.[39]

In subsequent title VII affirmative action challenges, the Court has analyzed the facts according to the *Weber* standard, upholding plans for training and promoting minorities but striking down those that require the layoff or discharge of whites. *Weber* represented a step forward, as there is nothing intrinsically offensive in eliminating all-white crafts. Said differently, Brian Weber did not have a federal or constitutional right to benefit from a discriminatory company or union policy. The discontinuance of such policies does not relegate white males like him into a caste; it simply ends their long-standing quotas.

### Fullilove v. Klutznick

In May 1977, Congress enacted the Public Works Employment Act, which authorized a $4 billion appropriation for federal grants to be made by the secretary of commerce to state and local governmental entities for use in local public works projects. The act contained a minority business enterprise (MBE) provision requiring that

> [e]xcept to the extent that the Secretary determines otherwise, no grant shall be made under this Act for any local public works project unless the applicant gives satisfactory assurance to the Secretary that at least 10 per centum of the amount of each grant shall be expended for minority business enterprises. For the purposes of this paragraph, the term "minority business enterprise" means a business at least 50 per centum of which is owned by minority groups, or in case of a publicly owned business, at least 51 per centum of the stock of which is owned by minority group members. For purposes of the preceding sentence, minority group members are citizens of the U.S. who are Negroes, Spanish-speaking, Orientals, Indians, Eskimos, and Aleuts.

Since the mid-1970s, similar provisions in federal and state contracting have been under assault for being quotas and the source of substantial fraud. But as with the remedial policy in *Weber*, we must ask: What facts made the government decide to incorporate it? Motive matters. If the motive was to discriminate on the basis of race, that is, to promote racial caste, we should, and must, oppose such provisions. But if the motive was to ensure that racial minorities receive some small portion of the billions of dollars spent annually in government contracts or to ensure that such contractors do not underutilize minority or female workers, we should support them enthusiastically.

Earl Fullilove and associations of construction contractors and subcontractors brought an action in federal court in New York against representatives of the United States Department of Commerce and the state of New York, as actual or potential grantees under the act, alleging that the MBE provision violated the equal protection component of the Fifth Amendment's due process clause and various federal statutes, including title VI of the Civil Rights Act of 1964. The district court upheld the validity of the MBE provision, and the Court of Appeals for the Second Circuit affirmed, expressly rejecting the contention that the set-aside requirement violated equal protection and also rejecting the plaintiffs' statutory claims.

In *Fullilove v. Klutznick*, although not agreeing to one opinion, the Court affirmed the lower federal courts' holding that the federal minority business enterprise provision of the Public Works Employment Act did not violate the equal protection clause or federal statutes.[40] Six justices, including Chief Justice Burger who had dissented in *Weber*, concurred in the judgment of the Court, and three dissented.[41]

Burger declared the issue to be whether Congress had the power to enact the MBE set-aside provision. The Court noted its usual deference given to Congress:

> A program that employs racial or ethnic criteria, even in a remedial context, calls for close examination; yet we are bound to approach our task with appropriate deference to the Congress, a co-equal branch charged by the Constitution with the power to "provide for the ... general Welfare of the United States" and "to enforce, by appropriate legislation" the equal protection guarantees of the Fourteenth Amendment.[42]

The Court's references in this passage point out that the Constitution gives Congress enumerated powers to legislate for the general welfare of the nation and to protect the equal protection rights of all persons.

Burger then considered whether the limited use of racial criteria was a constitutional means of achieving congressional objectives:

As a threshold matter, we reject the contention that in the remedial context the Congress must act in a wholly "color-blind" fashion. In *Swann v. Charlotte–Mecklenburg Board of Education*, we rejected this argument in considering a court-formulated school desegregation remedy on the basis that examination of the racial composition of student bodies was an unavoidable starting point and that racially based attendance assignments were permissible so long as no absolute racial balance of each school was required. In *McDaniel v. Barresi*, citing *Swann*, we observed that: "[I]n this remedial process, steps will almost invariably require that students be assigned 'differently because of their race.' Any other approach would freeze the status quo that is the very target of all desegregation processes." And in *North Carolina Board of Education v. Swann*, we invalidated a state law that absolutely forbade assignment of any student on account of race because it foreclosed implementation of desegregation plans that were designed to remedy constitutional violations. We held that "[j]ust as the race of students must be considered in determining whether a constitutional violation has occurred, so also must race be considered in formulating a remedy."[43]

Thus, in *Fullilove*, six justices explicitly rejected a rigid color blindness standard and approved a race-conscious set-aside. The Court explained that Congress's remedial powers were greater than those of any other governmental entity:

Here we deal, as we noted earlier, not with the limited remedial powers of a federal court, for example, but with the broad remedial powers of Congress. It is fundamental that in no organ of government, state or federal, does there repose a more comprehensive remedial power than in the Congress, expressly charged by the Constitution with competence and authority to enforce equal protection guarantees. Congress not only may induce voluntary action to assure compliance with existing federal statutory or constitutional antidiscrimination provisions, but also, where Congress has authority to declare certain conduct unlawful, it may, as here, authorize and induce state action to avoid such conduct.[44]

Thus, Congress can force compliance with its antidiscrimination policies by making private contractors or state grantees provide affirmative action set-asides to remedy past and continuing discrimination in the construction industry.

Burger, in an opinion joined by *Bakke*'s author, Justice Powell, also rejected the "white innocence" theory presented in *Bakke*:

It is not a constitutional defect in this program that it may disappoint the expectations of nonminority firms. When effectuating a limited and properly tailored remedy to cure the effects of prior discrimination, such "a sharing of the burden" by innocent parties is not impermissible. The actual "burden" shouldered by nonminority firms is relatively light in this connection when we consider the scope of this public works program as compared with overall construction contracting opportunities. Moreover, although we may assume that the complaining parties are innocent of any discriminatory conduct, it was within congressional power to act on the assumption that in the past some nonminority businesses may have reaped competitive benefit over the years from the virtual exclusion of minority firms from these contracting opportunities.[45]

Along with the Court's rejection of white innocence, the opinion refers to Congress's ability to employ a limited remedy to cure the effects of "prior discrimination." The Court used the term *prior discrimination* to refer to general societal discrimination practiced in the construction–contracting industry. The Court did not require Congress to prove specific, localized discrimination to justify the minority set-aside, as the Court had intimated in *Bakke*.[46]

*Fullilove* raised many new questions regarding the constitutionality of affirmative action set-aside programs. For example, did the Court believe that this set-aside was constitutional because it was sponsored by Congress but that a state could not treat its citizens in the same way? Or did the Court consider that the set-aside was constitutional under any level of judicial scrutiny? Such confusion sprang from Burger's assertion that his opinion did not adopt the analysis used by members of the Court in *Bakke*. He added, "Our analysis demonstrates that the MBE provision would survive judicial review under either 'test' articulated in the several *Bakke* opinions."[47]

The dissenters in *Fullilove* used Justice John Harlan's dissent from *Plessy* to argue that the MBE provisions were unconstitutional. After recalling Justice Harlan's statement regarding color blindness, Justice Stewart wrote,

> Today, the Court upholds a statute that accords a preference to citizens who are "Negroes, Spanish-speaking, Orientals, Indians, Eskimos, and Aleuts" for much of the same reasons (as were given by the majority in *Plessy*). I think today's decision is wrong for the same reason that *Plessy* was wrong, and I respectfully dissent.[48]

For Justice Stewart, *Fullilove* was just like *Plessy*, and affirmative action was another form of invidious racial subordination. It did not matter that the MBE provision had been enacted by Congress rather than by the state of Louisiana. Stewart believed that the equal protection standard absolutely prohibited any racially categorized discrimination by government. He wanted to apply a rule of presumptive invalidity to all racial classifications and to scrutinize them as inherently suspect.[49] A majority of the current Court appears to agree with Stewart's dissent. However, those justices in the majority have not explained why Burger was wrong. Until they distinguish *Fullilove* on some legitimate basis, it will appear that they simply ignored precedent to achieve an ideological end.

### Wygant v. Jackson Board of Education

In 1972 the Jackson (Michigan) Board of Education, because of racial tension in the community that extended to its schools, considered adding a layoff policy to the collective bargaining agreement between the board and the teachers' union that would protect certain minority group members from layoffs, despite their lack of seniority. The board and union eventually agreed on the following provision:

> In the event it becomes necessary to reduce the number of teachers through layoff from employment by the Board, teachers with the most seniority shall be retained, except that at no time would there be a greater percentage of minority personnel laid off than the current percentage of minority personnel employed in the school at the time of the layoff.

In 1974, layoffs did become necessary. But the board retained tenured white teachers and laid off probationary minority teachers, thus failing to maintain, in accordance with the collective bargaining provision, the percentage of minority teachers existing at the time of the layoff. The union and two minority teachers sued in federal court, charging that the board's failure to adhere to the layoff provision violated title VII and the equal protection clause of the Fourteenth Amendment. The district court concluded that it lacked jurisdiction over the case because the plaintiffs had not filed an appropriate claim with the Equal Employment Opportunity Commission (EEOC).

The plaintiffs then went to state court, raising essentially the same claims, including one for breach of contract. The state court held that the board had breached its contract with the plaintiffs and that the layoff provision was a permissible remedy for the effects of past societal discrimination. The board thereafter adhered to the preferential layoff policy and laid off white teachers with greater seniority than that of the minority teachers it retained. Wendy Wygant and other white teachers who were laid off sued in federal court, alleging violations of the equal protection clause of the Fourteenth Amendment and state and federal statutes. This court ruled against the plaintiffs, holding that the preferential layoff policy was permissible under the equal protection clause as an attempt to remedy societal discrimination by providing role models for minority schoolchildren. The court of appeals affirmed.

In *Wygant v. Jackson Board of Education*, a fragmented Court reversed the lower federal courts' holdings that the collective bargaining agreement was constitutional. Justice Powell described the question before the Court as "whether a school board, consistent with the Equal Protection Clause, may extend preferential protection against layoffs to some of its employees because of their race or national origin." He then reviewed the Court's precedents regarding the appropriate standard of review and concluded, as he had in *Bakke*, that racial and ethnic distinctions of any sort were inherently suspect and thus called for the most exacting judicial examination to make sure that they did not conflict with constitutional guarantees.[50]

Powell also looked at whether the layoff provision was supported by a compelling state interest and whether the means chosen to satisfy that interest were narrowly tailored to achieve the state's purpose. The lower federal courts had held that the board's interest in providing minority role models for its minority students was sufficiently important to justify the racial classification embodied in the layoff provision.[51]

Ignoring *Fullilove*, Powell concluded that the Court had never held that societal discrimination alone was sufficient to justify a racial classification. Instead, the Court had insisted on a showing of prior discrimination by the governmental unit involved before allowing the limited use of racial classifications to remedy such discrimination. The role model theory used by the lower courts had no logical end point and allowed the board to engage in discriminatory hiring and layoff practices long past the point required for any legitimate remedial purpose. The layoff provision was thus not narrowly tailored to achieve a compelling interest because it unnecessarily trammeled on the rights of white teachers like Wendy Wygant.[52]

Justices Sandra Day O'Connor and Byron White concurred in the judgment of the Court but elaborated on it differently. O'Connor stated that because the layoff provision maintained levels of minority hiring that had no relation to remedying employment discrimination, it was not narrowly drawn to effectuate its remedial purpose. Justice White wrote that none of the interests asserted by the board justified the racially discriminatory layoff policy or saved it from the requirements of the equal protection clause.[53]

A dissenting Justice Marshall accused the Court of deciding the merits of the case prematurely, without an adequate factual record and appropriate regard for the historical context of discrimination in Jackson, Michigan. He would have remanded the case for additional findings. Justice Stevens explained why governmental race consciousness was not always unconstitutional, writing that the white teachers were not laid off because of their race but, rather, because of economic conditions in Jackson and the board's important interest in maintaining its newly integrated faculty.[54]

*Wygant* illustrates how the Court has distinguished affirmative action plans relating to training from those discharging or laying off whites. When we compare Justice Powell's opinions in *Bakke, Fullilove,* and *Wygant,* we get a glimpse of how difficult such cases have been for the Court.

### United States v. Paradise

In 1972, a class of black plaintiffs challenged the long-standing practice of the Alabama Department of Public Safety's systematic exclusion of blacks as state troopers. The federal district court in Alabama found that the department had engaged in a pattern of discrimination in hiring, ordered it to hire one black trooper for each white trooper hired until blacks constituted 25 percent of the state trooper force, and enjoined the department from engaging in any discrimination in its employment practices, including promotions. The Court of Appeals for the Fifth Circuit affirmed.

Two years later, the federal district court found that the department had delayed or frustrated full relief to the plaintiff class by artificially restricting the size of the trooper force and the number of new troopers hired and that there was a disproportionate failure of the blacks that were hired to achieve permanent trooper status. The court reaffirmed its 1972 order. In 1977, the plaintiffs sought supplemental relief from the department's promotion practices. Another two years passed. In a partial consent decree approved by the court, the department agreed (1) to develop within one year a promotion procedure that would be fair to all applicants and have little or no adverse impact on blacks seeking promotion to the rank of corporal and (2) that the promotion procedure would conform with the Federal Uniform Guidelines on Employee Selection Procedures.

The decree required that once the department set in place such a procedure for reaching the rank of corporal, it was to develop similar procedures for the other upper ranks.

In a second consent decree approved by the court in 1981, the department reaffirmed its commitment to implement a promotion procedure
with little or no adverse effects on blacks. But in a test administered to
262 applicants, of whom 60 were blacks, only 5 blacks were in the top
half of the promotion register, and the highest black candidate was ranked
eighty. In 1983, the plaintiffs asked the district court to require the
department to promote blacks to corporal at the same rate at which they
had been hired, one for one, until the department implemented a valid
promotion procedure. The court then ordered the department to submit
a plan to promote at least fifteen qualified persons to corporal that would
not have an adverse racial impact. The department proposed promoting
fifteen persons, of whom four would be black.

The court granted the plaintiffs' motion to enforce the 1979 and
1981 consent decrees. In addition, noting that twelve years after it had
condemned the department's racially discriminatory policies, the effects
of those policies remained pervasive, the court held that for a specified
period of time, at least half of those promoted to corporal must be black
if qualified black candidates were available. It also imposed a 50 percent
promotional requirement for the upper ranks, but only if there were
qualified black candidates, if a particular rank were less than 25 percent
black, and if the department had not developed and implemented a
promotion plan without adverse impact on the relevant rank.

Subsequently, the department promoted eight blacks and eight whites
under the court's order. Then the *United States* appealed the court's
order on the ground that it violated the Fourteenth Amendment's equal
protection guarantee. The Court of Appeals for the Eleventh Circuit
affirmed the district court's order.

In *United States v. Paradise,* by a vote of five to four, the Supreme Court
affirmed the lower courts' decision, holding that the race-conscious relief
met even strict scrutiny analysis. Justice Brennan wrote that "it is now
well established that government bodies, including courts, may constitutionally employ racial classifications essential to remedy unlawful treatment of racial or ethnic groups subject to discrimination." He found that
the government had a compelling interest in remedying the past and
present discrimination by a state actor, namely, the Department of Public
Safety, which for four decades had excluded blacks from all positions:

"Such egregious discriminatory conduct was unquestionably a violation of the Fourteenth Amendment." [55]

The United States conceded that the court's order served a compelling interest, but it charged that the order was not narrowly tailored to accomplish its purposes. Brennan disagreed, pointing out several factors relevant to determining whether race-conscious remedies were appropriate, including "the necessity for relief and the efficacy of alternative remedies; the flexibility and duration of the relief, including the availability of waiver provisions; the relationship of the numerical goals to the relevant labor market; and the impact of the relief on the rights of third parties." [56] He found that the court's order met each factor and thus was narrowly tailored to achieve the court's goal of eliminating the effects of the department's "long term, open, and pervasive discrimination." [57]

Justice O'Connor and three others dissented, writing that the promotional quota was not narrowly tailored because it was not "manifestly necessary" to comply with the court's orders. She also accused the plurality of adopting a standardless view of the term *narrowly tailored* far less stringent than that required by strict scrutiny.[58] Most of all, O'Connor objected to the court's imposition of a racial quota "without first considering the effectiveness of alternatives that would have a lesser effect on the rights of nonminority troopers." [59]

*Paradise* brings to mind another quota system that has been only recently repudiated. Hundreds of similar cases involving the exclusion of minorities and women from employment in police and fire departments around the country have gone through the courts. *Paradise* thus raises important questions about what government can do to eliminate discriminatory employment policies, as well as the impact of those policies on future hiring, training, and promotion opportunities. Under current seniority rules, those white men who were hired without competing against minorities and women now have the inside track for advancement, not because of merit, but because of past race and gender privilege.

### City of Richmond v. Croson Co.

In 1983, the Richmond (Virginia) City Council adopted, in an ordinance, a minority business utilization set-aside plan, which required non-minority-owned prime contractors awarded city construction contracts to subcontract at least 30 percent of the dollar amount of the contract to one or more minority business enterprises from anywhere in the United States, with each such enterprise to be at least 51 percent owned and controlled by United States citizens who are blacks, Spanish-speaking, Asians, Native Americans, Inuits, or Aleuts. In the public hearing that preceded the ordinance's adoption, there was no direct evidence of race discrimination on the part of the city in awarding contracts or any evidence that the city's prime contractors had discriminated against minority-owned subcontractors. Instead, the proponents relied on a study indicating that even though the city's general population was half black, only 0.67 percent of the city's prime contracts had been awarded to minority businesses in the five years from 1978 to 1983. It also established that various contractors' associations had virtually no minority businesses within their membership and that the city's legal adviser had indicated that in light of *Fullilove*, the ordinance would be constitutional.

After the ordinance was adopted, the city issued an invitation to bid on a project for the plumbing at the city jail. The only bidder was a company that, despite having contacted some minority subcontractors, submitted a proposal that did not include sufficient minority subcontracting to satisfy the ordinance. Although the company requested a waiver of the set-aside requirement, the city denied the request and informed the company that it had decided to rebid the project. J. A. Croson Company then brought an action in a federal district court in Virginia, insisting that the ordinance violated the Fourteenth Amendment's equal protection clause. The district court, however, upheld the plan in all respects. The Court of Appeals for the Fourth Circuit affirmed, but this opinion was vacated and remanded by the Supreme Court for further consideration in light of the Court's ruling in *Wygant*. On remand, the court of appeals reversed the district court on the ground that the ordinance was invalid under the equal protection clause.

*City of Richmond v. Croson* divided the Court to an even greater extent than prior affirmative action cases had, producing six separate opinions. As shown, the facts in *Croson* were strikingly similar to those in *Fullilove*, except that the set-aside was sponsored by the city of Richmond and the percentage set-aside for minority-controlled businesses was thirty.[60]

Justice O'Connor announced the Court's judgment invalidating the Richmond set-aside. The first obstacle was the Court's opinion in *Fullilove* which upheld a congressional set-aside plan. The questions that Justice Burger left open, including whether a state set-aside plan also was constitutional, were now squarely before the Court. O'Connor distinguished *Fullilove* on the grounds that Congress had a specific constitutional mandate to enforce the dictates of the Fourteenth Amendment, section 5 being a positive grant of legislative power authorizing Congress to exercise its discretion in determining whether and what legislation was needed to secure its guarantees. On the other hand, O'Connor found section 1 of the Fourteenth Amendment to be a constraint on state power. Thus, unlike Congress, the states could undertake only those efforts to remedy discrimination that were consistent with section 1.[61]

In order to meet these constraints, Richmond had to specify the private discrimination it sought to remedy:

> Thus, if the city could show that it had essentially become a "passive participant" in a system of racial exclusion practiced by elements of the local construction industry, we think it clear that the city could take affirmative steps to dismantle such a system. It is beyond dispute that any public entity, state or federal, has a compelling interest in assuring that public dollars, drawn from the tax contributions of all citizens, do not serve to finance the evil of private prejudice.[62]

O'Connor's opinion suggests that the problem in this case was not affirmative action per se but, rather, the poor evidentiary showing of specific private discrimination in the local construction industry.[63]

O'Connor next addressed the proper standard of review, pointing out that strict scrutiny was essential to determining whether a racial classification was benign or, instead, motivated by illegitimate notions of racial inferiority or racial politics. Her opinion appears to acknowledge a distinction between benign racial classifications and those based on notions of racial inferiority or racial politics,[64] but significantly, O'Connor did not reject the notion that some racial classifications—those not steeped in stereotype or racial prejudice—were legitimate. She did not champion color blindness!

O'Connor specifically identified the defects of the Richmond plan: "[S]ocietal discrimination, without more, is too amorphous a basis for imposing a racially classified remedy."[65] Also, state and local agencies could not rely on congressional findings of national discrimination.[66] Instead, they had to "establish the presence of discrimination in their own bailiwicks, based either upon their own factfinding processes or upon determinations made by other competent institutions."[67] O'Connor did not believe that the evidence presented by the city identified discrimination in the Richmond construction industry.[68]

O'Connor intentionally limited the *Croson* analysis to blacks:

The foregoing analysis applies only to the inclusion of blacks within the Richmond set-aside program. There is *absolutely no evidence* of past discrimination against Spanish-speaking, Oriental, Indian, Eskimo, or Aleut persons in any aspect of the Richmond construction industry. . . . It may well be that Richmond has never had an Aleut or Eskimo citizen. The random inclusion of racial groups that, as a practical matter, may never have suffered from discrimination in the construction industry in Richmond suggests that perhaps the city's purpose was not in fact to remedy past discrimination.[69]

Unlike the *Fullilove* majority, the *Croson* majority found the overinclusiveness of the minority set-aside provision to be fatally flawed.

Another factor that distinguished *Fullilove* from *Croson* was that Congress had carefully examined and rejected race-neutral alternatives before enacting the MBE provision. In *Croson*, O'Connor found no evidence that the Richmond City Council had considered any race-neutral alternatives. Therefore, the Richmond plan failed both parts of the equal protection analysis.[70]

The *Croson* decision established the constitutional requirements for those state and local governments that wish to distribute public contracts more widely. That is, in order to specify a racial preference, a local government must either show specific evidence of past local discrimination or prove a significant statistical disparity between the number of qualified minority contractors willing and able to perform services and the number actually employed.[71]

Justice Marshall wrote a long dissent, explaining why race-conscious remedial policies should be subject to less rigorous review by the Court: "[I]t is a welcome symbol of racial progress when the former capital of the Confederacy acts forthrightly to confront the effects of racial discrimination in its midst."[72] The dissenters regarded the set-aside provision in *Croson* as indistinguishable from its model in *Fullilove*. Moreover, they believed that "a profound difference separates governmental actions that themselves are racist, and governmental actions that seek to remedy the effects of prior racism or to prevent neutral governmental activity from perpetuating the effects of such racism."[73]

**Metro Broadcasting v. FCC**

When the Federal Communications Commission (FCC) compares competing applications for a new radio or television broadcast station license, it awards an enhancement credit for ownership and participation by members of minority groups, defined by the FCC as "those of Black, Hispanic Surnamed, American Eskimo, Aleut, American Indian, and Asiatic American extraction." In addition, the FCC promotes minority ownership of broadcast stations through its "distress sale" policy, under which a licensee whose qualifications to hold a broadcast license have come into question may, if certain conditions are met, assign its license to an FCC-approved minority enterprise without the hearing ordinarily required before a license may be assigned.

Metro Broadcasting sought a review of an FCC order awarding a new television license to Rainbow Broadcasting in a comparative proceeding, in which the action was based on the ruling that the substantial enhancement granted to Rainbow because of its minority ownership outweighed the factors favoring Metro. Ultimately, the Court of Appeals for the D.C. Circuit affirmed the grant of the license to Rainbow. In a companion case, Shurberg Broadcasting sought a review of an FCC order approving Faith Center's distress sale of its television license to Astroline Communications Company, a minority enterprise. That court invalidated the distress sale policy, ruling that it deprived Shurberg of its right to equal protection.

In *Metro Broadcasting,* the Supreme Court consolidated these two cases, questioning whether these FCC policies violated the equal protection component of the Fifth Amendment.[74] In a five-to-four opinion written by Justice Brennan, the Court held that the policies did not violate equal protection principles.[75]

Justice Brennan's opinion paralleled the principal opinion of *Fullilove* insofar as the earlier opinion had summarized the Court's historical deference to Congress and the various sources of power available to Congress to enact the minority preference policies. But then Brennan added the following qualifier:

> A majority of the Court in *Fullilove* did not apply strict scrutiny to the race-based classification at issue. Three Members inquired "whether the objectives of th[e] legislation are within the power of Congress" and "whether the limited use of racial and ethnic criteria . . . is a constitutionally permissible means for achieving the congressional objectives." . . . Three other Members would have upheld benign racial classifications that "serve important governmental objectives and are substantially related to achievement of those objectives." . . . We apply that standard today. We hold that

benign race-conscious measures mandated by Congress—even if those measures are not "remedial" in the sense of being designed to compensate victims of past governmental or societal discrimination—are constitutionally permissible to the extent that they serve important governmental objectives within the power of Congress and are substantially related to achievement of those objectives.

Five members of the Court agreed that the standard of review for congressional affirmative action was intermediate scrutiny. Under this approach, programs are constitutionally permissible if they serve important governmental objectives within the power of Congress and are substantially related to the achievement of those objectives.[76]

Justice Brennan, who had joined Marshall's dissent in *Croson*, distinguished it from *Fullilove*. Because *Croson* did not concern congressional action, its reasoning could not be used to undermine *Fullilove*. In fact, Brennan argued that most of the language and reasoning of *Croson* reaffirmed the lesson of *Fullilove:* that race-conscious classifications adopted by Congress to address racial and ethnic discrimination are subject to a standard different from that applied to similar classifications enacted by state and local governments.[77]

The majority in *Metro* found that Congress's interest in enhancing broadcast diversity was at the very least an important governmental objective. Specifically, Brennan suggested that diversity on the airwaves served important First Amendment values. He wrote that the minority ownership policies were substantially related to achieving diverse programming, and he cited studies by the Congressional Research Service (CRS) and the FCC to support his view.[78] He also noted a correlation between minority ownership and minority hiring:

> [W]hile we are under no illusion that members of a particular minority group share some cohesive, collective viewpoint, we believe it a legitimate inference for Congress and the Commission to draw that as more minorities gain ownership and policymaking roles in the media, varying perspectives will be more fairly represented on the airwaves.[79]

In addition to the absence of stereotyping, Justice Brennan found that the minority preference policies were put in place after race-neutral efforts by Congress and the FCC had failed. He insisted the policies in dispute were aimed directly at barriers that minorities face in entering the broadcast industry. The policies were also of appropriate scope and duration. Justice Brennan wrote that Congress and the FCC also had evaluated the policies. Finally, the burden imposed by the policies was slight, since they affected only a small fraction of licenses.[80]

Justice O'Connor's dissent in *Metro Broadcasting* was far more revealing than her majority opinion in *Croson*. She criticized the majority for departing from fundamental principles under the equal protection clause and the strict scrutiny standard of review,[81] and she also seemed intent on eliminating the term *benign racial classification* from equal protection jurisprudence:

> The Court's reliance on "benign racial classifications," . . . is particularly troubling. " 'Benign' racial classification" is a contradiction in terms. Governmental distinctions among citizens based on race or ethnicity, even in the rare circumstances permitted by our cases, exact costs and carry with them substantial dangers. To the person denied an opportunity or right based on race, the classification is hardly benign. . . .
>
> . . . We are a Nation not of black and white alone, but one teeming with divergent communities knitted together by various traditions and carried forth, above all, by individuals. Upon that basis, we are governed by one Constitution, providing a single guarantee of equal protection, one that extends equally to all citizens.[82]

Although Justice O'Connor still seemed to accept that race-based remedial measures could be constitutional in certain situations, she could not accept the equation of "benign" and "remedial." Because the majority had employed a less strict standard of review, she believed it must have intended a different meaning for those terms: "A lower standard [of review] signals that the Government may resort to racial distinctions more readily. The Court's departure from our cases is disturbing enough, but more disturbing still is the renewed toleration of racial classifications that its new standard of review embodies."[83]

### Adarand Constructors, Inc. v. Pena

The case of *Adarand Constructors, Inc. v. Pena* arose after the federal Department of Transportation awarded the prime contract for a highway construction project in Colorado to Mountain Gravel and Construction. Mountain solicited bids from subcontractors for the guardrail portion of the contract. Adarand, which specializes in guardrail work, submitted the lowest bid. Gonzales Construction, another subcontractor in the guardrail business, also submitted one of the lower bids. Under the terms of the prime contract, Mountain would receive a bonus of $10,000 from the government if it hired subcontractors certified as small businesses controlled by socially or economically disadvantaged individuals, as defined in the Small Business Act (SBA).[84]

The SBA defines socially disadvantaged individuals as those who have been subjected to racial or ethnic bias because of their membership in a group without regard to their individual qualities. It defines economically disadvantaged individuals as socially disadvantaged individuals whose ability to compete in the free-enterprise system has been impaired because of diminished capital and credit opportunities compared with those of others in the same business area who are not socially disadvantaged. Under the SBA, black, Latino, Asian, and Native Americans are presumed to be socially disadvantaged. A related provision extends the same presumption to women. In practice, a third party who objects to this presumption in a particular case can come forward and establish that a particular business is not disadvantaged.[85]

Gonzales had been certified as a small, socially and economically disadvantaged business; Adarand had not. Therefore, Mountain awarded the subcontract to Gonzales. Adarand then brought suit in federal court, insisting that the federal government's practice of giving to general contractors on government projects a financial incentive to hire subcontractors controlled by socially and economically disadvantaged individuals and also the government's use of race-based presumptions in identifying such individuals violate the equal protection component of the Fifth Amendment's due process clause: "No person shall . . . be deprived of life, liberty, or property, without due process of law."[86] The district court ruled for the government. The Court of Appeals for the Tenth Circuit affirmed in light of the Supreme Court's holdings in *Fullilove* and *Metro*. Adarand appealed to the Supreme Court, and Court watchers waited to learn the fate of affirmative action.

Despite a wide-ranging set of opinions in *Adarand*, the Court reduced the issue to one key point: the level of scrutiny that applies when any governmental actor adopts a race-based policy. Would the Court apply the *Croson* or the *Metro* standard? Justice O'Connor reviewed the Court's split opinions from prior cases and concluded that *Croson* was a better precedent than *Metro Broadcasting*. She had written the majority opinion in *Croson* and a vehement dissent in *Metro Broadcasting*, which she described as a "surprising turn" and inconsistent with the Court's ruling in *Croson*.[87] It seems curious, given O'Connor's own employment history—the only job she could get after graduating at the top of her class from

Stanford Law School was as a legal secretary—that she would not understand the difference between government programs that are racist or sexist and those that seek to compensate for racism or sexism.

Nonetheless, O'Connor cast the pivotal vote, and as implied in her dissent in *Metro Broadcasting,* she enlisted *Adarand* to overrule *Metro* and implicitly *Fullilove.* To achieve her goal, O'Connor had to ignore much of her *Croson* opinion, especially the parts in which she distinguished *Fullilove.* O'Connor's opinion is remarkable for how it deftly recasts the Court's prior affirmative action decisions into inconclusive plurality opinions, with less force than those in which a majority of the Court adopted one opinion. Of course, *Croson* was a plurality opinion as well.

The Court held simply that all explicit racial classifications—whether imposed by a federal, state, or local government—must be subjected to strict scrutiny. That result had been predicted since O'Connor wrote her dissent in *Metro.* The larger story of the case, however, is Justice O'Connor's legal craftsmanship:

> [T]he Court's cases through *Croson* had established three general propositions with respect to governmental racial classifications. First, skepticism: "any preference based on racial or ethnic criteria must necessarily receive a most searching examination," *Wygant.* . . . Second, consistency: "the standard of review under the Equal Protection Clause is not dependent on the race of those burdened or benefited by a particular classification," *Croson.* And third, congruence: "equal protection analysis in the Fifth Amendment area is the same as that under the Fourteenth Amendment," *Bolling.* Taken together, these propositions lead to a conclusion that any person, of whatever race, has a right to demand that any governmental actor subject to the Constitution justify any racial classification subjecting that person to unequal treatment under the strictest judicial scrutiny.[88]

Here O'Connor did far more than review precedent. By piecing together comments from carefully selected cases, she revised and transformed their context and meaning. Her opinion implies that racial classifications were first an issue in the 1940s. What about *Dred Scott* or *Plessy?* What about all the desegregation and voting cases? O'Connor was like a gifted muralist, painting over America's blighted racial history, altering to gray what for many had been black and white. The specific facts of cases lost their focus, creating the misimpression that in each the Court faced an instance of invidious racial discrimination. Yet as shown in the earlier discussions of those cases, the Court's analysis was heavily driven by facts, and the decisions were anything but consistent. As a result of

O'Connor's revisionism, the Court majority could insist that any racial classification was produced by caste or oppression and that none was benign or remedial.

For a justice who usually relies on precedent as a cardinal principle of constitutional analysis, O'Connor went out of her way to explain why *Metro* was a "surprising turn."[89] She charged that the Court in *Metro* turned its back on *Croson*. But one could just as effectively argue that in *Croson*, O'Connor turned her back on *Fullilove*. If one applied O'Connor's consistency and congruence analysis to its logical end, she should have followed *Fullilove* in her opinion in *Croson*. Then *Metro* would have been consistent, too, and *Adarand* would have been unnecessary.

O'Connor explained why strict scrutiny of all governmental racial classifications is essential:

> Absent searching judicial inquiry into the justification for such race-based measures, there is simply no way of determining what classifications are in fact motivated by illegitimate notions of racial inferiority or simple racial politics. Indeed, the purpose of strict scrutiny is to "smoke out" illegitimate uses of race by assuring that the legislative body is pursuing a goal important enough to warrant use of a highly suspect tool. The test also ensures that the means chosen "fit" this compelling goal so closely that there is little or no possibility that the motive for the classification was illegitimate racial prejudice or stereotype.[90]

Fortunately, O'Connor admitted that some uses of racial classifications by the government are legitimate, which means that she does not apply a color-blind standard. Instead, she insisted on strict scrutiny to decide which racial classifications are constitutionally objectionable and which are not. Presumably, with the proper evidentiary record, O'Connor would uphold some narrowly tailored affirmative action policies:

> [W]e wish to dispel the notion that strict scrutiny is "strict in theory, but fatal in fact." The unhappy persistence of both the practice and the lingering effects of racial discrimination against minority groups in this country is an unfortunate reality, and government is not disqualified from acting in response to it. When race-based action is necessary to further a compelling interest, such action is within constitutional constraints if it satisfies the "narrow tailoring" test this Court has set out in previous cases.

*Adarand* was remanded to the court of appeals to apply the appropriate legal standard. This means that among other things, the lower court must determine whether Congress has a compelling interest for its subcontractor compensation clause presumptions, whether it has considered race-neutral alternatives, and whether the program is limited so that it will last no longer than the discriminatory effects it is designed to eliminate.[91]

Four justices dissented in *Adarand,* insisting that the majority had ignored controlling precedent. Justices Stevens, Stephen Breyer, Ruth Bader Ginsburg, and David Souter believed that

> as a matter of constitutional and democratic principle, a decision by representatives of the majority to discriminate against the members of a minority race is fundamentally different from those same representatives' decision to impose incidental costs on the majority of their constituents in order to provide a benefit to a disadvantaged minority.[92]

This point has been forcefully argued by leading constitutional scholars for nearly thirty years.[93]

As for the difference between laws designed to benefit a historically disfavored group and laws designed to burden such a group, Justice Ginsburg, citing Stephen Carter, wrote:

> [T]o say that two centuries of struggle for the most basic of civil rights have been mostly about freedom from racial categorization rather then freedom from racial oppression, is to trivialize the lives and deaths of those who have suffered under racism. To pretend ... that the issue presented in *Bakke* was the same as the issue in *Brown* is to pretend that history never happened and the present doesn't exist.[94]

*Adarand*'s initial reverberations have already been heard. For example, after nearly three decades of giving federal courts broad discretion to end educational segregation, the same five justices agreed more recently that federal judges have narrow remedial powers in school desegregation cases. The same group also ruled that the Justice Department cannot direct the states to maximize the number of majority–minority districts in accordance with the Voting Rights Act of 1965.[95] It may not be long before those justices reinterpret the nature and scope of that act.

It will take several years for Americans to learn the full meaning of *Adarand.* Perhaps this case will not mean the end of race-based affirmative action, but it will be much more difficult to justify race-based remedial affirmative action policies, except when the government admits and establishes that it has participated in identifiable discrimination against specific persons or when the plaintiff proves invidious discrimination. Indeed, the majority opinion implies that such remedial policies are presumptively invalid not simply in the employment context but also in housing, education, and voting. Another issue left open by *Adarand* is whether the Court will extend its congruence/consistency/skepticism theory to gender-based affirmative action or whether such policies will continue to be reviewed under a less rigorous standard.

My purpose for sketching several of the leading affirmative action cases is to highlight their factual context, specifically the discriminatory circumstances leading to the adoption of the remedial policies. These cases show that affirmative action policies have indeed made a difference, improving the opportunities of many persons who before them were categorically excluded because of race or gender quotas. None of the remedial policies adopted in these case examples had the purpose or effect of producing white caste or of excluding all whites from employment or education or from competing for public contracts.

The sharp ideological division in the Court regarding race-based affirmative action is characterized by competing visions of the meaning of racial equality under the Constitution. For some members of the Court, equal protection permits the government to act affirmatively to dismantle the legacy of slavery, discrimination, and racial supremacy in the United States. These justices believe that in order to treat some persons equally, one must treat them differently, and they do not consider such different treatment to be invidious racial discrimination. Justice Blackmun was the most prominent advocate of this view:

> I suspect that it would be impossible to arrange an affirmative action program in a racially neutral way and have it successful. To ask that this be so is to demand the impossible. In order to get beyond racism, we must first take account of race. There is no other way. And in order to treat some persons equally, we must treat them differently. We cannot—we dare not— let the Equal Protection Clause perpetuate racial supremacy.[96]

For other members of the Court, racial equality and nondiscrimination mean that the government should not classify persons by race, except in dire emergencies or when the government itself has caused or permitted identifiable discrimination to occur in its locale. They believe that to treat persons equally, one must treat them the same. Justice O'Connor is the chief advocate of the latter view: "[T]he guarantee of equal protection cannot mean one thing when applied to one individual and something else when applied to a person of another color."[97]

For now, in affirmative action cases, as goes O'Connor, so goes the Court. Unfortunately, she has never explained why eliminating racial caste is not presumptively a compelling governmental interest justifying the adoption of remedial affirmative action. Why isn't racial caste in America considered a national emergency? Clearly, for those who exist in its worsening conditions, no issue is more important. For other Americans, racial caste is a disease killing their future as well.

### THE POLITICS OF AFFIRMATIVE ACTION: MYTH OR REALITY?

For the past three decades, federal affirmative action programs have run the gamut from outreach and hortatory efforts to encourage federal agencies and contractors to use minority- or women-owned businesses to specific mandates to hire women and minorities consistent with stated goals, timetables, and set-asides. Accordingly, the Community Reinvestment Act requires certain banks to conduct and record efforts to reach out to underserved communities. The Foreign Service maintains a minority internship program. The Environmental Protection Agency sponsors a mentor–protégé program to encourage prime contractors to develop relationships with small and disadvantaged businesses. The Small Business Act requires each federal agency to set goals for contracting with small and disadvantaged businesses. The Federal Communications Commission—until *Adarand*—had used race and gender as considerations in the sale of broadcast licenses. And the Intermodal Surface Transportation Efficiency Act authorizes the payment of subcontractor compensation bonuses to prime contractors who use socially disadvantaged businesses.[98]

According to a 1995 study of affirmative action commissioned by President Bill Clinton, such programs are designed to promote inclusion, prevent future discrimination by employers, and provide employers with a practical way to gauge their own progress in employing minorities and women.[99] The Department of Labor, through the Office of Federal Contract Compliance Programs (OFCCP), continues to promote equal employment opportunities among private businesses that have federal contracts. The provisions of Executive Order 11,246 apply to contractors and subcontractors with contracts of more than $10,000 per year.

OFCCP regulations contain separate requirements for construction and nonconstruction firms. Nonconstruction firms with fifty or more employees or contracts totaling $50,000 must develop and maintain a written affirmative action plan. As part of the plan, the contractor must conduct a workforce analysis of each job title, determine the workforce availability of women and minorities for each job group, and conduct a utilization analysis to determine whether women or minorities are being underutilized. If the contractor discovers that minorities or women are being underutilized, it must devise ways of overcoming this and to make a good-faith effort to carry them out. Construction firms are not required to maintain written plans but must show good-faith efforts to meet demographic goals for minorities and nationwide goals for women.[100] The Labor Department or the OFCCP may require goals for hiring minorities and women, but quotas are explicitly prohibited.

Given the prohibition of quotas, "goal setting" is used to target and evaluate the effectiveness of affirmative action efforts and to eradicate and prevent discrimination. Numerical benchmarks are established in light of the availability of qualified applicants in the job market or the employer's workforce. Significantly, a contractor's failure to achieve its affirmative action goal is not a violation of Executive Order 11,246, but the failure to make a good-faith effort is.[101]

The OFCCP conducts compliance reviews. In 1994, it undertook approximately four thousand reviews, accounting for roughly 3 percent of nonconstruction and 1.5 percent of the construction firms. If the OFCCP finds a violation, it attempts to conciliate with the contractor. A contractor in violation of Executive Order 11,246 may have its contracts terminated or suspended, though such actions are rare.[102]

Federal affirmative action programs affect more two million federal employees. Each federal civilian agency is required to establish plans to foster equal opportunities for minorities and women. The Equal Employment Opportunity Commission (EEOC) has advisory authority and review responsibility for such plans. By means of "management directives," the EEOC requires agencies to determine whether minorities and women are underrepresented in various employment categories. Most recently, the commission proposed that no agency set goals. Instead, agencies are required to report the discharge or separation rates of minorities, women, and persons with disabilities.[103]

Citing numerous empirical studies, the Clinton report concluded that affirmative action does create opportunity. As for fairness, the report found little evidence to support the charge that white males have suffered widespread reverse discrimination. Moreover, employers are free to use race-neutral strategies to achieve their affirmative action goals. Overall, the report describes the current affirmative action requirements as flexible, minimally intrusive, transitional, and balanced. The goals and timetables policy rests on references to the relevant pool of applicants, and no law requires an employer to hire unqualified employees.

So why all the fuss? What is really behind the recent vigorous attack on affirmative action? There are at least two factors: money and racial politics. In 1993, just under 193,000 construction and nonconstruction businesses employing 26 million people were covered by the provisions of Executive Order 11,246. These businesses received contracts totaling more than $160 billion. Thus, part of the reason for the assault is the amount of money involved and who will receive it. Remedial affirmative action policies tell employers that those who make good-faith efforts to employ minorities and women, or, in some instances, to use small businesses, will have a competitive advantage in winning contracts over those who do not. Some of these contractors apparently are unwilling to make the required efforts. Without the affirmative action mandate, we can only guess whether they would (or would not) employ minorities and women, or small businesses. History gives us reason to be skeptical. Beyond money, affirmative action also serves as a good wedge issue that wins votes.

Modern affirmative action has been under attack ever since the late 1960s when President Nixon instituted the Philadelphia Plan. The political firestorm throughout the country today evolved from the triumphs and defeats of those seeking to preserve Executive Order 11,246 and those fighting it. Since then, the surest way to assault policies emanating from Executive Order 11,246 has been to brand them quotas.[104] Executive Order 11,246 followed closely on the heels of the Civil Rights Act of 1964, which during congressional debates had been attacked as a quota bill: "The bill would discriminate against white people," insisted a senator from Mississippi. Former Presidents Nixon, Ronald Reagan, and George Bush each campaigned against quotas, and Bush made a similar charge regarding the Civil Rights Act of 1991, which Congress enacted to reverse a series of Supreme Court decisions overruling established law.[105]

As Nicholas Lemann observed, what was once a cause among conservatives is now one of the central issues in the national elections. Every high-profile American politician has taken a stand on affirmative action. In Maryland, an undergraduate student sued the state university for operating a scholarship program solely for black students. After the federal appellate court held that the program was invalid, the Supreme Court denied review.[106] In Alabama, the city of Birmingham continues its litigation with white and black firefighters regarding the legality of consent decrees containing hiring goals to increase the number and rank of black firefighters.[107] In a separate case involving the at-large election of

Alabama judges, after a federal judge endorsed a settlement proposal that would permit the appointment of half a dozen black judges to the state's appellate courts, The Court of Appeals for the Eleventh Circuit reversed.[108]

In Texas, four white applicants sued the state law school in Austin for its admissions procedures permitting a subcommittee to evaluate all applications from minority students, charging that it violated the principles of *Bakke*. The federal trial court agreed that a separate review was unconstitutional. The federal appellate court questioned *Bakke* and rejected Justice Powell's conclusion that race could be one of many factors employed to achieve educational diversity.[109] And in California, Glynn Custred and Tom Wood, two middle-aged white academics, introduced a ballot initiative that, if supported by a majority of California voters, would ban all state-sponsored affirmative action. California has become known for its recent citizen initiatives on many subjects, including taxes, crime victims, insurance, and immigration. The latest reads:

> Neither the State of California nor any of its political subdivisions or agents shall use race, sex, color, ethnicity or national origin as a criterion for either discriminating against, or granting preferential treatment to, any individual or group in operation of the State's system of public education or public contracting.[110]

After Pat Buchanan and William Buckley praised the initiative, affirmative action moved from the back room to the head table for public judgment. If Custred and Wood secure the necessary number of signatures to place the California Civil Rights Initiative (CCRI) on the ballot, it will face the voters on the same day that President Clinton does. Since it is crucial for a presidential candidate to win California's fifty-four electors, there is no avoiding the forthcoming debate. What are the arguments for and against affirmative action? What competing interests are at stake? And which politicians will say anything to get elected?

The tone of the latest attack on affirmative action appears vituperative, with politicians or commentators contending that affirmative action is a first cousin of Jim Crow, antithetical to meritocratic decision making; that the Constitution guarantees equality of opportunity, not equal results; that class is a better proxy for past discrimination than race is; and even that affirmative action was a bad idea from the start.

Many affirmative action critics make no attempt to educate the public about the various policies encompassed under the affirmative action label.

Rather, they insist that every affirmative action policy is a disguised quota and every victim is either a white male who was more qualified than the minority or female hired[111] or a "superstar" minority who is tainted or stigmatized by the erroneous assumption that he or she advanced because of affirmative action.[112] Therefore, in the next several years, Americans should expect more virulent statements or ads attacking affirmative action, like the one circulated by Senator Jesse Helms from North Carolina at the end of his 1990 reelection campaign. The ad plays on white fears— "You really needed that job, you were the best qualified," ominously intones the voice-over, showing a pair of white hands clutching and then crumpling a rejection letter. "But they had to give it to a minority because of a racial quota," the ad explains, showing a pair of black hands grasping a letter of appointment.[113] Apparently, this not-so-subtle race baiting appeals to some of the American electorate, because Helms came from behind to defeat his black challenger. The genius of the ad is that it appeals not just to overt racists but also—and more important—to people who do not think of themselves as racist.

Although rarely stated in polite company, the inference created by such race baiting is that the huge gulf between the economic and political opportunities and wealth of blacks and whites existing today in this country is the result of some inherent deficiency in blacks: "They" are irresponsible, lazy, given to vice or crime, or just plain inferior to whites. And in any event, whites today are neither privileged by America's race-conscious history nor otherwise responsible for its current racial caste.

Such statements regarding the character and capacity of African Americans or other minorities are at once shocking and debilitating to many proponents of affirmative action. It is difficult to read or hear such statements without a sense of rage or, even more, to respond when one thinks that their purveyors are disingenuous, dishonest, or too ensconced in privilege to care about injustice.[114] But this rage only impedes communication, polarizing already antagonized relations.

A response is further complicated by the fact that not all whites enjoy the fruits of racial privilege or embrace theories of racial supremacy, explicit or implicit. What does one say to those whites who have not hit pay dirt but instead look up from near the bottom of the United States' economic well? Critics assert that such "innocent" persons also have a right to nondiscrimination. Why should they lose jobs for the sins and advantages of others? One answer was suggested by Justice Powell in *Bakke*, a diversity approach that, among many factors, can also include economic disadvantage as a relevant factor in decision making. There is ample room under the remedial affirmative action tent for persons who have endured economic disadvantage. But Powell did not insist that economic disadvantage was the sole legitimate factor.

## Casting Stones

Opponents of remedial affirmative action policies present numerous arguments against them, including legal, moral, and policy rationales and allegations that they unfairly burden innocent victims and otherwise hurt society.[115] Legally, they argue that affirmative action violates the Fourteenth Amendment of the Constitution or titles VI or VII of the 1964 Civil Rights Act. Morally, critics contend that affirmative action is unfair to employers in general and displaced workers in particular. Other critics argue that affirmative action harms its beneficiaries and exacerbates racial enmity.

In light of America's long history of white racial privilege, the rising tide against remedial affirmative action is truly remarkable. First, it mischaracterizes and thereby vilifies remedial affirmative action policies. Critics of affirmative action attack as illegitimate preferences only those policies from the last three decades designed to give equal opportunity to minorities and women and say nothing about prior racial preferences and quotas, especially for white men, that led to exclusion and inequality. Americans cannot close their eyes to the other eighteen decades of their constitutional history when a rigid color line was the rule and white men and their families were America's affirmative action babies.[116] Remedial affirmative action was taken only after experience showed that white men would not voluntarily comply with antidiscrimination policies. Is there any evidence that in the absence of affirmative action policies, white men now will stop discriminating against minorities and women?

Second, critics argue that affirmative action has failed, that it helps the wrong, privileged minorities and hurts the wrong, disadvantaged whites. It deprives white males of equal opportunity. It stigmatizes recipients, implies their inferiority, and increases racial polarization. Every affirmative action policy is a quota in disguise. It violates the rule of nondiscrimination and meritocratic decision making. Finally, it leads to the hiring of unqualified persons and lowers the quality of production or other standards.

None of these claims, each of which I will address, withstands scrutiny.

### Affirmative Action Has Failed

It is difficult to understand how anyone who compares the American workplace or academy today with that of thirty years ago could believe that remedial affirmative action has failed. In fact, affirmative action has opened many doors that were closed by law or custom to minorities and white women solely on the basis of their race or gender. Consider, for example, the textile belt of the Carolinas, where white men once held a monopoly on mill jobs. Not so today; whites and blacks work side by side. At the Sara Lee textile mill in Greenwood, South Carolina, two-thirds of the more than four hundred employees are minorities. One-third of the mill's management are minorities, mostly blacks. Some point to the temporary suspension of several U.S. fabric contracts as the catalyst for some of these changes. The change in the color of mill workers may explain in part why Helms's ad struck a nerve in the Carolinas. But the mill jobs never should have been reserved for white men in the first place.

Other reports confirm that white women have made some of the greatest gains during the affirmative action era. A US West employee, Nancy Davis, is one such beneficiary of that company's effort to comply with a court-ordered agreement to open traditionally male jobs to women. After eighteen months, jumping over male coworkers with more experience, Davis became one of Denver's first women to manage a telephone crew of seventeen men and one woman. The company claims it has brought more women and minorities into high-level management than many similar companies have. Notably at US West, white women have made far greater gains than have minority men or minority women.

Historically, minorities and white women were restricted to low-wage jobs; some were forbidden to hold title to land; and some were barred from entering certain occupations at all. Whole industries and job classifications were open, in effect, only to white men. There was no system of merit. Many white men did not have to compete against blacks, Latinos, Asians, or white women. Police and fire departments forbade minorities and women to apply. Even college-educated blacks could obtain no better job than that of bellboy, janitor, elevator operator, or chauffeur. Craft and industrial jobs were closed. Women were restricted to part-time jobs with lower pay and fewer benefits.

Remedial affirmative action was established along with other laws to eliminate our system of white male domination. As a result of affirmative action, there has been an influx of blacks, other minorities, and white women into graduate and professional degree programs, industry positions, crafts, and public agency employment previously held almost exclusively by white men. Today we have minority and white female lawyers, doctors, engineers, police officers, state troopers, firefighters, and bus drivers. Such jobs are no longer the sole preserve of white men.

Similarly, federal contractors and agencies that formerly hired few if any minorities or women now employ many more. According to one study, the employment share of black males in federal contractor firms increased from 5.8 percent in 1974 to 6.7 percent in 1980. In noncontractor firms, the increase was more modest, from 5.3 percent to 5.9 percent. In federal agencies, the overall and white-collar employment of women and minorities has steadily increased, but both groups continue to be disproportionately employed in clerical or low-grade positions. In 1993, 86 percent of clerical jobs were held by women, and 40 percent were held by minorities. That same year, only 13 percent of the Senior Executive Service employees were women, and 8.5 percent were minorities. In 1949, 0.9 percent of military officers were black; today, that percentage is approximately 7.5. Because of occupational and educational desegregation, the gap in the median incomes of blacks and whites, as well as that between men and women, has shrunk.[117]

In much the same way that people opposed school desegregation, many have sought to bypass federal mandates for affirmative action. But mere defiance of and resistance to the law cannot serve as evidence that affirmative action has not worked. At most, they show that some Americans will ignore, resist, and circumvent the law in order to maintain privilege. Affirmative action could and, if permitted, will be more successful.

None of this means, of course, that racial (or gender) caste has ended since the inception of affirmative action or that there have not been some perhaps unanticipated negative effects. The resentment of some white males is one cost. Other effects include the disproportionate benefit of affirmative action for white women, as well as the growing divergence between the number of black female managers compared with the number of black males in, for instance, America's banking industry. Also, competition among Latinos, Asians, and blacks for affirmative action preferences has, in some communities, pitted these groups against one another. But these effects are not simply by-products of affirmative action; they underscore why America must do more, not less, to create opportunity. The question should not be whose ox is gored but, rather, how we do it and share it.

### Affirmative Action Helps and Hurts the Wrong People

Critics of affirmative action who assert that it helps and hurts the wrong people overlook the fact that affirmative action was not established as a subsistence program for the poor. Instead, it was designed initially to persuade persons receiving federal contracts to stop discriminating against minorities and white women who were qualified and available to do the relevant work but who were nevertheless passed over solely because of their race or sex. Their exclusion from entire categories of jobs increased their risk of poverty. But affirmative action was an antidiscrimination policy. Now that many of the exclusionary policies have been eliminated, more minorities and women with the necessary qualifications are being employed in higher-paying jobs. White men, who continue to obtain a large share of such jobs, simply no longer have the iron grip on these jobs that they once held. Although remedial affirmative action will not by itself eliminate poverty, it can diminish the racial and gender caste caused by occupational and educational segregation and tracking. When that happens, poverty rates for minorities and women will decline.

Moreover, there is something suspicious about the charge that affirmative action helps "privileged" minorities in America and hurts economically disadvantaged minorities and whites. As someone who benefited from affirmative action programs at Duke and UCLA during the 1970s and 1980s, I know that some of the students who were helped by affirmative action programs were whites. Others were women, and still others were persons of color. Neither school had affirmative action programs for blacks only.

In addition, many of my minority contemporaries at those schools were only first- or second-generation college students, most with modest resources. Like me, they borrowed money to finance college. But, critics state, some were the sons and daughters of doctors and lawyers who could not have been victims of discrimination. That is simply wrong: Until 1963, a prestigious school like Duke did not recruit or admit any black, no matter who his or her parents were or what their income was. Likewise, Vivian Malone-Jones and James Hood did not end the University of Alabama's color barrier until 1963. They weren't excluded because of poverty; they just were not white enough. Thus, even though Justice Thurgood Marshall, an honors graduate from Lincoln University, came from a home with both parents working, he was excluded from the University of Maryland School of Law just because it did not admit any blacks.

Race and class have been and are independent bases for discrimination; they cannot be combined. Justice Antonin Scalia and others who maintain that class is a better proxy for discrimination live a lie, refusing to admit that even rich blacks experience racial discrimination when they move to white neighborhoods, try to join social clubs, or compete for business. So, even if Justice Scalia believes his father never earned a dime off the sweat of a black man, he should admit that being classified white gave his father and him opportunities in America closed to most blacks, whatever their economic status.

As for the charge that affirmative action hurts disadvantaged whites, many remedial policies, such as those examined in *Adarand*, already include social or economic disadvantage as a relevant factor. This practice also is consistent with Justice Powell's diversity model in *Bakke*. If an affirmative action plan does not include social or economic disadvantage as a relevant factor in decision making, its absence is not an argument against all affirmative action but, rather, one for a broader plan.

In addition, plaintiffs like Brian Weber, Paul Johnson, or Randy Pech cannot be described as poor white male victims of affirmative action. Weber, for example, very likely benefited from an official policy at Kaiser that only white union men would work in certain crafts. Kaiser and the union preferred to hire and promote white men. Thus Weber claimed more seniority than newly hired black workers had. But he had greater seniority only because of past discrimination against blacks and so should not be able to rest a reverse discrimination claim on the effects of racial discrimination that benefited him. Paul Johnson, who sued the Santa Clara County (California) Department of Transportation for promoting a woman ahead of him, benefited from a culture in which only men did transportation road crew work, which best positioned them for the more lucrative position of road dispatcher. And Pech lost the guardrail bid not solely because of his race but because his had not been certified as a socially or economically disadvantaged business. It is simply wrong to charge that no white could so qualify. What Weber, Johnson, Pech, and other supposed victims of remedial affirmative action must recognize is that whites-only hiring, promotion, and training opportunities directly or indirectly benefited them while limiting blacks, other minorities, and women.

Rarely do critics of affirmative action openly set working-class whites against middle- or upper-class whites in the way that they pit working-class people of color against middle- or upper-class people of color, or minorities against poor whites. This ploy is as old as time: Divide the workers by pitting them against one another. Poor and middle-class white men have been taught for decades that if minorities or white women advance, they will not, and not surprisingly, they have responded by supporting exclusive economic and political monopolies.

Ironically, when Allan Bakke was denied admission to medical school, he had much more competition from other white applicants, some with scores lower than his, than he did from minority applicants.[118] Nonetheless, he didn't frame his complaint in terms of merit, but in terms of unfair preferences for minorities. A claim of merit would have implicated the applications of the eighty-four white students who were admitted when Bakke was rejected. He must have known that he could not win on the basis of merit. If Davis's medical school had admitted one hundred white students with lower ratings than Bakke's, he would have had no claim. For him, it probably would have been acceptable if all one hundred medical students at Davis were white, no matter what their ratings. But no black with lower ratings than his deserved admission.

### Affirmative Action Denies White Males Equal Opportunity

Affirmative action has not meant that white men have unequal opportunities; rather, it has appropriately mandated an end to prior quotas, preferences, and monopolies for white men only. None of the current affirmative action policies in this country excludes white men from any occupation, limits them to unskilled jobs, or denies them educational opportunities. None prevents whites from voting or dilutes their voting strength below that of their percentage of the population. Instead, remedial affirmative action does little more than tell federal agencies and private employers that compete for billions of dollars in government contracts that they must study their labor market demographics to make sure they are not underutilizing qualified minorities and women. Where they find underutilization, they must make good-faith efforts to eliminate it. That does not seem like much to require, given the past practices of such agencies or contractors.

In addition, any candid scrutiny of national statistics regarding access to higher education, employment, housing, political representation, or the allocation of public contracts shows that white men are not routinely losing opportunities to less-qualified minorities or women.[119] That is another myth.

Minorities and women—and especially minority women—remain in caste. One study confirms that blatant discrimination is still a continuing problem in the labor market. Random testing throughout the country by professional discrimination "testers"—persons trained to present themselves similarly and to ask certain questions—reveals that employers faced with white and minority candidates with similar credentials are less likely to interview or offer a job to a minority or female applicant:[120]

- Two pairs of male testers visited the offices of a nationally franchised employment agency on two different days. The black tester in each pair received no job referrals. However, the white testers who appeared minutes later were interviewed by the agency, coached on interviewing techniques, and referred to and offered jobs as switchboard operators.
- A black female tester applied for employment at a major hotel chain in Virginia and was told that she would be called if it wished to pursue her application. Although she never received a call, an equally qualified white counterpart who appeared a few minutes later was told about a vacancy for front desk clerk, was interviewed, and was offered the job.
- A black male tester inquired about an ad for a sales position at a Maryland car dealership. He was told that the way to enter the business would be to start by washing cars. A white counterpart, with identical credentials, was immediately interviewed for the sales job. Similar results were found in tests involving Latino and Asian testers.

Consider another 1995 study sponsored by former President Bush and former Senator Robert Dole:[121]

- White males continue to hold 97 percent of the senior management positions in Fortune 1000 industrial and Fortune 500 service industries. Only 0.6 percent of the senior management are black, 0.3 percent are Asian, and 0.4 percent are Latino.
- There are only two women CEOs in Fortune 1000 companies.
- The fears and prejudices of lower-rung white male executives were

listed as a principal barrier to the advancement of women and minorities.

- Black unemployment remains fragile, especially in an economic downturn, when it leads the downward spiral. For example, in the 1981/1982 recession, black employment dropped by 9.1 percent, but white employment fell by only 1.6 percent.
- An average woman with a master's degree earns the same amount as does an average man with an associate degree. Although college-educated black women have reached earnings parity with college-educated white women, college-educated black men earn 76 percent of the earnings of their white male counterparts. Latina women earn less than 65 percent of the income earned by white men at the same educational level.

There is a perception today that whites, especially men, do not have equal opportunities. But that idea conflicts with what we see around us. At the University of Alabama where I work, more than 96 percent of the faculty are white, and nearly 75 percent are men. As stated earlier, white men continue to earn a disproportionate number of all college and professional degrees. According to the *Chronicle of Higher Education*, in 1992, whites earned 84.5 percent of all doctoral degrees, and men earned 63 percent. Based on reports from approximately 3,300 colleges, 456,316 of the 520,551 full-time faculty in 1991/1992 were white.[122]

White men still run the economic and political institutions in America. They still are overrepresented in the upper levels of industry, government, and the academy. Their employment share, especially at the top, has diminished only slightly. Since those at the top are visible, one must wonder who or what fuels the perception that white males are losing opportunities. According to the Bush/Dole study, mid-level white executives were the main barrier to the advancement of minorities and women. Perhaps they feel most threatened. Are they responsible for perpetuating the myth of inequality?

This perception also arises in part from the way affirmative action has in fact diminished the unfair monopolies that white men once enjoyed. Americans must never forget that no job or title has a race or gender. Therefore, it is not normal that only two women are CEOs of Fortune 1000 companies. Since current policies do not exclude white men from economic and political opportunities, how can anyone say they are unfair?

### Affirmative Action Stigmatizes Its Beneficiaries and Worsens Racial Balkanization

One hears all the time how affirmative action supposedly stigmatizes its beneficiaries by implying that they cannot succeed without affirmative action, thereby lowering their self-esteem or making others question their competence. Some critics link affirmative action to increased racial polarization, balkanization, and racial tension. This is only wordplay.

Minorities and women did not gain equal educational and employment opportunities without affirmative action. Dred Scott, Homer Plessy, Myra Bradwell, and Virginia Minor all were victims of white male privilege during the nineteenth century, well before remedial policies were enacted to aid people like them. Their exclusion was not about their ability relative to that of white men; it was about preserving quotas for white men. Thus, it is unclear why a policy that ends white male privilege would stigmatize women or minorities.

Such contentions about stigma wrongly cast affirmative action as the villain, the source of contemporary racial enmity. Of course, this assumes that if it were not for affirmative action, such perceptions of inferiority and stigma would not exist and there would be no racial balkanization. But our history is littered with examples demonstrating that the exclusion of blacks, other minorities, and white women from economic and political opportunities was justified by theories of white male supremacy and minority and female inferiority. Long before Presidents Roosevelt, Eisenhower, Kennedy, Johnson, and Nixon adopted contemporary affirmative action policies, whites—especially white men—excluded minorities and women from economic and political participation through their own programs of affirmative action.

Ethnic balkanization has much more to do with racially restrictive covenants, preferential zoning practices, and discrimination by lending institutions and realtors than with remedial affirmative action. It simply is inaccurate to attribute racial enmity and current segregation to remedial affirmative action. Rather, they stem from a long record of perverse racial animus toward blacks and gender patronization of white women that we cannot deny.[123] Affirmative action is not a disease; it is a remedy that needs more time to work.

Not surprisingly, no one ever has claimed that the numerous racial quotas for whites stigmatized them or that such policies caused racial balkanization or antipathy. Imagine that when Americans go to a white male doctor or dentist today, they are asked whether he went to a school that excluded blacks, women, or other minorities or whether he was admitted under a quota. Since Americans don't ask such questions, why does Justice Scalia think that they would ask such questions about minority doctors who have gained opportunities under remedial policies?[124] Isn't this just another part of the privilege of whiteness—that even the most extensive record of racial privilege is not demeaning or stigmatizing, white men are presumed worthy or qualified, and minorities and women are unworthy and unqualified?

### Affirmative Action Is Quotas, Pure and Simple

Strict race quotas have not been a component of many affirmative action policies since the Supreme Court decided *Bakke* in 1978. That decision made it clear that race could not be the sole criterion for decisions by the government, without a finding of invidious discrimination attributable to the government. Thus, it is dishonest to use inflammatory code words to describe a policy that does no more than require broad and open advertising and recruitment for new hires, recording and reporting efforts to diversify the workforce, or setting goals for workplace diversification based on labor market demographics. And even in cases when a decision maker has used a quota, it is not a justification for abandoning all affirmative action but, rather, only proof that *Bakke*'s principle has been violated.

Quotas have both weaknesses and strengths. They should not operate as ceilings for minorities or women. A wise administrator would not have set aside sixteen places at Davis's medical school. Likewise, UCLA should not have set aside 40 percent of the admissions slots in the law school for diversity admits. Both schools probably did the most they believed they could do, and with good intentions. However, there was an effective alternative with little of the intense emotion that has been coupled with even the appearance of a quota: the diversity approach championed by Justice Powell. Few schools have followed Powell's prescription, which is why the University of Texas School of Law was vulnerable to a lawsuit in 1992. Suppose that all 100 new medical students at Davis and all 350 new law students at UCLA were diversity admits. Some would be white, black, Native American, Asian, and Latino. Some would be persons with disabilities. Some would be female. Some would be young, others older. Some would be first-generation college students, some fifth. But no program would be all-white or all-black or all-male or all-female unless no one else applied. As Powell believed, under a diversity model, every applicant would be compared with every other one.

Why haven't more schools done what Powell suggested? Is it too much work for faculty or administrators to read every file carefully? Would alumni oppose a complete diversity model? Or do those who run America's colleges and universities have only a lukewarm interest in ending educational and occupational segregation? Whatever the reason, it is clear that many institutions have yet to try a real diversity plan.

On the other hand, without realistic numerical goals, there is no way to ensure that some portion of a public benefit like higher education accrues to minorities and women who, without it, often get left out. Educational opportunity is a key ingredient to success in our society. When a state's principal universities disproportionately enroll whites or men, it tracks others into less rewarding positions, sometimes into caste. The government should be able to eliminate caste.

Under the mandate of affirmative action, it is assumed that economic and political opportunities will be opened to people with diverse demographic characteristics. Thus, if a society offers one hundred jobs, affirmative action means that whites will not be given all of them. And therein lies the rub and the best explanation for the aggressive campaign against affirmative action.

**Affirmative Action Violates the Merit Rule**

Critics of affirmative action never explain how remedial antidiscrimination policies violate the rule of nondiscrimination- or merit-based decision making. First, employers who refused to employ minorities and women before they were compelled by law to do so did not use meritocratic hiring criteria. Far from it: minorities and women were told that either they need not apply or they could work only in low-paying positions. Merit was equivalent to whiteness and maleness, with an additional class modifier for some positions. Affirmative action, however, requires that formerly all-white jobs be open to others.

Opponents of affirmative action rarely offer a proposal that addresses the economic and political opportunities, privileges, and wealth that many whites have obtained because of past race-conscious preferences. They also rarely note the inherent unfairness to minorities and white women of not adopting remedial policies. Too much of the fairness analysis in affirmative action commentary overlooks the innocence of minorities and white women who remain frozen out without remedial affirmative action.

Because of historical racial preferences for whites, several generations of whites have attended the best schools, taken the best jobs, lived in the best communities, and controlled almost all the political and economic power in this country. They have thereby been able to pass this accumulated wealth to subsequent generations. On the other hand, that same race consciousness for whites has limited the accumulation of wealth for blacks, who control the least amount of this country's political and economic power. Far fewer blacks have been able to transfer wealth to subsequent generations. The result is modern racial caste.[125] Many opponents of remedial affirmative action say nothing about the connection between our discriminatory history and current racial caste.

Moreover, it is an exaggeration to pretend that employment decisions today are made exclusively on the basis of merit. Recall the news programs that show by hidden camera what happens when two applicants with identical credentials, one black and one white, inquire about the same job: The black applicant is told the job has been filled. A few minutes later the white applicant is interviewed and offered the job. Such tests reveal consistent results throughout the country.

Jobs are filled as much, if not more, by whom you know or how you look, rather than what you know or what you can do. Thus, segregated housing, schools, and social networks, as well as word-of-mouth advertising by those already on the job influence hiring far more than does a comparison of résumés. Also, many whites making hiring decisions show a form of racial affinity to other whites that they do not afford to blacks. Many whites would have to overcome stereotypes of blacks before they would feel comfortable hiring them.

Some critics of affirmative action insist that it is reverse discrimination. But no affirmative action plan excludes white men from entire job categories; none relegates them to unskilled, part-time, or low-paying jobs. No plan denies white men access to educational opportunities or the chance to vote. What exactly, then, is reverse discrimination? It is a charade!

Through a kind of shell game, critics charge that using race (or gender) to ensure that some minorities (and women) are employed, promoted, or admitted is the same as using it to exclude them. In this way, then, intentionally drawing a majority black or Latino legislative district in

North Carolina, Texas, Georgia, or Florida is the same as drawing lines in Tuskegee, Alabama so that all but a handful of the five hundred blacks living there are excluded from voting. Similarly, critics insist that using race as one of several factors in college admissions is constitutionally the same as a whites-only admission policy. This is ridiculous. Affirmative action promotes inclusion, not racial supremacy. Nothing in the Constitution says that government or private employers cannot value diversity or promote occupational and educational integration. Indeed, the Court in *Bakke* held the opposite.

### Affirmative Action Advances Unqualified Persons and Lowers Productivity

Some affirmative action opponents charge that although they agree with affirmative action's abstract rationales, they translate into the hiring, promotion, or admission of incompetent people over more competent people, to the detriment of the company, school, the beneficiary, or even the national economy. This claim may be one of the most insidious charges against affirmative action.

What makes this claim pernicious is the implication that affirmative action is the only process by which unqualified persons can get hired, promoted, or admitted to college. If the question is whether affirmative action has meant that some people who are unqualified or less qualified have advanced, the answer is a firm yes. But it is also a qualified yes, qualified in the sense that incompetent or semicompetent people are promoted everywhere, all the time, over more deserving others. Affirmative action is not immune, nor can it be, from this phenomenon.

There exists perhaps no better example of this phenomenon than former Vice President Dan Quayle. A mediocre student, an inarticulate speaker, a politician with such a suspect intellectual background that he was given a "reading list" by his advisers, Quayle spent four years a heartbeat away from the presidency due largely to the circumstances of his birth. No question Quayle was scrutinized and mocked, but he was rarely the object of outrage or resentment for his glaring lack of qualifications. A speech in which Quayle did not misspeak or a debate in which he was not humiliated by his opponent became a cause for celebration among his advisers, who spun barely competent performances into masterpieces of political oratory.

Imagine how Americans would respond to a black politician who couldn't spell *potato*, who bumbled his way through debates, who horribly mangled well-known sayings such as the United Negro College Fund credo, "A mind is a terrible thing to waste" (which Quayle converted into "What a waste it is to lose one's mind").[126] An inarticulate, poorly educated African American who was catapulted to high national office owing not to his family's political connections or his supposed ability to appeal to women (as Quayle was) but to affirmative action and his ability to draw black votes would be seen as a vindication of and a justification for every critique of affirmative action. Just as it is not difficult to imagine Jesse Helms saying, "You see, this is what affirmative action gets you," so it is inconceivable for a politician or talking head to dismiss openly a man such as Quayle with the words "You see, this is what white racial privilege gets you." I would argue that given the scrutiny that affirmative action has had to withstand, those hired, promoted, or admitted under affirmative action programs are perhaps less prone to the Quayle phenomenon.

No affirmative action policy requires any employer to hire or promote an unqualified worker. None requires a college to admit unqualified students. But the law does require that federal contractors take good-faith efforts to hire qualified minorities and women who are available in various occupational areas. Of course, there is pressure on employers to investigate labor statistics, determine utilization patterns, and correct problems of underutilization. But no policy compels any employer to hire persons without the proper training. Essentially, affirmative action goals are aspirational, not mandatory.

None of the arguments against affirmative action is ultimately persuasive. It is good policy and constitutional; without it, decision makers will revert to the old way of doing things, with minorities and women getting only crumbs.

## RACIAL REALISM

Statistical disparities in the United States between blacks and whites still mirror those reported by the Kerner Commission in 1968: we remain a nation of "two societies, one black, one white–separate and unequal." And even though there are many causes of the disparities in the lives of blacks and whites today, most experts believe that a central cause remains racial discrimination.[127]

Black children are born to unwed mothers three and one-half times more often than white children are. More than half of black families are headed by women, whereas fewer than one in five white families are. And of the families headed by women, 60 percent of the black families live in central cities, but less than half that number of white families do.

Blacks die of tuberculosis seven times more often than whites do; blacks die of AIDS, meningitis, anemias, kidney diseases, alcohol-induced causes, infant deaths, nutritional deficiencies, diabetes, and drug-induced causes at rates between two to three times the white rates. Blacks die from homicides at a rate six and one-half times greater than that for whites. Among young black males, murder is the leading cause of death. At the starting and finishing lines of life in the United States, blacks and whites have dramatically different experiences.

Important defining racial disparities exist throughout life. Four and one-half percent of blacks between the ages of twenty-five and thirty-four who completed college are unemployed, whereas only 2 percent of whites are. For persons in that same age range who did not complete high school, a full quarter of blacks are unemployed, as opposed to slightly more than 10 percent of whites. Similarly, of the black and white families living below the poverty line in the Northeast, Midwest, South, and West, the rate for blacks is four to five times greater than for whites.

Eighty-two percent of all blacks between the ages of twenty-five and thirty-five completed high school, but nearly 90 percent of all whites did. However, only 13 percent of blacks in that group completed four or more years of college, twice the percentage of whites who did. Blacks earned less than 6 percent of the bachelor's degrees conferred in 1989, and whites earned about 85 percent. Blacks also received only 3.5 percent of the doctorates conferred in 1989, and whites received 90 percent. Similarly, blacks earned 5 percent of the medical and law degrees granted in 1989, and whites earned 86 percent of the medical degrees and 90 percent of the law degrees.

Black families earn $580 for every $1,000 earned by white families. The 1990 median income for white families was $36,915, and for black families, $21,423. Working white men had a median income of $21,170; working black men, $12,868. White women had a 1990 median income of $10,317; black women, $8,328. Even when black men reach the same academic level as white men do, their incomes remain several steps behind that of their white counterparts. Interestingly, black women earn almost the same income as their white female counterparts with one to four years of college. Because women are underpaid in comparison to men anyway, it is easier for black women to gain equity. In 1990, white unemployment was 4 percent, for blacks, 11 percent. "To be black in America is to know that you remain last in line for so basic a requisite as the means for supporting yourself and your family."[128]

In 1989 a report by the Committee on the Status of Black Americans stated:

> [T]he great gulf that existed between black and white Americans in 1939 has only narrowed; it has not been closed. One of three blacks live in households with incomes below the poverty line. Even more blacks live in areas where ineffective schools, high rates of dependence on public assistance, severe problems of crime and drug abuse, and low and declining employment prevail.[129]

The committee concluded that foremost among the reasons for the present state of black–white relations are two continuing consequences of the nation's long and recent history of racial inequality: the negative attitudes toward blacks and the actual disadvantaged conditions under which many blacks live.

Given the pervasiveness of racial caste, Americans invariably wonder whether there is not something peculiar about blacks that has positioned them perpetually at the bottom of America's economic ladder. If so, what is the cause? Is it cognitive inferiority, as Charles Murray's book *The Bell Curve* would have us believe? An excessive victim mentality, as Shelby Steele writes in *The Content of Our Character?* Do blacks have a poor work ethic? Have they failed to embrace traditional American values, as implied in Thomas Sowell's *Race and Culture?*[130]

Murray's thesis is that cognitive ability is a better predictor than discrimination is of socially undesirable behaviors such as having children out of marriage, welfare dependency, unemployment, or poverty. Since whites have higher cognitive ability than blacks do, he asserts, they engage in socially desirable behaviors, less unemployment, greater educational attainment, fewer out-of-wedlock babies, and so forth. I agree with Murray that America is a land of at least two nations, but I don't believe that the division is between smart people and dumb people. Instead, shouldn't Murray ask why America has educational tracks, black schools, and white schools? My life experience has shown me that I was not dumb, only undereducated and undernurtured. When I should have been mastering reading and language skills, I was starving and perfecting theft.

Murray fails to tell his readers that America has a unique history of denying blacks equal opportunities for cognitive development. But he cannot overlook the long-standing American policy not to educate blacks and other minorities equally with whites. How, then, can he be sure that if whites were undereducated in the way that blacks have been, they would not have the scores they do today on intelligence tests? And if he is correct that cognitive ability is 40 to 80 percent heritable, it should matter to him and other Americans that my mother, her parents, and their parents were colored persons excluded from equal public education.

Shelby Steele's writing is likewise flawed because he makes no attempt to ground it in America's history. He writes as though whites have measured themselves or others by the content of their character rather than by the color of their skin. Not so in Ohio. Not so in America. It is difficult for Steele to use the words of Martin Luther King Jr., a man who literally gave his life fighting white privilege, in a book that argues that blacks make excessive claims to victimhood. Steele recasts King's ideas by making fleeting references to America's history of white supremacy. King understood far better than Steele does that all blacks are victims of whites-only policies. Indeed, King believed that theories of racial supremacy were dangerous for all Americans. Steele's book is at best a placebo that makes some people feel better about America's current racial crisis. But like a placebo, it lacks substance. The issue isn't whether blacks manipulate whites' guilt. Rather, it is whether America can survive its racial caste, whatever its causes.

Thomas Sowell's global tour of occupational segregation in no way diminishes the significance of white privilege in the United States. Nor does it disprove that whites-only policies from as recently as the 1960s still reverberate throughout the country. Sowell's thesis is that culture and values, more than environment, explain poverty or prosperity. Some cultures, he claims, have better skills, work habits, savings propensities, and attitudes toward education and entrepreneurship. Thus, in Sowell's mind, cultural values have the same function as cognitive ability does for Murray: Smarter people have better cultural values.

Like Murray, Sowell writes as if America's history never happened: there was no racial discrimination in education or employment. Sowell should know that culture did not keep Thurgood Marshall out of the University of Maryland's law school and that poor attitudes did not keep Autherine Lucy out of the University of Alabama. Poor cultural values or work habits did not keep blacks out of all-white unions or white jobs or keep them from participating in the political process. Sowell's "world perspective" does little to explain why so many whites in the United States have directed their racial prejudice against blacks for so long.

Murray, Steele, and Sowell simply don't understand racial prejudice or admit its significance. Racial prejudice has flourished because of the advantages and material benefits it yields to those who practice it. Prejudice also provides an excuse or rationalization for the exploitation of blacks.[131] Jonathan Kozol *(Savage Inequalities)*, Sylvester Monroe *(Brothers)* and Alex Kotlowitz *(There Are No Children Here)* graphically described the life-and-death consequences of racial prejudice. But surprisingly little has been written about the costs of racial prejudice to those in the dominant group—whites. What are the costs to America from black teenage unemployment, malnutrition, disease, violence, and crime? How much time and money are spent on controversies and litigations in which one party claims discrimination while the other attempts to prove none exists? Murray, Steele, and Sowell write as if racial prejudice is imaginary. Not so. It inhibits our nationhood.

Since we Americans cannot turn back the clock to 1619, 1787, 1896, or 1965 and begin again at the same, unweighted starting line, we must ask what we can do now under the Constitution to remedy the current effects of pervasive racial caste. Surely, the answer isn't that we can't do anything.

## ELIMINATING CASTE

Remedial affirmative action arose in response to America's sordid history and tradition of white racial privilege. Because it is remedial in nature, it is not constitutionally equivalent to past policies promoting white supremacy. Moreover, the Supreme Court has said numerous times that the equal protection clause does not demand that things that are different be treated under the law as though they are the same. Therefore, since remedial affirmative action does not promote racial supremacy, as prior whites-only policies did, it does not violate the Constitution's equality mandate.

Critics of remedial affirmative action should recall the words of Justice Harlan, who wrote after the Civil War amendments were adopted that "[t]here is no caste here. Our Constitution is color blind, and neither knows nor tolerates classes among citizens." They should explain why the Constitution, especially the equal protection clause of the Fourteenth

Amendment, prohibits governmental policies designed to eliminate racial caste.

The current attack on affirmative action threatens to enlarge the gulf in this country in political and economic power among the races and between the sexes. The principal problem in this country is racial caste, a product of this nation's racial preferences favoring whites, especially white men, to varying degrees, for nearly four centuries. Indeed, the greatest tragedy of America's history is its romance with theories of white supremacy, including the incorporation of such principles into the American Constitution.

Critics of affirmative action present no workable policy alternative to reduce racial caste. Some declare they would support a class-based affirmative action plan. But that would do little about race-based discrimination, especially for persons who are not poor. Others would have such plans be voluntary. But since nothing prevents voluntary efforts now, that would not be a solution either. If someone criticizes a policy, shouldn't he or she offer a better alternative? One has the feeling with critics of affirmative action that their alternative is to do nothing except maintain the status quo.

Moreover, Americans should support class-based affirmative action as well as—and separate from—race- or gender-based plans. Class-based plans alone will not remedy race and gender discrimination. If America is to keep its goal of remedial affirmative action, it must adopt policies ensuring that minorities and women have equal opportunities. Only that will reduce caste. Whether or not white Americans admit it, too many of them frequently use nonwhiteness as a negative disqualifier. Therefore, the question is why they cannot or should not use nonwhiteness as a positive qualifier to desegregate educational and occupational tracks and thereby reduce racial caste.

Justice Powell offered one solution to racial caste and the color blindness trap in his *Bakke* opinion. Powell's concern was that every applicant to Davis's medical school receive the same treatment. The Harvard plan achieved that end in two ways: every applicant could compete for every slot, and race was one of many factors considered by the committee. This model eliminated any charges of quotas. It also made sure that no applicant was excluded from the pool solely on the basis of race. In addition, every admitted student was a diversity admit, so there was no unnecessary labeling of students. What's wrong with a diversity approach? Why can't employers or admissions officers decide on a range of parameters and apply them to everyone?

What offended the Constitution in *Bakke* was the creation of two admissions policies and the quota for minorities. But suppose a university stated the following:

> This school is committed to diversity. Any student with a 2.5 or higher overall grade point average and a score of 1000 or above on the SAT or 18 or above on the ACT can apply for admission. In addition to these numbers, the applicant can submit letters of recommendation and a personal essay describing his or her family history. Applicants may also be interviewed by the admissions staff or by an alumni representative. Based on all these data, each application will be rated on a scale of 1 to 100.

In this scenario, every applicant competes for every place. There are no quotas. But the school can still achieve educational diversity, and no individual could claim denial of equal protection of the law.

I see no reason that the San Francisco Fire Department, the Alabama state troopers, Kaiser, US West, or Sara Lee Mills cannot establish similar criteria for hiring or promotion. Nothing in the American Constitution requires any employer to follow a numeric hiring scheme. Antidiscrimination laws do no more than forbid employers from arbitrarily excluding prospective employees because of invidious discrimination.

Another solution available to the Court is to apply its difference model for gender discrimination cases to race-based affirmative action cases. For more than twenty years, the Court has consistently held that a gender classification "must be reasonable, not arbitrary, and must rest upon some ground of difference having a fair and substantial relation to the object of the legislation, so all persons similarly circumstanced shall be treated alike."[132]

According to that review standard, the Court has upheld statutes favoring women in situations in which societal discrimination against them has left them disadvantaged. For example, the Court validated a Florida statute that granted a $500 property tax exemption for widows but not for widowers. It concluded that the statute rested on a "ground of difference having a fair and substantial relation to the object of the legislation"—the reduction of the disparity between the economic capabilities of a man and a woman. The Court did not require the state to prove that a particular woman had been discriminated against but instead recounted how society's "male-dominated culture" reduced the economic opportunities available to women. The Court also upheld a federal statute that permitted women, when computing their retirement benefits under Social Security, to deduct three more lower-earning years than a male wage earner could. The Court wrote: "Reduction of the disparity in the economic condition between men and women caused by the long history of discrimination against women has been recognized as an important governmental objective."[133]

It would not be a significant step for the Court to apply its difference model to race cases. Stated simply, if the equal protection clause does not require gender blindness, why must Americans interpret it to require color blindness? Why can't the government enact policies to eliminate the economic disparities between blacks, other minorities, and white women and white men? Surely, societal discrimination against blacks has been no less harmful than that against women, so why a double standard? Doesn't America's still-prevailing racial caste prove that in some situations there is a difference between whites and minorities that could justify remedial affirmative action for minorities? In the current cases, it is conceivable that in a case like *Adarand* or *Croson*, the Supreme Court might uphold a gender-based plan but strike down the same plan if it were race based. There is no justification for that anomaly in the Constitution or American history.

Application of either the diversity theory or the difference model would enable the Court to advance the central purpose of the Fourteenth Amendment—the elimination of racial caste. Ultimately, as we evaluate the arguments for and against affirmative action, we must decide whether the Constitution champions inequality or equality. The American Constitution should do as much to eliminate racial caste as it once did to protect slavery, segregation, and white supremacy.

Before Americans can have a color-blind society or government, they must repudiate myths of racial supremacy and affirmatively dismantle racial caste. When they have done so, race will no longer be the obstacle it has become. But until they do, color blindness will be a problem in America.

## AFTERWORD

**B**ecause my family still lives in Columbus, I visit several times a year. Family gatherings today are happy, festive times. Dee no longer works but spends much of her time visiting her family. She has nearly two dozen grandchildren and a half-dozen great-grandchildren. My siblings and I help support her financially. She still cooks regularly, but now at home for my brothers or sisters who would rather eat her cooking than their own.

All my sisters and brothers have better lives today. They have small families and work in various occupations. Two work at the same hospital; one does cosmetology; one manages a pizza place; one works at a paint-and-glass factory; one directs food services at a retirement center; and one drives a city bus. One has served time for check forgery. I have some fear that one other is headed in that direction, and there seems little that I can do about it because he believes that that life is his best option. None of them had the affirmative action opportunities that I did. Duke and UCLA could accommodate only a few people like me. Similar affirmative action programs have always been limited. We need more programs, not fewer.

I also visit the teachers, parents of close friends, and employers, both black and white, who cared for me and helped me escape my ghetto. And

I see my best friends, most of whom also left Columbus, who kept me preoccupied with noncriminal activities. I owe all of them my life. You see, it wasn't just affirmative action, or just welfare, or just hard work on my part that got me out. My brothers and sisters, teachers, employers, friends, and their parents all made sacrifices for me. I stand on their gifts.

Yet whenever I visit, I am also reminded of cruel deprivation that no child should endure, especially in a land as rich as ours. I cannot drive past my old houses and not recall how little we had, and I cannot forget the freezing nights or empty refrigerators. I cannot forget the long days when I was weary from hunger. When I see my old schools, I remember how poor my primary education was and how as a teenager, I was just learning to read.

I grew up hating Columbus, hating the squalid conditions in which I lived. My disdain increased when I saw all around me comfort and opulence, especially in white Columbus. Had I done something to deserve those horrid circumstances? Was I inferior? I did not understand then that I was suffering in part because some Ohioans continued to promote white privilege and to ignore the ghetto. I learned about Ohio's legacy of white supremacy only by leaving black Columbus.

I often wonder whether those early white Ohioans could have known that the racial privileges that they assigned themselves would produce so much despair for blacks. If they could have seen into the future, would they have acted differently? If you could go back in time, faced with their choices, what would you do? Unfortunately, few white Ohioans learn in local history classes about their state's endorsement of white supremacy. Therefore, many would probably deny that they have benefited from racial privileges. But I suspect few have asked their fathers, mothers, or grandparents whether they benefited from racial privileges. It is as if many of them believe that by not thinking or talking about them, such privileges never existed. This conspiracy of silence sustains white supremacy as effectively as prior law does.

How many Americans living today have benefited, directly or indirectly, from some form of affirmative action or preferential treatment, including preferences for relatives, alumni, financial donors, veterans, or those based on religion, class, sex, or race? I don't think many Americans have examined their own lives for preferences. But their failing to do so prevents a candid discussion about the merits of remedial affirmative action. It also makes possible the false ideas that all preferences are the same and that without them merit will prevail.

Some Americans believe in a recent myth called *merit:* neutral qualifications such as grades and standardized test scores. Today, merit means that those who have the best grades and scores are the smartest, deserving the best opportunities. Why is it at all shocking that on average, blacks have lower grades or test scores, given their past cumulative educational deprivation and the continued underfunding of their schools? More important, how could grades and test scores be considered neutral factors in America? And why the reliance on merit today when for centuries America's graduate schools were filled with white men who had no more ability than many blacks or women did? Did giving them training hurt them or stigmatize them? The continuing reliance on grades and scores will extend, not eliminate, caste. American history has convinced me that without affirmative action, merit will again be equated primarily with whiteness and maleness, leaving most Americans at the back door.

Have national leaders like Bob Dole, Newt Gingrich, or Bill Clinton benefited from affirmative action preferences? Are they, as Stephen Carter refers to himself, "affirmative action babies"? I would like to ask each of them if they—or their parents, or their parents' parents—benefited from preferences or if they ever have bothered to think or ask about it. Is it possible that all the race, gender, religion, or class preferences down through America's history somehow missed them? Why don't they talk about them? Their silence implies that they are not products of preferences, and to discuss preferences, of course, would require them to determine whether they benefited from those for whites only or for males only. Then they would have to concede that modern affirmative action is fundamentally different from previous preferences for white men. Why don't they admit that eliminating white supremacy is not the same as promoting it? Isn't it obvious that valuing America's diversity is not the same as valuing only its whiteness?

Clinton, Dole, and others want us to believe that they earned all that they have, that they worked hard and played by the rules, and that they are self-made. Do you really believe that? And doesn't that imply that those who have not "made it" have not worked hard and don't deserve any more than they have? Don't you know a lot of people who work hard and who nonetheless are poor? Is it possible that some of them are victims of caste?

What about Clarence Thomas, Thomas Sowell, or Shelby Steele? Have they navigated life without benefiting from remedial preferences? Did they go to graduate schools that did not use preferences? Do they talk about the benefits that affirmative action gave them? Did Antonin Scalia, Sandra Day O'Connor, or any other member of the Supreme Court get there without benefit of preferences? Has any American escaped the effects of America's caste legacy?

If the critics of remedial affirmative action took a long, hard look in the mirror, I suspect they would find that along life's way, they or someone they depended on benefited from a caste-producing preference or a remedial preference. Why is it so difficult for them to distinguish between the two? Some of them do not consider their past privileges to fall within their definition of affirmative action, and they argue that affirmative action is harmful and stigmatizing. Is that true? When was the last time that you heard someone claim that preferences stigmatized white men, who for two centuries were America's perennial favorites? Have you ever heard that affirmative action harms the self-esteem of athletes or the children of rich people? Affirmative action cannot be defined in one way for minorities but in another way for others. And we cannot forget that remedial affirmative action is designed to eliminate caste, nothing more. Why would it be stigmatic?

Without affirmative action, I could easily have been trapped by racial caste. I needed opportunities to improve myself, to hone my intellect and skills. I needed (but did not have) a school board that cared as much about black children like me as it did about white children in the Columbus schools, a board that cared whether I too became a knowledgeable, skilled, productive citizen, one that would not allocate more money to white schools than to black schools or would fund schools in a way that produced huge disparities in per pupil expenditures. I needed a school board that was committed to racial equality and more teachers who believed that black children could learn anything white children could learn, who demanded hard work and academic excellence from themselves and all their students, not teachers who thought black children were inferior and going nowhere. I needed a local welfare agency that cared whether I was hungry when I went to school or if I had heat in my home during the cold winters, not one staffed by social workers who resented that my mother had so many children and received welfare. I needed an agency to help me deal with my feelings of shame and embarrassment about my family's poverty. I needed help, not spite or blame.

It is a miracle that anyone survives such an upbringing. In fact, an increasing number of Americans do not, and the growing dangers of racial caste put all of us at risk. Every day, I experienced many of the symptoms of racial caste while growing up in black Columbus, and I know both the anger and the hopelessness that it engenders. No one can tell me that people who grew up in ghettos had equal opportunity. I could just as easily have grown up to be a pimp or drug dealer. I did not. My rescuer was remedial affirmative action.

Somehow, those days of despair did not make me hate white people. I sometimes wonder why, but I think that my experiences with whites at Johnson Park, Duke, and UCLA are part of the reason. I still want to live in an integrated America, but I constantly reflect on why so many whites have treated so many blacks so inhumanely throughout our history, only now to insist that nothing can be done about racial caste, that we should be color blind, and that remedial affirmative action is unfair. Such whites take no responsibility for the racial caste that is killing innocent people. James Baldwin wrote about such whites that "it is the innocence which constitutes the crime."[1] It takes deliberate indifference, ignorance, and gall to say to blacks that there is just one race in America or that modern racial caste cannot be traced to conduct by whites.

Affirmative action opened doors for me that were closed to blacks such as Thurgood Marshall, Autherine Lucy, Lloyd Gaines, and Ada Sipuel, all of whom were excluded from graduate or professional schools in Maryland, Alabama, Missouri, and Oklahoma during the 1930s through the 1950s, despite their proven ability, solely because those universities were for whites only. Because of the courage of Vivian Malone-Jones, James Hood, and the thousands of others who challenged their denial of equal educational opportunities throughout the country, I did not face identical barriers.

Affirmative action has also worked for many others, including some current members of the Supreme Court who seem to have forgotten that their race or gender once presumptively disqualified them from a position on the Court. Justice Thurgood Marshall, who broke the color barrier on the Court in 1967, supported remedial affirmative action and frequently noted for his colleagues the distinction between it and preferences promoting caste.

Similarly, Charles Daye, a distinguished law professor at the University of North Carolina, Chapel Hill, is correct when he explains that remedial affirmative action gave him an opportunity to attend Columbia Law School in the late 1960s but that it did not make him an honors graduate. He earned that distinction and every outstanding grade it required.[2]

Remedial affirmative action gave me a chance for a productive life. But I had to make something of it, knowing that the price of failure was high! Unlike Justice Clarence Thomas and others, I am not ashamed that I benefited from remedial affirmative action. It helped me improve my life. I have confidence and self-esteem and gained more, in part, by completing college and law school. Moreover, unlike Stephen Carter, I am not an "affirmative action baby" who now, belatedly, disdains it and its supposed stigma. More accurately, I am one of America's "racial caste babies," who somehow survived a ghetto and who supports remedial policies designed to eliminate caste. I would never pull up the ladder that helped me climb out of racial poverty.

The United States cannot survive another century of white supremacy and black caste; it cannot survive the continuation of substantially segregated educational and occupational tracks, segregated communities, or the myriad schemes currently used to dilute minority political power. They make a mockery of the idea of racial equality while weakening the country politically and economically.

America cannot continue to treat some of its citizens as throwaways. There are no "extra" people. The country must find a way to offer everyone rewarding life opportunities, and as long as such opportunities remain limited, it cannot continue acting as if the best opportunities are for whites or men only. Put simply, Americans must share. People of color, white women, and other working poor in America will either have access to the best educational and employment opportunities that have long been the prerogative of white male elites, or Americans will likely see a return to the marches and riots that indelibly scarred the United States during the 1960s. Now, as then, many of its cities show signs of great racial tension. As the aftermath of the Rodney King beating trial illustrated, they can explode at any moment. White males are not the only Americans who are angry.

I want so much to be proud of America. But I cannot if I am viewed as nothing more than a vulgar caricature. I want a dollar in my hand to buy the same thing that a white person can. I want to buy a house or car under the same credit requirements set for whites. I want to move into any community and have neighbors welcome me with a casserole, not a burning cross or a For Sale sign. I want schools for black children that are as well funded and rigorous as those for whites. I want America to repudiate its romance with white supremacy. I want America to celebrate its diversity, not just its whiteness. I want every privilege of whiteness extended to Americans with darker skin. I want to sing America's national anthem and not feel betrayed. I want to salute its flag and know that the principles it supposedly symbolizes extend to Americans with darker skin. I want America's Constitution's protection and eloquence to apply to me, too. In a word, I want to belong. I cannot respect a country that treats me with disdain; I cannot be America's problem.

ℓ℘

# NOTES

······································································································································································

NOTES TO PREFACE

1. Adarand Constructors, Inc. v. Pena, 115 S.Ct. 2097 (1995).

2. Payne v. Tennessee, 501 U.S. 808, 844 (1991).

3. Daniel C. Maguire, *A New American Justice* (Garden City, N.Y.: Doubleday, 1980), 3.

4. Justice Harlan pointed out this irony as early as 1883, when he wrote
    With all respect for the opinion of others, I insist that the National Legislature may, without transcending the limits of the Constitution, do for human liberty and the fundamental rights of American citizenship, what it did, with the sanction of this court, for the protection of slavery and the rights of the masters of fugitive slaves.
The Civil Rights Cases, 109 U.S. 3, 50–53 (1883) (Harlan, J., dissenting).

5. Plessy v. Ferguson, 163 U.S. 537, 558 (1896) (Harlan, J., dissenting).

6. Harlan could not have meant that it was unconstitutional for the government to take race into account, because he acknowledged that the Civil War amendments were in fact adopted to secure for the newly freed blacks all the civil rights enjoyed by whites, and he also had written thirteen years earlier:
    If the constitutional Amendments be enforced, according to the intent with which, as I conceive, they were adopted, there cannot be in this Republic, any class of human beings in *practical* subjection to another class, with power in the latter to dole out to the former just such privileges as they may choose to grant.

**185**

The Civil Rights Cases, 109 U.S. at 59–62 (Harlan, J., dissenting) (emphasis added).

7. Plessy, 163 U.S. at 558–61.

8. Regents of the University of California v. Bakke, 438 U.S. 265, 289–90, 291 (1978). Justice Powell agreed with four other members of the Court that race could be one of many factors considered by admissions officers in their selection among applicants for medical school (265, 325–26, opinion of Brennan, J.).

9. One recent definition of the color blindness principle holds that a state may use the criterion of race only when it acts to undo the effects of its own discrimination or when it acts in a social emergency, such as a prison race riot. See City of Richmond v. J. A. Croson Co., 488 U.S. 469, 521–24 (1989) (Scalia, J., concurring in judgment).

10. The writer who has most significantly influenced my thinking regarding race is William E. B. Du Bois (1868–1963). My concluding sentence is paraphrased from Du Bois's prophetic words published in 1903:

> The problem of the twentieth century is the problem of the color-line,— the relation of the darker to the lighter races of men in Asia and Africa, in America and the islands of the sea. It was a phase of this problem that caused the Civil War; and however much they who marched South and North in 1861 may have fixed on the technical points of union and local autonomy as a shibboleth, all nevertheless knew, and we know, that the question of Negro slavery was the real cause of the conflict.

See W. E. B. Du Bois, *The Souls of Black Folk* (New York: New American Library, 1969) (1903), 54–55. For a concise, informative bibliographic essay and selected bibliography for Du Bois, see Manning Marable, *W. E. B. Du Bois: Black Radical Democrat* (Boston: Twayne, 1986), 267–80.

NOTES TO PART ONE

1. Helen Tunnicliff Catterall, *Judicial Cases Concerning American Slavery and the Negro*, vol. 5 (New York: Octagon Books, 1968), 2.

2. See Gray v. Ohio, 4 Ohio 353 (1831); Williams v. School District, 1 Wright's Ohio Reports 578 (Ohio 1834).

3. Monroe v. Collins, 17 Ohio St. 665 (1867). See also Jeffries v. Ankeny, 11 Ohio 372 (1842); Thacker v. Hawk, 11 Ohio 376 (1842); Lane v. Baker, 12 Ohio 237 (1843); Ex parte Robinson, 6 McLean 355 (Ohio 1855); Ex parte Sifford, 22 Fed. Cas. 105 (1857).

4. Van Camp v. Logan, 9 Ohio St. 406 (1859).

5. Ibid., 408–10.

6. Ibid., 411–14.

7. Ibid., 415–25.

8. James Baldwin, *The Fire Next Time* (New York: Dial Press, 1963), 118.

9. Ian F. Haney López, *White by Law: The Legal Construction of Race* (New York: New York University Press, 1996), 10.

10. Cheryl Harris, "Whiteness as Property," *Harv. L. Rev.* 106 (1993): 1707, 1725. See also López, *White by Law*, 10–19.

11. Andrew Hacker, *Two Nations: Black and White, Separate, Hostile, Unequal* (New York: Scribner, 1992).

12. *A Citizen's Guide to the Federal Budget* (Washington, D.C.: U.S. Government Printing Office, 1996), 8; *Budget of the United States Government, Fiscal Year 1996* (Washington, D.C.: U.S. Government Printing Office), 25–30.

13. Kathe Sandler, *A Question of Color* (San Francisco: California Newsreel, 1992).

14. See, for example, Missouri v. Jenkins, 115 S.Ct. 2038, 2061–73 (1995).

15. Peggy McIntosh, "White Privilege and Male Privilege: A Personal Account of Coming to See Correspondences Through Work in Women's Studies," in Margaret Anderson and Patricia Hill Collins, eds., *Race, Class, and Gender* (Belmont, Calif.: Wadsworth, 1995), 76–87.

16. W. E. B. Du Bois, *The Souls of Black Folk* (New York: New American Library, 1969) (1903), 45.

17. I borrowed the language for this pledge from concepts in an article by William Van Alstyne, "Rites of Passage, the Supreme Court, and the Constitution," *U. Chi. L. Rev.* 46 (1979): 723, 809–10.

18. See generally Derrick A. Bell Jr., *Race, Racism and American Law*, 3rd ed. (Boston: Little, Brown, 1992) (currently the only national law school casebook analyzing racism in the United States). See also John Hope Franklin, *From Slavery to Freedom*, 7th ed. (New York: Knopf, 1994); Clayborne Carson et al., *The Eyes on the Prize, Civil Rights Reader: Documents, Speeches, and Firsthand Accounts from the Black Freedom Struggle, 1954–1990* (New York: Viking Press, 1991); Donald Nieman, *Promises to Keep* (New York: Oxford University Press, 1991); A. Leon Higginbotham Jr., *In the Matter of Color* (New York: Oxford University Press, 1978); C. Vann Woodward, *The Strange Career of Jim Crow* (New York: Oxford University Press, 1974); Leon Friedman, *The Civil Rights Reader* (New York: Walker Press, 1967).

19. Andrew Kull, *The Color-Blind Constitution* (Cambridge, Mass.: Harvard University Press, 1992).

20. Adarand, 115 S.Ct. at 2119.

21. See Anthony Downs, *U.S. Commission on Civil Rights, Racism in America and How to Combat It* (Washington, D.C.: U.S. Government Printing Office, 1970), 5–6.

22. Ibid., 7.

23. Charles Lawrence, "The Id, the Ego, and Equal Protection: Reckoning with Unconscious Racism," *Stan. L. Rev.* 39 (1987): 317, 330.

NOTES TO PART TWO

1. New York Trust Co. v. Eisner, 256 U.S. 345, 349 (1921).

2. Winthrop D. Jordan, *White over Black: American Attitudes Toward the Negro 1550–1812* (Chapel Hill: University of North Carolina Press, 1968), 4–11. See also Ronald Sanders, *Lost Tribes and Promised Lands* (Boston: Little, Brown, 1978), which traces the early history of contacts between Africans and Europeans.

3. Jordan, *White over Black*, 8–32.

4. George M. Frederickson, *The Black Image in the White Mind* (Middletown, Conn.: Wesleyan University Press, 1971).

5. Marlon T. Riggs, *Ethnic Notions* (San Francisco: California Newsreel, 1987), traces the evolution of black caricatures over a century.

6. Garner v. Louisiana, 368 U.S. 157, 179–81 (1960) (Douglas, J., concurring).

7. Ulrich B. Phillips, *American Negro Slavery* (New York: Appleton, 1918), 41–45, 309. See also William A. Dunning, *Reconstruction, Political and Economic 1865–1877* (New York: Harper Torchbooks, 1907). Eric Foner provides a forceful critique of the Dunning school in his *Reconstruction: America's Unfinished Revolution 1863–1877* (New York: Harper & Row, Publishers, 1988), xix–xxvii.

8. John Hope Franklin, *From Slavery to Freedom*, 7th ed. (New York: Knopf, 1994).

9. Richard Delgado, "Storytelling for the Oppositionists and Others: A Plea for Narrative," *Mich. L. Rev.* 87 (1989): 2411, 2417.

10. Scott Clark, "When 'Wait' Means 'Never': American Tolerance of Racial Justice," *Nat'l Black L.J.* 13 (1993): 123.

11. A. Leon Higginbotham Jr., *In the Matter of Color* (New York: Oxford University Press, 1978), 19–60 (Virginia), 61–99 (Massachusetts), 100–50 (New York), 151–215 (South Carolina), 216–66 (Georgia), and 267–310 (Pennsylvania); Franklin, *Slavery to Freedom*, 56–67.

12. Higginbotham, *Matter of Color*, 19.

13. Kenneth M. Stampp, *The Peculiar Institution: Slavery in the Ante-Bellum South* (New York: Vintage Books, 1956), 5–6.

14. Higginbotham, *Matter of Color*, 20. See also Jordan, *White over Black*, 44–48.

15. Higginbotham, *Matter of Color*, 21. Higginbotham concludes that the weight of the historical evidence suggests that the first blacks in colonial America were identified and treated as servants rather than slaves.

16. Franklin, *Slavery to Freedom*, 56.

17. Eugene Genovese, *Roll Jordan Roll: The World the Slaves Made* (New York: Vintage Books, 1976), 31.

18. Stampp, *Peculiar Institution*, 5.

19. Franklin, *Slavery to Freedom*, 56–57.

20. Helen Tunnicliff Catterall, *Judicial Cases Concerning American Slavery and the Negro*, vol. 1 (New York: Octagon Books, 1968), iv–v.

21. Ibid., 53–54. For a summary of Virginia cases between 1624 and 1875, see ibid., 76–265, and also Higginbotham, *Matter of Color*, 19–60.

22. Higginbotham, *Matter of Color*, 22–23.

23. Loving v. Virginia, 388 U.S. 1 (1967).

24. Higginbotham, *Matter of Color*, 24.

25. United States v. Armstrong, no. 95–157 (U.S. 1996).

26. McCleskey v. Kemp, 481 U.S. 279, 285, 325–37 (1987).

27. Professors David C. Baldus, Charles Pulaski, and George Woodworth performed the study and published their findings in several related works. Baldus et al., *Equal Justice and the Death Penalty* (Boston: Northeastern University Press, 1990), 80–139, 198–228, 306–425. This book presents the results of two overlap-

ping empirical studies of post-Furman legislative reforms regarding whether the new standards and guidelines to channel the exercise of jury discretion were effective and whether comparative proportionality review by state appellate courts ensured that death-sentencing systems were operating in a consistent, nondiscriminatory fashion. The authors found that although the levels of arbitrariness and racial discrimination in capital sentencing had declined since 1972, there still was evidence of a racial disparity in the application of the death penalty and of arbitrary, excessive sentences (1–6, 394–425). For a summary of other statewide studies, see ibid., 229–65.

28. McCleskey, 481 U.S. at 287. See also Baldus et al., *Equal Justice*, 400–8.

29. McCleskey, 481 U.S. at 297, 298, 313, 319. Here the Court applied the difficult-to-prove standard set out in cases following *Washington v. Davis*, 426 U.S. 229 (1976), and *Personnel Adm'r of Massachusetts v. Feeney*, 442 U.S. 256, 279 (1979).

30. McCleskey, 481 U.S. at 329–36 (Brennan, J., dissenting) (citing Ga. Penal Code, part 4, title 1, div. 4, §§ 4704, § 4249 (1861). See generally Higginbotham, *Matter of Color*, 24–25; Paul Finkelman, "The Crime of Color," *Tulane L. Rev.* 67 (1993): 2063, 2064–66.

31. Higginbotham, *Matter of Color*, 25.

32. Catterall, *Judicial Cases*, vol. 1, 79.

33. Higginbotham, *Matter of Color*, 26.

34. Catterall, *Judicial Cases*, vol. 1, 77.

35. Ibid., 78.

36. Franklin, *Slavery to Freedom*, 56–59; Catterall, *Judicial Cases*, vol. 1, 59.

37. See William W. Hening, *Hening's Statutes at Large*, vol. 1 (New York: R. and W. and G. Bartow, 1823), 540. According to the 1659 act,

> Dutch and all strangers of Christian nations are allowed free trade if they give bond and pay import of ten shillings per hogshead laid upon all tobacco exported to any foreign dominions; always provided that if Dutch or other foreigners shall import any Negro slaves they, the said Dutch or other foreigners, shall for the tobacco really produced by the said Negroes, pay only the impost of two shillings per hogshead, the like being paid by our own nation.

38. Higginbotham, *Matter of Color*, 37. See also Franklin, *Slavery to Freedom*, 74.

39. Kenneth Stampp wrote that "the master class, for its own purposes wrote chattel slavery, the caste system and color prejudice into American custom and law." Stampp, *Peculiar Institution*, 23.

40. William W. Hening, Hening's *Statutes at Large*, vol. 2 (New York: R. and W. and G. Bartow, 1823), 492. The 1680 act proved to be ineffective, and so it was followed by additional provisions in 1682:

> Whereas the act of 1680 on Negro insurrection has not had the intended effect, it is enacted that church wardens read this and the other act, twice every year, in the time of divine service, or forfeit each of them six hundred pounds of tobacco, and further to prevent insurrections no master or overseer shall allow a Negro slave of another to remain on his plantation above four hours without leave of the slave's own master.

41. William W. Hening, Hening's *Statutes at Large*, vol. 3 (New York: R. and W. and G. Bartow, 1823), 459. Another section of the 1705 law gave the master greater control over the life of his slave:

> And if any slave resist his master, or owner, or other person, by his or her order, correcting such slave, and shall happen to be killed in such correction, it shall not be accounted felony; but the master, owner, and every such other person so giving correction, shall be free and acquit of all punishment and accusation for the same, as if such accident had never happened.

42. For a comprehensive collection of nineteenth-century slave statutes, see Paul Finkelman, *Statutes on Slavery: The Pamphlet Literature* (New York: Garland, 1988), and Paul Finkelman, *State Slavery Statutes: A Guide to the Micro-Fiche Collection* (New York: Garland, 1989). This collection reviews in part all slave codes from the fifteen southern states enacted between 1789 and 1865, covering more than 7,100 statutes. For a summary of Virginia's slave codes, see *Revised Code of Virginia* (2 vols. with supp.) (1819).

43. Franklin, *Slavery to Freedom*, 69–70.

44. Henry Steele Commager, *Documents of American History* (New York: Appleton-Century-Crofts, 1968), 103. Virginia's bill of rights was presented on June 12, 1776. The first section provided

> 1. That all men are by nature equally free and independent, and have certain inherited rights, of which, when they enter into a state of society, they cannot by any compact deprive or divest their posterity; namely, the enjoyment of life and liberty, with the means of acquiring and possessing property, pursuing and obtaining happiness and safety.

45. The Declaration of Independence, ¶¶ 1 and 2 (U.S. 1776).

46. Thomas Jefferson, *Writings* (New York: Penguin Books, 1984), 267. Jefferson's *Notes on the State of Virginia* contains repeated references to white superiority and black degradation. See Jefferson, *Writings*, 256–75.

47. Derrick Bell elegantly described this conception of involuntary sacrifice. See Derrick A. Bell Jr., *Race, Racism and American Law*, 3rd ed. (Boston: Little, Brown, 1992), 34–36.

48. The leading authority on records of the Constitutional Convention is Max Farrand, *The Records of the Federal Convention of 1787*, 4 vols. (New Haven, Conn.: Yale University Press, 1937); a list of the delegates attending the Convention is in vol. 3, app. B, 555. See also James H. Hutson, *Supplement to Max Farrand's The Records of the Federal Convention of 1787* (New Haven, Conn.: Yale University Press, 1987); Arthur Taylor Prescott, *Drafting the Federal Constitution* (New York: Greenwood Press, 1968), especially 22–36, his lively, contemporaneous sketches of the delegates; James Madison, *Notes of Debates in the Federal Convention of 1787* (Athens: Ohio University Press, 1966).

49. By June 13, there were nineteen resolutions. See Farrand, *Records*, vol. 1, 18–23, 235–37; Madison, *Notes*, 23–33, 115–17.

50. Farrand, *Records*, vol. 1, 249–57; Madison, *Notes*, 121–29. On June 18, Alexander Hamilton proposed another plan, national in nature but different from the Virginia plan. For example, members of the federal senate, executive, and judi-

ciary would serve without pay. See Farrand, *Records*, vol. 1, 282–93; Madison, *Notes*, 129–39.

51. Derrick A. Bell Jr., *And We Are Not Saved: The Elusive Quest for Racial Justice* (New York: Basic Books, 1987), 22–24, 34–35. Bell cites the historian William Wiecek for the following list of direct and indirect accommodations to slavery that can be found in the Constitution:

1. Article I, Section 2: representatives in the House were apportioned among the states on the basis of population, computed by counting all free persons and three-fifths of the slaves (the "federal number," or "three-fifths," clause);
2. Article I, Section 2, and Article I, Section 9: two clauses requiring, redundantly, that direct taxes (including capitations) be apportioned among the states on the foregoing basis, the purpose being to prevent Congress from laying a head tax on slaves to encourage their emancipation;
3. Article I, Section 9: Congress was prohibited from abolishing the international slave trade to the United States before 1808;
4. Article IV, Section 2: the states were prohibited from emancipating fugitive slaves, who were to be returned on demand of the master;
5. Article I, Section 8: Congress was empowered to provide for calling up the states' militia to suppress insurrections, including slave uprisings;
6. Article IV, Section 4: the federal government was obliged to protect the states against domestic violence, including slave insurrections;
7. Article V: the provisions of Article I, Section 9, clauses 1 and 4 (pertaining to the slave trade and direct taxes) were made unamendable;
8. Article I, Section 9, and Article I, Section 10: these two clauses prohibited the federal government and the states from taxing exports, one purpose being to prevent them from taxing slavery indirectly by taxing the exported product of slave labor.

See William M. Wiecek, *The Sources of Antislavery Constitutionalism, 1760–1848* (Ithaca, N.Y.: Cornell University Press, 1977), 62–63.

52. Farrand, *Records*, vol. 1, 201; Madison, *Notes*, 103. See, for example, the delegate Gerry's comments: "Why should blacks, who are property in the South, be counted in the rule of representation more than cattle & horses of the North?" Also see the motion by Wilson and Pinckney to calculate taxes and representation

> in proportion to the whole number of white and other free citizens and inhabitants of every age, sex and condition, including those bound to servitude for a term of years, and three-fifths of all other persons not comprehended in the foregoing description, except Indians not paying taxes.

This language is remarkable. The terms *white, free,* and *three-fifths* illustrate that our organic law employed race labels to delineate superior rights for whites over blacks. Thus, from the very beginning, our Constitution embraced race-conscious privileges advantaging whites.

Subsequent iterations of the Virginia plan by the Committee of the Whole, the Committee of Detail, and the Committee of Style substantially modified what had been article III, but each included the compromise to count five slaves as three persons for purposes of determining proportional representation in the national legislature.

This compromise is only one example of race-conscious affirmative action agreed to at Philadelphia. White men agreed that black slaves would count partially in determining the number of each state's representatives in Congress and the amount of direct taxes owed. They also decided that the new Constitution would not ban slavery or prohibit it before 1808, would prohibit states from emancipating fugitive slaves, and empower Congress to put down insurrections, including slave uprisings.

53. Farrand, *Records*, vol. 1, 559–97; Madison, *Notes*, 256–82.

54. The final draft of article I, section 2, clause 3, reads in part:

> Representatives and direct taxes shall be apportioned among the several states which may be included within this Union, according to their respective numbers, which shall be determined by adding the whole number of free persons, including those bound to service for a term of years and excluding Indians not taxed, three-fifths all other persons. (art. I, § 2, cl. 3)

55. Farrand, *Records*, vol. 1, 561; Madison, *Notes*, 259.

56. Farrand, *Records*, vol. 1, 562–66; Madison, *Notes*, 260–61.

57. Farrand, *Records*, vol. 1, 580; Madison, *Notes*, 268.

58. Delegate Williamson made a similar point when he approved of the ratio of three-fifths. Farrand, *Records*, vol. 1, 580–88; Madison, *Notes*, 269–76.

59. Farrand, *Records*, vol. 1, 586–97; Madison, *Notes*, 275–82.

60. Farrand, *Records*, vol. 1, 592–97; Madison, *Notes*, 277–80.

61. Farrand, *Records*, vol. 1, 605; Madison, *Notes*, 286. Mr. Wilson moved "that a Republican form of Government shall be guarantied to each State & that each State shall be protected against foreign & domestic violence." The motion passed unanimously. See Farrand, *Records*, vol. 2, 47–49; Madison, *Notes*, 322.

62. Farrand, *Records*, vol. 2, 106; Madison, *Notes*, 362.

63. Farrand, *Records*, vol. 2, 176–89, 220; Madison, *Notes*, 385–96, 409.

64. Farrand, *Records*, vol. 2, 221–23; Madison, *Notes*, 413. The quotation continues:

> And what is the proposed compensation to the Northern States for a sacrifice of every principle of right, of every impulse of humanity. They are to bind themselves to march their militia for the defence of the Southern States; for their defence against those very slaves of whom they complain ... the Legislature will have the indefinite power to tax them by excises, and duties on imports: both of which will fall heavier on them than on the Southern inhabitants; for the bohea tea [a black tea] used by a Northern freeman, will pay more tax than the whole consumption of the miserable slave, which consists of nothing more than his physical subsistence and the rag that covers his nakedness. On the other side the Southern States are not to be restrained from importing fresh supplies of wretched Africans, at once to increase the danger of attack, and the difficulty of defence; nay they are to be encouraged to it by an assurance of having their votes in the National Government increased in proportion, and at the same time to

have their exports & their slaves exempt from all contributions for the public service. . . . For what then are all these sacrifices to be made? He would sooner submit himself to a tax for paying for all the Negroes in the U. States, than saddle posterity with such a Constitution.

65. Farrand, *Records*, vol. 2, 364–65; Madison, *Notes*, 502–3.

66. Farrand, *Records*, vol. 2, 369–72; Madison, *Notes*, 503–6.

67. Farrand, *Records*, vol. 2, 372–73; Madison, *Notes*, 506–7.

68. Farrand, *Records*, vol. 2, 373; Madison, *Notes*, 507.

69. Farrand, *Records*, vol. 2, 374–75; Madison, *Notes*, 507–9. The committee members appointed were Langdon, King, William Sam Johnson of Connecticut, William Livingston of New Jersey, George Clymer of Pennsylvania, Dickinson, L. Martin, James Madison of Virginia, Williamson, C. C. Pinckney, and Baldwin.

70. Farrand, *Records*, vol. 2, 400; Madison, *Notes*, 522.

71. Farrand, *Records*, vol. 2, 415–16; Madison, *Notes*, 531–32.

72. Farrand, *Records*, vol. 2, 443, 453–54; Madison, *Notes*, 545–46, 552.

73. Farrand, *Records*, vol. 2, 553, 585–603; Madison, *Notes*, 608, 616–27.

74. Farrand, *Records*, vol. 2, 632–33; Madison, *Notes*, 650–62.

75. Frederick Douglass, "What to the Slave Is the Fourth of July," cited in Alice Moore Dunbar, ed., *Masterpieces of Negro Eloquence* (New York: Bookery Publishing, 1914), 46–48. For contemporary treatments of the thoughts of Douglass, see Waldo E. Martin Jr., *The Mind of Frederick Douglass* (Chapel Hill: University of North Carolina Press, 1984), and William S. McFeely, *Frederick Douglass* (New York: Norton, 1991).

76. Thurgood Marshall, "Reflections on the Bicentennial of the U.S. Constitution," *Harv. L. Rev.* 101 (1987): 1, 2, 5.

77. 3 Stat. 545 and 3 Stat. 645 (1820). The Missouri Compromise of 1820 provided in part:

> And be it further enacted, That in all that territory ceded by France to the United States, under the name of Louisiana, which lies north of thirty-six degrees and thirty minutes north latitude, not included within the limits of the state, contemplated by this act, slavery and involuntary servitude, otherwise than in the punishment of crimes, whereof the parties shall have been duly convicted, shall be, and is hereby, forever prohibited: Provided always, That any person escaping into the same, from whom labour or service is lawfully claimed, in any state or territory of the United States, such fugitive may be lawfully reclaimed and conveyed to the person claiming his or her labour or service as aforesaid.

78. 9 Stat. 462 (1850), repealed by 13 Stat. 200 (1864). The Fugitive Slave Act of 1850 provided that if a fugitive slave escaped into any state or territory in the United States, the slave could be reclaimed by the slave's owner or the owner's agent. In addition, the act gave the slave owner a right of action in the U.S. circuit courts to reclaim fugitive slaves.

Interestingly, section 5 of the act commanded good citizens to assist with the slave's recapture. Under section 6, the testimony of the alleged fugitive was inadmissible. Section 7 made it a criminal offense to hinder the arrest of or return of a slave.

79. 10 Stat. 277 (1854). The Kansas–Nebraska Act of 1854 provided that the territories of Kansas and Nebraska could organize into states and that the issue of slavery was to be decided locally under the doctrine of popular sovereignty.

80. 60 U.S. (19 How.) 691 (1857). This case was one of the most important ever decided by the Court. First, it was extremely rare for the Court to invalidate federal laws, and *Dred Scott* was a direct challenge to congressional power to regulate U.S. territories. In that sense, it compares with the importance of *Marbury v. Madison*, 5 U.S. (1 Cranch) 137 (1803). Second, in *Dred Scott*, the Supreme Court defined persons of African ancestry as noncitizens for purposes of suing in federal courts. The Court stated for the first time that blacks, whether slave or free, were not citizens within the meaning of the Constitution. Third, the *Dred Scott* decision reflected the deep division in the country over slavery and prompted the fears of many whites that it would expand throughout the country.

81. Don E. Fehrenbacher, *The Dred Scott Case* (New York: Oxford University Press, 1978), 239–49. See also Walter Ehrlich, *They Have No Rights: Dred Scott's Struggle for Freedom* (Westport, Conn.: Greenwood Press, 1979).

82. Fehrenbacher, *Dred Scott*, 250, 51–56.

83. 4 Mo. 354 (1837).

84. 10 How. 82, 13 L. 337 (1850).

85. See Emerson v. Scott, 15 Mo. 576 (1852).

86. Dred Scott, 60 U.S. (19 How.) 691 (1857).

87. Fehrenbacher, *Dred Scott*, 235.

88. Ibid., 323. For an interesting recent discussion of *Dred Scott* in which the author analyzes the legal status of blacks in Chief Justice Taney's home state, see David Skillen Bogen, "The Maryland Context of Dred Scott: The Decline in the Legal Status of Maryland Free Blacks 1776–1810," *Am. J. of Legal History* 34 (1990), especially 381, arguing that the rights of free blacks in Maryland worsened during this period.

There were several different opinions delivered by the Court. Chief Justice Taney's opinion is the most famous because of its characterization of persons of African descent. Justice Benjamin Curtis of Massachusetts presented the most persuasive challenge to Chief Justice Taney's view. See Dred Scott, 60 U.S. (19 How.) at 767 (Curtis, J., dissenting).

89. Dred Scott, 60 U.S. (19 How.) at 700 (emphasis added).

90. Dred Scott, 60 U.S. (19 How.) at 703–10. Chief Justice Taney wrote: "The court is of the opinion that, upon the facts stated in the plea of abatement, Dred Scott was not a citizen of Missouri within the meaning of the Constitution of the United States, and not entitled as such to sue in its courts."

91. Dred Scott, 60 U.S. (19 How.) at 702–21.

92. Dred Scott, 60 U.S. (19 How.) at 701–2 (emphasis added).

93. Dred Scott, 60 U.S. (19 How.) at 770–95 (Curtis, J., dissenting).

94. Roy P. Basler, ed., *The Collected Works of Abraham Lincoln*, vol. 3 (New Brunswick, N.J.: Rutgers University Press, 1953), 145–46.

95. Edward B. Callender, *Thaddeus Stevens: Commoner* (New York: AMS Press, 1972); Moorfield Storey, *Charles Sumner* (New York: AMS Press, 1972); David H. Donald, *Charles Sumner and the Coming of the Civil War* (New York: Knopf, 1960),

108; Ralph Korngold, *Thaddeus Stevens: A Being Darkly Wise and Rudely Great* (New York: Harcourt, Brace, 1955).

96. Eric Foner, *Freedom's Law Makers: A Directory of Black Officeholders During Reconstruction* (New York: Oxford University Press, 1993); Bruce A. Ragsdale and Joel D. Treese, *Black Americans in Congress 1870–1989* (Washington, D.C.: U.S. Government Printing Office, 1990); Ann Jenette Sophie McFarlin, *Black Congressional Reconstruction Orators and Their Orations 1869–1879* (Metuchen, N.J.: Scarecrow Press, 1976).

97. The Reconstruction period extended December 8, 1863, with Lincoln's Proclamation of Amnesty and Reconstruction to the withdrawal of troops from the South in 1877. See W. E. B. Du Bois, *Black Reconstruction in America, 1860–1880* (New York: Russell and Russell, 1935). See also Melvin Urofsky, *A March of Liberty: A Constitutional History of the United States* (New York: Knopf, 1988), 436; Eugene Gressman, "The Unhappy History of Civil Rights Legislation," *Mich. L. Rev.* 50 (1952): 1323.

98. Franklin, *Slavery to Freedom,* 228.

99. 14 Stat. 27 (1866). The complete act, along with other postwar civil rights statutes, can be found in Theodore Eisenberg, *Civil Rights and Employment Discrimination Law: Selected Statutes and Regulations* (Charlottesville, Va.: Miche, 1991).

100. Franklin, *Slavery to Freedom,* 225. See also Urofsky, *A March of Liberty,* 436–37.

101. Smith v. Allwright, 321 U.S. 649 (1944).

102. Terry v. Adams, 345 U.S. 461 (1953).

103. 18 Stat. 335 (1875).

104. 83 U.S. (16 Wall.) 36 (1873).

105. 92 U.S. 542, 548–55 (1876).

106. U.S. Const. Amend. XII:

> The person having the greatest number of votes for President, shall be the President, if such number be a majority of the whole number of Electors appointed; and if no person have such majority, then from the persons having the highest numbers not exceeding three on the list of those voted for as President, the House of Representatives shall choose immediately, by ballot, the President.

107. Foner, *Reconstruction,* 564–83. Perhaps the greatest irony in the racial history of blacks and whites in the United States is that blacks have had to turn to whites for protection against and relief from white supremacy and racial subordination. This fact certainly helps explain why three constitutional amendments and a half-dozen federal statutes failed to eradicate white supremacy and racial subordination. See Genovese, *Roll Jordan Roll,* 48–49.

108. 109 U.S. 3 (1883).

109. The Civil Rights Cases, 109 U.S. at 20–26.

110. Plessy v. Ferguson, 163 U.S. 537 (1896). Under the Louisiana statute, all railway companies had to provide equal but separate accommodations for whites and blacks or to partition a single coach. The conductor directed persons to the proper area. Failure to comply with the conductor's order was punishable by a fine of $25 or imprisonment for not more than twenty days. If the conductor

assigned a passenger to the wrong compartment, the conductor could be fined $25 or imprisoned for twenty days. The conductor could refuse to carry a passenger who refused to follow his order, without any risk of liability to the conductor or the railway company (540–41).

Plessy was apparently seven-eighths Caucasian and one-eighth African. He claimed that his African blood was not discernible, and so he took a vacant seat in the coach for whites. After he refused an order to move, Plessy was forcibly ejected and arrested (541).

111. Ibid., 543.

112. Ibid., 544.

113. Ibid., 548 (emphasis added).

114. Ibid., 555. Justice Harlan continued by saying that the Thirteenth, Fourteenth, and Fifteenth Amendments removed the race line from our government systems:

> They had, as this court has said, a common purpose, namely, to secure "to a race recently emancipated, a race that through many generations have [sic] been held in slavery, all the civil rights that the superior race enjoy." They declared, in legal effect, this court has further said, "that the law in the states shall be the same for the black as for the white; that all persons, whether colored or white, shall stand equal before laws of the states, and, in regard to the colored race, for whose protection the amendment was primarily designed, that no discrimination shall be made against them by law because of their color" (555–56, citations omitted).

115. Ibid., 556. The quoted language provides an interesting context for interpreting Justice Harlan's assertion that our Constitution is color blind. Justice Harlan was concerned about racial subordination and laws that implied inferiority of blacks. Similar language is quoted in *Strauder v. West Virginia*, 100 U.S. 303, 307–8 (1880).

116. Plessy, 163 U.S. at 556. In the context of the facts in *Plessy*, Justice Harlan must have meant that Louisiana could not enforce its statute because the statute violated the constitutional rights of black citizens to occupy the same public conveyance as whites if they chose to do so. However, if one removes Justice Harlan's statements from their context, they seem to establish a universal constitutional color blindness standard.

117. Ibid., 560.

118. Andrew Kull, *The Color-Blind Constitution* (Cambridge, Mass.: Harvard University Press, 1992), 151–63; William Van Alstyne, "Rites of Passage, the Supreme Court, and the Constitution," *U. Chi. L. Rev.* 46 (1979): 809.

119. For additional support for the view that Justice Harlan was concerned about racial subordination, see his dissent in the *Civil Rights Cases*, 109 U.S. 3, 35 (1883):

> But I hold that since slavery, as the Court has repeatedly declared, . . . was the moving or principal cause of the adoption of [the Thirteenth Amendment], and since that institution rested wholly upon the inferiority, as a race, of those held in bondage, their freedom necessarily involved immunity from and protection against, all discrimination against them, because of their race, in respect of such civil rights as belong to freemen of

other races. Congress, therefore, under its express power to enforce that amendment, by appropriate legislation, may enact laws to protect that people against the deprivation, because of their race, of any civil rights granted to other freemen in the same State, and such legislation may be of a direct and primary character.

120. Bakke, 438 U.S. at 326–27 (opinion of Brennan, White, Marshall, and Blackmun, JJ., concurring in part and dissenting in part).

121. 347 U.S. 483 (1954).

122. James M. Washington, ed., *A Testament of Hope: The Essential Writings of Martin Luther King, Jr.* (San Francisco: Harper & Row, 1986), 219.

123. W. E. B. Du Bois, *The Souls of Black Folk* (New York: New American Library, 1969), 54–55.

124. See C. Vann Woodward, *The Strange Career of Jim Crow* (New York: Oxford University Press, 1974), 6–7.

125. Address of Booker T. Washington at the Atlanta Exposition in 1895, cited in Thomas Reed, ed., *Modern Eloquence* (Philadelphia: John D. Morris, 1900), 1136–40.

126. Randall W. Bland, *Private Pressure on Public Law: The Legal Career of Justice Thurgood Marshall 1934–1991*, 2nd ed. (Lanham, Md: University Press of America, 1993), 3. Regarding Marshall's youth in Baltimore, see Michael D. Davis and Hunter Clark, *Thurgood Marshall* (New York: Carol Publishing Group, 1992), 30–46. See also Carl T. Rowan, *Dream-Makers, Dream-Breakers* (Boston: Little, Brown, 1994); Mark Tushnet, *Making Civil Rights Law: Thurgood Marshall and the Supreme Court* (New York: Oxford University Press, 1994).

127. Bland, *Private Pressure on Public Law*, 3–4; Davis and Clark, *Thurgood Marshall*, 30–46.

128. Roberts v. City of Boston, 59 Mass. (Cush.) 198 (1850).

129. Brown v. Board of Education, 347 U.S. 483 (1954).

130. Murray v. Maryland, 182 A.2d 590 (1936).

131. Tushnet, *Making Civil Rights Law*.

132. 321 U.S. 649 (1944). See also Terry v. Adams, 345 U.S. 461 (1953).

133. 334 U.S. 1 (1944).

134. See Boynton v. Virginia, 364 U.S. 454 (1960); McLaurin v. Oklahoma, 339 U.S. 637 (1950); Sweatt v. Painter, 339 U.S. 629 (1950); Sipuel v. Board of Regents of University of Oklahoma, 332 U.S. 631 (1948); Missouri ex rel. Gaines v. Canada, 305 U.S. 337 (1938).

135. Lucy v. Adams, 350 U.S. 1 (1955).

136. 347 U.S. 483 (1954).

137. Brown v. Board of Education, 347 U.S. at 493–95.

138. Perhaps the most famous criticism came from Herbert Wechsler, "Toward Neutral Principles of Constitutional Law," *Harv. L. Rev.* 73 (1959): 15. Professor Wechsler wrote, "[Courts] must be genuinely principled, resting with respect to every step that is involved in reaching judgment on analysis and reasons quite transcending the immediate result that is achieved."

139. Cooper v. Aaron, 358 U.S. 1, 17 (1958).

140. Clayborne Carson et al., *The Eyes on the Prize, Civil Rights Reader: Documents,*

*Speeches, and Firsthand Accounts from the Black Freedom Struggle, 1954–1990* (New York: Viking Press, 1991), 97–106. See also Tony A. Freyer, *The Little Rock Crisis: A Constitutional Interpretation* (Westport, Conn.: Greenwood Press, 1984).

141. Carson et al., *Eyes on the Prize,* 37–43.

142. Leon Friedman, *The Civil Rights Reader* (New York: Walker Press, 1967), 63–70.

143. Seth Cagin and Philip Dray, *We Are Not Afraid: The Story of Goodman, Schwerner and Chaney and the Civil Rights Campaign for Mississippi* (New York: Macmillan, 1988).

144. See, for example, Van Alstyne, "Rites of Passage," 809, arguing in support of color blindness; Paul Brest, "Foreword: In Defense of the Antidiscrimination Principle," *Harv. L. Rev.* 90 (1978): 1, 1–2, 16–23, arguing against the color blindness standard; John Hart Ely, "The Constitutionality of Reverse Racial Discrimination," *U. Chi. L. Rev.* 41 (1974): 723, arguing against use of a strict color blindness model when a political majority discriminates against itself; John Kaplan, "Equal Justice in an Unequal World: Equality for the Negro—The Problem of Special Treatment," *Nw. U.L. Rev.* 61 (1966): 363, arguing against use of race as the basis for special treatment for blacks in the employment context.

145. See also Charles Fried, "Metro Broadcasting, Inc. v. FCC: Two Concepts of Equality," *Harv. L. Rev.* 104 (1990): 107, 110–11, critiquing the group-rights conception of equal protection analysis; Randall Kennedy, "Racial Critiques of Legal Academia," *Harv. L. Rev.* 102 (1989): 1745, contending that recent race-conscious scholarship of authors such as Bell, Matsuda, and Delgado lacked merit; Morris B. Abram, "Affirmative Action: Fair Shakers and Social Engineers," *Harv. L. Rev.* 99 (1986): 1312, arguing against affirmative action; and Randall Kennedy, "Persuasion and Distrust: A Comment on the Affirmative Action Debate," *Harv. L. Rev.* 99 (1986): 1327, arguing in favor of limited affirmative action.

146. See also T. Alexander Aleinikoff, "A Case for Race-Consciousness," *Colum. L. Rev.* 91 (1991): 1060, 1062–63, maintaining that America is not a color-blind society and that race has a deep social significance that continues to disadvantage blacks and other Americans of color; Neil Gotanda, "A Critique of 'Our Constitution Is Color-Blind,'" *Stan. L. Rev.* 44 (1991): 1, 1–3, examining the ideological content of the phrase "our constitution is color blind"; Donald Lively and Stephen Plass, "Equal Protection: The Jurisprudence of Denial and Evasion," *Am. U. L. Rev.* 40 (1991): 1307, 1312–46, discussing how equal protection jurisprudence is characterized by patterns of denial and evasion; Alan Freeman, "Antidiscrimination Law: The View from 1989," *Tulane L. Rev.* 64 (1990): 1407, 1408–9, arguing that the U.S. Supreme Court has enshrined a vision of America that normalizes existing patterns of inequality and hierarchy; Duncan Kennedy, "A Cultural Pluralist Case for Affirmative Action in Legal Academia," *Duke L.J.* 1990: 705, 705–12, discussing the political and cultural arguments for affirmative action in legal academia; Gary Peller, "Race Consciousness," *Duke L.J.* 1990: 758, 760, exploring the ideological roots of the critical race theory movement; Patricia J. Williams, "Metro Broadcasting, Inc. v. FCC: Regrouping in Singular Times," *Harv. L. Rev.* 104 (1990): 525, discussing the significance of and necessity for group claims in our legal system and the costs of pitting individual rights against

group interests at a moment in history when such categories as race and class intersect so that race defines class; Kimberlé Williams Crenshaw, "Race, Reform, and Retrenchment: Transformation and Legitimation in Antidiscrimination Law," *Harv. L. Rev.* 101 (1988): 1331, 1334–35, criticizing both neoconservative scholars and critical legal studies scholars for failing to analyze the significance of race in the legal and political subordination of blacks; David A. Strauss, "The Myth of Colorblindness," *Sup. Ct. Rev.* 1986: 99, 100–13, discussing the doctrinal consistency between affirmative action and antidiscrimination principles; Laurence H. Tribe, "In What Vision of the Constitution Must the Law Be Color-Blind," *J. Marshall L. Rev.* 20 (1986): 201, 203, examining Justice Harlan's view that the Fourteenth Amendment prohibits government laws enshrining white supremacy); Suzanna Sherry, "Selective Judicial Activism in the Equal Protection Context: Democracy, Distrust and Deconstruction," *Geo. L.J.* 73 (1984): 89, 91–99, analyzing the implications of replacing the suspect classifications doctrine with a disfavored class doctrine in the contexts of race and gender cases; and Alan Freeman, "Legitimizing Racial Discrimination Through Antidiscrimination Law: A Critical Review of Supreme Court Doctrine," *Minn. L. Rev.* 62 (1978): 1049, showing how antidiscrimination law has, at the same time, outlawed racial discrimination and legitimized the subordinate status of blacks.

147. Gotanda, "A Critique," 1–3. See also Kull, *Color-Blind Constitution*, 112–30, 151–63.

148. See Van Alstyne, "Rites of Passage," 809–10; Kaplan, "Equal Justice in an Unequal World," 379.

149. See Alexander M. Bickel, *The Morality of Consent* (New Haven, Conn.: Yale University Press, 1975), 133.

150. Strauss, "Myth of Colorblindness," 100–3. He concluded that the failure to engage in race-conscious affirmative action may sometimes be unconstitutional.

151. See Crenshaw, "Race, Reform, and Retrenchment," 1358–64; Gotanda, "A Critique," 45–52; Aleinikoff, "A Case for Race-Consciousness," 1062–63.

152. See Andrew Hacker, *Two Nations: Black and White, Separate, Hostile, Unequal* (New York: Scribner, 1992), 4.

153. Gotanda, "A Critique," 46.

154. Gotanda, "A Critique," 26; Hacker, *Two Nations*, ix.

155. Shelby Steele, *The Content of Our Character: A New Vision of Race in America* (New York: Harper Perennial, 1990), 57–75; Thomas Sowell, *Race and Culture: A World View* (New York: Basic Books, 1994); Dinesh D'Souza, *Illiberal Education: The Politics of Race and Sex on Campus* (New York: Free Press, 1991).

156. See Hacker, *Two Nations*, 6.

157. See Walter Goodman, "Looking Racism in the Face in St. Louis," *New York Times*, September 26, 1991, C22. The program is also available on video: *True Colors* (Deerfield, Ill.: MTI Film and Video, 1991).

158. See Brest, "Foreword," 14–15.

159. See Williams, "Metro Broadcasting," 528–33; Strauss, "Myth of Colorblindness," 114–15; Hacker, *Two Nations*, 19–22.

160. Compare, for example, the work of Professor Peter Westen, "The Empty Idea of Equality," *Harv. L. Rev.* 95 (1982): 537, 542–43, arguing that statements of

equality logically and necessarily collapse into simpler statements of rights so that the additional step of transforming simple statements of rights into statements of equality not only involves unnecessary work but also engenders profound confusion; Kenneth Karst, "Why Equality Matters," *Ga. L. Rev.* 17 (1983): 245, 247–48. Karst contends that the equal citizenship principle that is the core of the Fourteenth Amendment does have substantive content; that is, a person should be treated by an organized society as a respectable, responsible, and participating member of the national community. Karst says the principle is violated when the organized society treats someone as an inferior, as part of a dependent caste, or as a nonparticipant. He expanded this discussion of equality in his *Belonging to America: Equal Citizenship and the Constitution* (New Haven, Conn.: Yale University Press, 1989). See also Erwin Chemerinsky, "In Defense of Equality: A Reply to Professor Westen," *Mich. L. Rev.* 81 (1983): 575, 576. Chemerinsky argues that the concept of equality is morally necessary because it compels us to care about how people are treated in relation to one another, is analytically necessary because it presumes that people should be treated alike and puts the burden of proof on those who wish to discriminate, and finally is rhetorically necessary because it is a powerful symbol that helps convince people to safeguard their rights, which otherwise would not be protected. Kent Greenawalt, "How Empty Is the Idea of Equality?" *Colum. L. Rev.* 83 (1983): 1167, 1168–69. Greenwalt states that rather than banish the concept of equality from moral and legal argument, it is more promising to gain a fuller understanding of the significance of existing concepts of equality. Peter Westen replied to some of these commentators' critiques of his seminal article in "On 'Confusing Ideas': Reply," *Yale L.J.* 91 (1982): 1153; Peter Westen, "The Meaning of Equality in Law, Science, Math and Morals: A Reply," *Mich. L. Rev.* 81 (1983): 604; Peter Westen, "To Lure the Tarantula from Its Hole: A Response," *Colum. L. Rev.* 83 (1983): 1186.

161. Hacker, *Two Nations*, 17–49, 93–106, 134–46, 179–98. See also Gunnar Myrdal, *An American Dilemma* (New York: Harper & Row, 1962) (1944), who discusses how the Negro problem is intertwined with all other social, economic, political, and cultural problems in America and his optimism about future race relations in America. Gerald David Jaynes and Robin M. Williams Jr., eds., *A Common Destiny: Blacks and American Society* (Washington, D.C.: National Academy Press, 1989), examine the unfinished agenda of a nation still struggling to come to terms with the consequences of its history of relations between blacks and whites.

NOTES TO PART THREE

1. See Brown v. Board of Education 347 U.S. 483 (1954) and Swann v. Charlotte–Mecklenburg Board of Education 402 U.S. 1 (1971).

2. See Jones E. Jones Jr., "The Origins of Affirmative Action," *U.C. Davis L. Rev.* 2 (1988): 383, 389–403. See also Jones E. Jones Jr., "The Genesis and Present Status of Affirmative Action in Employment: Economic, Legal, and Political Realities," *Iowa L. Rev.* 70 (1985): 901; Jones E. Jones Jr., "Reverse Discrimination in Employment: Judicial Treatment of Affirmative Action Programs in the U.S.," *Howard L.J.* 25 (1982): 217; Ronald Turner, *The Past and Future of Affirmative*

*Action* (New York: Quorum Books, 1990), 4–5; Daniel C. Maguire, *A New American Justice* (Garden City, N.Y.: Doubleday, 1980), 27–51, 127–68; Gertrude Ezorsky, *Racism and Justice* (Ithaca, N.Y.: Cornell University Press, 1991), 9–27.

3. Herbert Hill, *Black Labor and the American Legal System* (Washington, D.C.: Bureau of National Affairs, 1977), 7–27. See also William B. Gould, *Black Workers in White Unions* (Ithaca, N.Y.: Cornell University Press, 1977); Alfred W. Blumrosen, Modern Law: *The Law Transmission System and Equal Opportunity* (Madison: University of Wisconsin Press, 1993), vii–viii, 289–317. Others contained a requirement that the applicant be a Christian or believer in God. Hill, *Black Labor,* 19–20. See also Herbert Hill and James E. Jones, eds., *Race in America: The Struggle for Equality* (Madison: University of Wisconsin Press, 1993), 263–369.

4. Hill, *Black Labor,* 274–308.

5. Ibid., 296.

6. John Hope Franklin, *From Slavery to Freedom,* 7th ed. (New York: Knopf, 1994), 455.

7. Jones, "Origins," 389–403.

8. Ibid., 392–94. See also Turner, *Past and Future,* 4–5.

9. Executive Order 8802, 3 C.F.R. 957 (1938–43 Comp.).

10. Jones, "Origins," 394.

11. Ibid., 395. See also President's Committee on Government Contracts, *Patterns for Progress: Final Report to President Eisenhower* (Washington, D.C.: U.S. Government Printing Office, 1960).

12. 3 C.F.R. 339 (1964–65 Comp.), reprinted in 42 U.S.C. § 2000e (1982); Jones, "Origins," 396.

13. Michael I. Sovern, *Legal Restraints on Racial Discrimination* (New York: Twentieth Century Fund, 1966).

14. Jones, "Origins," 396–97. Sovern, *Legal Restraints,* 110–13.

15. Civil Rights Act of 1964, Pub. L. No. 88–352, 78 Stat. 241 (1964). For current statutes see 42 U.S.C. 2000a–2000h (St. Paul: West Publishing, 1994).

16. Civil Rights Act of 1964, Pub. L. No. 88–352, 78 Stat. 241 (1964) (see 42 U.S.C. 2000e–5(g)).

17. 3 C.F.R. 339 (1964–65 Comp.). Executive Order 11,246 was amended to cover discrimination on the basis of sex or religion by Executive Order 11,375, which states that "the contractor will take affirmative action to ensure that applicants are employed, and that employees are treated during employment, without regard to their race, color, religion, sex or national origin."

18. Jones, "Origins," 398; Sovern, *Legal Restraints,* 227–28.

19. Jones, "Origins," 399–402.

20. See Contractors Ass'n of E. PA v. Secretary of Labor, 442 F.2d 159, 165 (3d Cir.), cert. denied, 404 U.S. 854 (1971).

21. Ibid., 171–77.

22. Ibid., 173.

23. Bakke, 438 U.S. 265, 269–81 (1978).

24. Ibid., 281–87.

25. Ibid., 285–86, citing Representative Emanuel Celler, chairman of the House Judiciary Committee, 110 Cong. Rec. 1519 (1964).

26. Bakke, 438 U.S. at 287.

27. Ibid., 289–91. To trace the development of the levels of scrutiny reflected in modern race cases, one has to go back at least to 1938 when the Court decided *United States v. Carolene Products*, 304 U.S. 144 (1938). In a now famous footnote, Justice Harlan F. Stone wrote that the presumption of constitutionality that applied to legislation adopted to achieve public health concerns might have a narrower scope of operation when legislation appears on its face to be within a specific prohibition of the Constitution or when the legislation is directed at particular religious, national, or racial minorities. Justice Stone implied that such legislation may call for a correspondingly more searching judicial inquiry. Carolene Products, 304 U.S. at 152, n. 4.

Six years later, in *Korematsu v. United States*, 323 U.S. 214 (1944), Justice Hugo Black said for the Court, "[A]ll legal restrictions which curtail the civil rights of a single racial group are immediately suspect. That is not to say that all such restrictions are unconstitutional. It is to say that Courts must subject them to the most rigid scrutiny" (216).

The Court has stated that under the strict scrutiny test, a government practice or statute that restricts "fundamental rights" or that contains "suspect classifications" is subject to "strict scrutiny" and can be justified only if no less restrictive alternative is available. See San Antonio Independent School District v. Rodriquez, 411 U.S. 1, 16–17 (1973).

28. Bakke, 438 U.S. at 292.

29. Ibid., 294.

30. The Civil Rights Cases, 109 U.S. at 24–27.

31. Bakke, 438 U.S. at 295 n. 34 (citations omitted).

32. Ibid., 298. Justice Powell failed to understand that someone bears the burden of our society's racial subordination. And he did not explain why someone in Bakke's position should be exempt from bearing some portion of the burden. The fact is that Bakke did not bear a burden greater than the burden of a black applicant who under Davis's admissions policies had virtually zero chance of gaining one of the eighty-four "open" slots in the first-year class. Davis's admissions policies favored Allan Bakke because he had the kind of credentials sought in applicants.

*Bakke* is an excellent example of government's use of race-neutral criteria that clearly subordinates blacks and other minorities. When selecting its admissions criteria, Davis knew, or should have known, that virtually no blacks would satisfy them. The result is that blacks remain closed out of many professions under the guise of color blindness race neutrality.

33. Ibid., 306–7.

34. Ibid., 317. Since 1978, most colleges and universities have operated some form of diversity admissions programs.

35. Ibid., 317–19.

36. United Steelworkers of America v. Weber, 443 U.S. 193 (1979).

37. Ibid., 197–99, 208, 201, 202, 203. By 1978, the black unemployment rate was 129 percent higher than the white rate (204, n. 4).

38. Ibid., 208–9.

39. Ibid., 217–19, 254–55.

40. Fullilove v. Klutznick, 448 U.S. 448, 453–54, 492 (1980).

41. Chief Justice Burger announced the judgment in an opinion, joined by Justices White and Powell. Justice Powell also wrote a separate concurrence, and Justice Marshall concurred separately in the judgment, joined by Justices Brennan and Blackmun. Justice Stewart dissented, joined by Justice Rehnquist. Justice Stevens dissented separately.

42. The MBE provision was added to the act after $2 billion had already been distributed and minority applicants had raised questions about the fairness of the distribution procedures. Presumably, a significant portion of the first $2 billion went to non-minority-controlled businesses (either contractors or subcontractors). The sponsor of the amendment stated that its objective was to direct funds into the minority business community, which could not be expected to benefit significantly from the public works program as formulated. See Fullilove, 448 U.S. at 459, n. 20, and 472.

43. Ibid., 482 (citations omitted). Recall that Chief Justice Burger wrote the majority opinion in *Swann.*

44. Ibid., 483 (citation omitted).

45. Ibid., 484.

46. The Court concluded that given the broad powers of Congress and the means chosen to achieve its objectives, the MBE provision did not violate the Constitution. Chief Justice Burger suggested that the constant administrative review system and the waiver provision that permitted a grantee or contractor to demonstrate a good-faith effort to comply with the set-aside gave reasonable assurance that the program would operate constitutionally. Ibid., 490.

47. Ibid., 492. Chief Justice Burger appeared to apply close scrutiny and appropriate congressional deference in deciding *Fullilove.* However, his language suggests that the issue of which standard of review should apply to affirmative action cases remained unresolved.

48. Ibid., 523 (Stewart, J., dissenting).

49. Ibid.

50. Wygant v. Jackson Board of Education, 476 U.S. 267, 270–72, 269–70, 273–74 (1986).

51. Ibid., 274.

52. Ibid., 274, 275–77, 279–84.

53. Ibid., 284 (O'Connor, J., concurring in part and concurring in the judgment), 294 (White, J., concurring in the judgment), 295.

54. Ibid., 295 (Marshall, J., joined by Brennan and Blackmun, JJ., dissenting); 313 (Stevens, J., dissenting), 318–20.

55. United States v. Paradise, 480 U.S. 149, 153–66, 167, 166, 167 (1987).

56. Ibid., 171.

57. Ibid., 171–72.

58. Ibid., 171–72, 196 (O'Connor, J., joined by Rehnquist, C.J., and Scalia, J., dissenting) (Justice White dissented separately), 197.

59. Ibid., 201. Justice O'Connor argued that nonracial remedies were available to the district court, including appointing a trustee to monitor the department or holding the department in contempt (200–1).

Two years later in a similar case involving black and white firefighters in Birmingham, Alabama, five justices held that white firefighters who claimed that they were being denied promotions in favor of less qualified blacks were not precluded from challenging the employment decisions made in accordance with consent decrees from prior litigation to which they were not parties. See Martin v. Wilks, 490 U.S. 755, 758–69 (1989).

60. 488 U.S. 469 (1989). For a summary of each opinion, see 469–75, 477–86. The Richmond City Council (with a black majority) issued a bid request for plumbing fixtures at the city jail. Croson bid for the job and attempted to comply with the set-aside by securing the partnership of an MBE. When the bids were opened, Croson was the only bidder; however, the MBE that Croson had selected could not obtain the necessary credit approval. Thereafter, Croson sought a waiver from the city of the minority set-aside provision. After the city refused the waiver request and decided to rebid the project, Croson sued. Both lower federal courts applied the reasoning of *Fullilove* and concluded that the same result should follow in *Croson*.

However, since *Fullilove*, the Court had decided *Wygant*, in which the Court had invalidated a collective bargaining agreement under the equal protection clause. The agreement provided that if layoffs became necessary in the Jackson school district, at no time would a greater percentage of minority teachers be laid off than the percentage of minority teachers employed in the school at the time of the layoff. Accordingly, when layoffs became necessary, Wygant and others were laid off before minority teachers with less seniority. There was no majority opinion. When the U.S. Supreme Court noted probable jurisdiction in *Croson*, it vacated the Fourth Circuit's judgment and ordered reconsideration in light of *Wygant* (see Wygant, 476 U.S. at 267).

On reconsideration of *Croson*, in light of *Wygant*, the Fourth Circuit invalidated the Richmond set-aside program. It was again appealed to the U.S. Supreme Court.

61. Croson, 488 U.S. at 486, 490, 491–92. Justice O'Connor said that section 2 of the Fifteenth Amendment had been given a similar reading. She did not argue that a state or local subdivision could not eradicate the effects of private discrimination. In fact, she argued the opposite, but she wrote that the power must be exercised in a manner consistent with section 1 of the Fourteenth Amendment.

62. Ibid., 492 (citations omitted).

63. Justice O'Connor, like Justice Powell in *Bakke*, appeared to accept the reasoning in *Washington v. Davis* for what must be proved to establish racial discrimination. Past industrywide discrimination was not sufficient. Since *Croson*, the government has had to show that there has been discrimination in the local market against the persons to benefit from the set-aside. Ibid., 493–98.

64. Ibid., 493. Four of the justices in *Wygant* had also argued for strict scrutiny.

65. Ibid., 497. The proponents of the Richmond plan had argued that only 0.67

percent of all prime contracts had gone to minority businesses. Although the minority population was 50 percent, there were very few minority businesses in the local or state contractors' associations. Congress had made substantial findings showing how the effects of past discrimination had stifled minority participation in the construction industry nationally (504).

66. Ibid., 504.

67. Ibid., 502. Since the *Croson* decision, numerous states and city governments have undertaken or commissioned *Croson* disparity studies to determine whether there is evidence of local discrimination in the letting of public contracts. Frequently, the studies are performed by accountancy experts who bid on the projects. Justice O'Connor wrote that to prove discrimination, one had to focus on the disparity between the number of minority businesses qualified to undertake the task and the percentage of total city construction dollars received by minority firms.

68. Ibid., 505–6.

69. Ibid., 506 (emphasis added).

70. Ibid., 507. It seemed equally significant to the Court that five of the nine city council members in Richmond were black. The Court suggested several times that the black political majority was playing racial politics, yet the Court never quite explained why the percentage of public contracts for blacks was so small. Also, it seems ironic that the Court would underscore the race of the majority of council members while espousing the doctrine of color blindness. The members of the Court, like the rest of us, are simply not color blind.

To justify a racial classification, the government must show that the classification serves a compelling state interest and that the means are narrowly tailored to achieve the state's objective (511).

71. Ibid., 509.

72. Ibid., 528, 551–54.

73. Ibid., 551–52.

74. Metro Broadcasting v. FCC, 497 U.S. 547, 455 (1990). The two policies under dispute were (1) a program awarding applicants for new licenses an enhancement for substantial minority ownership and (2) the minority "distress sale" program, permitting the transfer of a limited category of existing radio and television broadcast stations only to minority-controlled firms. Congress enacted the policies after it found that minorities owned less than 1 percent of all radio and television stations (456).

75. Ibid., 459–62. The plaintiffs in the consolidated cases were Metro Broadcasting of Orlando and Shurberg Broadcasting of Hartford, each of which had lost a bid to obtain a television station. Metro Broadcasting challenged the award of a station to a firm that received an enhancement under the first policy because it was 90 percent Latino owned. Shurberg challenged the award of a television station to a minority-controlled entity via a distress sale program under the second policy.

76. Ibid., 462–63 (citations omitted).

77. Ibid., 463–64. The Court then announced that the FCC's policies were

constitutional under the intermediate standard of review because they served the important governmental objective of broadcast diversity and the policies were substantially related to that objective.

78. Ibid., 465–68. Justice Brennan borrowed from Justice Powell's reasoning in *Bakke* regarding the benefits of a diverse student body to argue that both broadcast diversity and student diversity serve important governmental interests. Justice Brennan reasoned that the general public benefited from wider information sources. He deferred to congressional findings on the correlation between minority ownership and diverse programming:

> The judgment that there is a link between expanded minority ownership and broadcast diversity does not rest on impermissible stereotyping. Congressional policy does not assume that in every case minority ownership and management will lead to more minority-oriented programming or to the expression of a discrete "minority viewpoint" on the airwaves. Neither does it pretend that all programming that appeals to minority audiences can be labeled "minority programming" or that programming that might be described as "minority" does not appeal to nonminorities. Rather, both Congress and the FCC maintain simply that expanded minority ownership of broadcast outlets will, in the aggregate, result in greater broadcast diversity. A broadcasting industry with representative minority participation will produce more variation and diversity than will one whose ownership is drawn from a single racially and ethnically homogeneous group (472).

See also ibid., 473, n. 31–32.

79. Ibid., 474 (citations omitted).

80. Ibid., 478, 481–85.

81. Ibid., 486–87 (O'Connor, J., dissenting). Chief Justice Rehnquist and Justices Scalia and Kennedy joined in her dissent. But O'Connor's criticism seems disingenuous. First, the facts of *Metro Broadcasting* are much more like those of *Fullilove* than those of *Croson*. Second, as in *Fullilove,* the majority in *Metro Broadcasting* deferred to congressional sources of power and evidentiary findings. Third, the reasoning presented in *Metro Broadcasting* tracks that presented by the principal opinion in *Fullilove* and meets most of the criticism against Richmond's set-aside plan that Justice O'Connor made in *Croson*.

82. Ibid., 491–92.

83. Ibid., 491–93.

84. Adarand Constructors, Inc. v. Pena, 115 S.Ct. 2097, 2102–4 (1995).

85. Ibid., 2103–4.

86. Ibid., 2104–6.

87. Ibid., 2097, 2106–12.

88. Ibid., 2111.

89. Ibid.

90. Ibid., 2112.

91. Ibid., 2118.

92. Ibid., 2122–23, 2133–36.

93. Paul Brest, "Foreword: In Defense of the Antidiscrimination Principle,"

*Harv. L. Rev.* 90 (1978): 16–23; John Hart Ely, "The Constitutionality of Reverse Discrimination," *U. Chi. L. Rev.* 41 (1974): 727–39.

94. Adarand, 115 S.Ct. at 2136.

95. See Missouri v. Jenkins, 115 S.Ct. 2038 (1995); Miller v. Johnson, 115 S.Ct. 2475 (1995).

96. Bakke, 438 U.S. at 407 (Blackmun, J., separate opinion).

97. Croson, 488 U.S. at 494.

98. Text of "Affirmative Action Review" Report to President Clinton Released July 19, 1995, Daily Lab. Rep. (BNA) No. 139, at D-30 (July 20, 1995) (special supplement).

99. Ibid.

100. Ibid.

101. Ibid.

102. Ibid.

103. Ibid.

104. Griggs v. Duke Power Co., 401 U.S. 424 (1971).

105. Nicholas Lemann, "What Happened to the Case for Affirmative Action?" *New York Times Magazine,* June 11, 1995, 36–66.

106. Podberesky v. Kirwan, 38 F.3d 147 (4th Cir. 1994), cert. denied, 115 U.S. 2001 (1995).

107. Birmingham Fire-Fighters Ass'n 117 v. City of Birmingham, 31 F.3d 1548 (11th Cir. 1994).

108. White v. Alabama, 867 F. Supp. 1571 (M.D. Ala. 1994), 74 F.3d 1058 (11th Cir. 1996)

109. Hopwood v. Texas, 861 F. Supp. 551 (W.D. Tex. 1994), 78 F.3d 932 (5th Cir. 1996).

110. Lemann, "What Happened," 39–40.

111. See, for example, Johnson v. Santa Clara County Transportation Agency, 480 U.S. 616 (1987).

112. Stephen L. Carter, *Reflections of an Affirmative Action Baby* (New York: Basic Books, 1991), 47–69.

113. Rich Connell and Sonia Nazario, "Affirmative Action: Fairness or Favoritism?" *Los Angeles Times,* September 10, 1995, part A, 1.

114. Maguire, *New American Justice,* 27–38.

115. Dan Maguire presents a comprehensive list of the myriad arguments against affirmative action and a critique of each. See ibid., 32–38, 167–88.

116. See Carter, *Reflections,* 4–5.

117. Connell and Nazario, "Affirmative Action," 1. See also Report to President Clinton.

118. Maguire, *New American Justice,* 174.

119. See *Chronicle of Higher Education,* Almanac Issue, September 1, 1995, 5–33, which confirms that

  • In 1992, more than 90 percent of full-time faculty at American universities were white.

  • In 1992, nearly 119,000 of the 137,000 executive administrators were white.

• In 1993, whites earned 26,700 doctorates, and blacks earned 1,352.
• In 1993, whites earned 60,830 professional degrees, and blacks earned 4,100.

120. Report to President Clinton.

121. Federal Glass Ceiling Commission, *Good for Business: Making Full Use of the Nation's Human Capital* (Washington, D.C.: U.S. Governmentt Printing Office, March 1995).

122. Ibid., 18, 33.

123. Donald Lively and Stephen Plass, "Equal Protection: The Jurisprudence of Denial and Evasion," *Am. U. L. Rev.* 40 (1991): 1307, 1312–46.

124. Antonin Scalia, "The Disease as Cure: In Order to Get Beyond Racism We Must First Take Account of Race," *Wash. U. L. Q.*, 1979: 147, 152.

125. Andrew Hacker, *Two Nations: Black and White, Separate, Hostile, Unequal* (New York: Macmillan, 1992). See also Gerald David Jaynes and Robin M. Williams Jr., eds., *A Common Destiny: Blacks and American Society* (Washington, D.C.: National Academy Press, 1989).

126. Robin Abcarian, "Quayle's Opportunity: A Terrible Thing to Waste," *Los Angeles Times*, May 22, 1992, Part E, 1.

127. *Report of the National Advisory Commission on Civil Disorders* (Washington, D.C.: U.S. Government Printing Office, 1968), 1. See also Hacker, *Two Nations*, ix; Jaynes and Williams, eds., *A Common Destiny*, 5.

128. Hacker, *Two Nations*, 223–36, 104.

129. Jaynes and Williams, eds., *A Common Destiny*, 3.

130. Charles Murray and Richard J. Herrnstein, *The Bell Curve: Intelligence and Class Structure in American Life* (New York: Free Press, 1994); Shelby Steele, *The Content of Our Character: A New Vision of Race in America* (New York: Harper Perennial, 1990); Thomas Sowell, *Race and Culture: A World View* (New York: Basic Books, 1994).

131. Arnold M. Rose, *The Roots of Prejudice* (Paris: UNESCO, 1951).

132. Reed v. Reed, 404 U.S. 71, 76 (1971).

133. Kahn v. Shevin, 416 U.S. 351, 353–55 (1974), and Califano v. Webster, 430 U.S. 313, 317 (1977). For a fuller discussion of gender blindness, see Bryan K. Fair, "Foreword: Rethinking the Colorblindness Model," *Nat'l Black L.J.* 13 (1993): 73–81.

NOTES TO AFTERWORD

1. James Baldwin, *The Fire Next Time* (New York: Dial Press, 1963), 20.

2. Charles Daye, "On Blackberry Picking, Generations of Affirmative Action, and Less Dangerous Enterprises: An Open Letter to Stephen Carter," *Stanford L. Rev.* 45 (1993): 485. This is a discussion of Stephen Carter's *Reflections of an Affirmative Action Baby* (New York: Basic Books, 1991).

# INDEX